John Spencer has been an active researcher of ghosts and the paranormal for over twenty years. He is a member of the Ghost Club, the Society for Psychical Research (SPR) and the Association for the Scientific Study of Anomalous Phenomena (ASSAP). He has been a team leader on many highly successful vigils, and a member of several others for English Heritage. He is also at the forefront of exploratory work with hypnosis and the paranormal.

Tony Wells is by profession a freelance computer consultant working for a range of blue-chip companies. He became interested in scientific investigation of the paranormal some years ago, and now spends several evenings a month on ghosthunts with colleagues – including John Spencer. He is an active member of the SPR and ASSAP. In 1993 he started running evening classes on the paranormal – the first of their kind in the UK. He also works with psychics and mediums in development circles, performing experiments such as table-tilting and creating artificial ghosts.

GHOSTWATCHING

*JOHN SPENCER
AND TONY WELLS*

Virgin

First published in Great Britain in 1994 by
Virgin Books
an imprint of Virgin Publishing Ltd
332 Ladbroke Grove
London W10 5AH

Copyright © John Spencer and Tony Wells 1994

The right of John Spencer and Tony Wells to be identified as the authors of this work has been asserted by them in accordance with the Copyright Designs and Patents Act 1988

This book is sold subject to the condition that it shall not, by way of trade or otherwise, be lent, resold, hired out or otherwise circulated without the publisher's prior written consent in any form of binding or cover other than that in which it is published and without a similar condition including this condition being imposed upon the subsequent purchaser. All rights reserved.

A catalogue record for this book is available from the British Library

ISBN 1 85227 469 7

Typeset by CentraCet Ltd, Cambridge
Printed and bound in Great Britain by
Mackays of Chatham Ltd,
Lordswood, Kent

Contents

List of illustrations — vii
Acknowledgements — ix
Introduction — 1

PART ONE – THE WORLD OF GHOSTS

1. Origins and History of Ghosts — 7
2. Ghosts That Ignore You — 18
3. Ghosts That Interact with You — 37
4. Ghosts with an Attitude — 64
5. Ghosts of the Living — 86
6. Other Ghost Phenomena; Associated Phenomena — 96
7. The Ghosts in the Machine? — 111

PART TWO – GHOSTWATCHING

8. Vigils — 127
9. Dealing with Witnesses — 157
10. Banishing Ghosts — 173
11. Working at the Frontiers of Science — 201

PART THREE – SO YOU WANT TO BE A GHOSTWATCHER?

12. Getting the Team Together — 215
13. Finding People and Places to Research — 226
14. Are You Psychic? — 234

Contents

APPENDICES
A – Organisations 251
B – Sample Interview Questionnaire 254
C – Style of Reporting 257
D – Equipment 260

References and additional recommended reading 271
Index 275

Illustrations

Harry Price setting up controls for investigation of the Crawley Case, December 1945 (*Mary Evans/Harry Price Collection, University of London*)
The ruins of Borley Rectory, 5 April 1944, showing the alleged 'flying brick' (*Mary Evans/Harry Price Collection, University of London*)
Charlton House, south London, site of the authors' group experiments and evening classes (*Tony Wells*)
A reputedly haunted staircase in Charlton House (*Tony Wells*)
Rochester Castle, Kent (*Tony Wells*)
The Environmental Monitoring Unit (EMU) module set up at the Waldorf Restaurant, Maidstone (*Tony Wells*)
Robin Lawrence, ghost researcher, on site in Dover Castle (*John Spencer*)
Interior of St John's Tower, Dover Castle (*John Spencer*)
The Ancient Ram Inn, Gloucestershire, site of reputedly the most haunted room in England (*John Spencer*)
The Bishop's Room at the Ancient Ram Inn (*John Spencer*)
The Home of Compassion, Thames Ditton, where ghostly nuns have often been seen (*John Spencer*)
Hampton Court, scene of many royal hauntings (*John Spencer*)
A demonstration of how *not* to go ghostwatching (*Simon Earwicker*)
The Long Gallery at Charlton House, site of experiments in table rapping (*John Spencer*)

Illustrations

One of the famous 'Bélmez faces' which appeared on a kitchen floor in Spain in 1971 (*Mary Evans Picture Library*)

Acknowledgements

The authors would like to thank all the individuals who have helped with the construction of this book including: Maurice Townsend and Mike Lewis of the Association for the Scientific Study of Anomalous Phenomena; Eleanor O'Keeffe of the Society for Psychic Research; Alan Wesencraft, the Honorary Librarian of the magnificent Harry Price Library in the University of London's Senate House; the very helpful staff at both the Harpenden and Lewisham Libraries; Robin Lawrence who has organised so many excellent ghosthunts at so many castles; Dave Thomas for his contribution on the Media and Blue Bell Hill; Anne Spencer for helping provide case material and for checking the manuscript, and Jane Le Surf for helping with early drafts; Gavin Naden of the *South East London Mercury* for help with the publicity that obtained cases; to Chris and Philip Walton who have provided support.

We would also like to thank those in the various corporate bodies who have allowed us to spend so much time on their premises: English Heritage, Fort Amherst and Greenwich Council's Charlton House.

We must also thank the various witnesses who have allowed us to report their cases. Some have preferred to remain anonymous, but they of course know who they are.

We also acknowledge the debt to our families, who were patient with us.

And finally, of course, our thanks to the ghosts, without whom . . .

Introduction

GHOSTWATCHING IS EXCITING; it can also be physically exhausting and mentally challenging. For 90 per cent of the time the main requirement of a ghostwatcher is patience, because nothing is happening. But the other 10 per cent – when the action starts – can be extremely rewarding.

The subject of ghosts and associated phenomena has fascinated people for many years – probably since the dawn of history – and today interest is growing at a rapid pace. Perhaps this is because it is one of the few subjects left where the amateur can make a real and valuable contribution to a subject which may have tremendous long-term impact.

In parallel with this the availability of low-cost domestic video equipment makes it increasingly likely that someone will have a camera ready and primed when a ghost appears, increasing the material available for research. Similarly, security cameras are also increasing in number, and they too might record appearances.

The benefits of having this technology in widespread use are already beginning to be seen. The authors have worked on, or are aware of, several possible paranormal sightings recorded on video: a police video from a motorway camera that was released to us, two videos from shopping centre security cameras, and nineteen different camcorder recordings of the same incident – the appearance of a UFO – which occurred during an eclipse which many people were filming.

Ghost research deals with fundamental issues: the evidence of 'life' after death; the search for latent abilities, such as telepathy, within people; and the way we perceive the world.

It is divided into two complementary areas:
1. Are ghosts and related phenomena real?
2. If they are real, what do they represent?

Throughout this book, we have illustrated our search for the answers with examples of ghost experiences from real-life cases. Some of these cases were reported by people who had reputations to maintain; in the knowledge that their careers would not be enhanced by their making such disclosures, they nevertheless did so. With this in mind, and considering that their experiences fall in line with 'ordinary' people's statements, we conclude that at least some of the numerous accounts of ghosts must have some basis in fact.

This book describes two main areas: ghost phenomena themselves, and modern approaches to research. Ghosts represent not one single group of events, but rather a complex variety of different situations, probably with a variety of meanings, and certainly demanding a variety of techniques of research.

We should point out that we use the term 'ghost' very broadly, using it in a general sense which includes those phenomena which specialists refer to as spirits, apparitions, and so on. As such it encompasses a range of phenomena from sightings of figures to tables which rap by themselves and answer questions in a seemingly intelligent way. Because the term is so broad we have had to classify the subject according to general headings, as that will help the reader to understand the wider implications of the subject.

To research ghosts requires a balance between accepting witnesses' belief without cynical challenge, and remaining objectively sceptical as to interpretation and meaning. In his book *1984* George Orwell described the problem: 'Doublethink means the power of holding two contradictory beliefs in one's mind simultaneously, and accepting both of them.'

If the reader is left with the opinion that the authors

remain questioning of the phenomena we call 'ghosts' and the mechanisms that create them, this will be an accurate view. Any objective researchers who claim otherwise, and claim to know 'The Truth', are either trying to fool you or themselves.

HOW TO USE THIS BOOK

Part I, 'The World of Ghosts', includes many real-life cases and describes the variety of ghost and spirit phenomena according to their characteristics. Most ghost sightings are spontaneous and happen to people in an unexpected manner. This section is designed to provide reference information for the would-be ghostwatcher and anyone else interested in this research.

Part II, 'Ghostwatching', describes the authors', and others', practical experiences of ghost research. For adventurous ghostwatchers we describe techniques for generating some types of ghosts of your own.

Part III, 'So You Want to be a Ghostwatcher?', provides the information you will need if you want to become a researcher yourself – finding cases, dealing with witnesses, creating a team, getting the right equipment, and so on. The section also tells you how you can find out if you are psychic, and gives practical suggestions for developing psychic abilities.

And for the reader who doesn't want to be a ghostwatcher, but is just fascinated by the subject, we can promise you lots of surprises, and a few smiles at some of our worst disasters and our best successes.

A list of reference sources appears on p. 271. Numbers within the text indicate that fuller details of individual cases can be found in the work mentioned.

Part One

THE WORLD OF GHOSTS

1 Origins and History of Ghosts

GHOST PHENOMENA are inextricably linked with the question of survival of the spirit after death. Ghosts are perceived by the vast majority of people as manifestations of 'the return of the dead'. With our present state of knowledge we can only regard this as a theory. Even if the theory turns out to be correct, there is plenty of evidence to show that it is not the *only* truth – for example, in this book we examine reports of 'ghosts' that turn out to be living people.

Having said this, survival of the spirit is inextricably linked with religions in their various forms throughout the ages. All religions seem to include in their creeds a belief that there is some form of continuing existence after mortal, physical death. Perhaps this is, in fact, a basis of religion in general. Written accounts of previously oral traditions of the earliest cultures include references to some form of spiritual survival; we can assume that there is some likelihood that those cultures which have passed into history without leaving written references probably held similar beliefs. Certainly the burial traditions of our ancestors strongly suggest a belief in some sort of life beyond the grave, or at least a special taboo surrounding the dead.

For example, many of the earliest buried skeletons that have been discovered were found surrounded by jewellery and ornaments, much of it of considerable value. Other graves have included more mundane articles – utensils and food. Many of these presumably belonged to the deceased in

Ghostwatching

life, and apparently held a special taboo that prevented them being taken away or stolen after death. It is of course also possible that these objects were intended for the deceased's use in the afterlife; we know that this was the intention of similar burial rituals in later cultures such as that of the Egyptians.

Red ochre – a type of clay containing haematite – has been found sprinkled over the remains of Paleolithic peoples. It is thought highly likely by anthropologists that this was intended to strengthen the deceased for his life after death; the red ochre is associated with the colour of blood. The Magdalenian skeleton of Hoteaux in the Ain was covered in red ochre; that found in Sordes in the Landes was similarly coated. Modern Australian aborigines consider the red clays and rocks to be symbolic of strong blood. It is possible therefore that these early peoples believed in a survival of spirit.

Many of these earliest bodies have been found in a 'trussed-up' position; the 'old man' of Chancelade in the Dordogne, a body from the Magdalenian period, is an example. Anthropologists have concluded that our ancestors might have been making an attempt to ensure that the dead person did not come back to walk amongst the living. It seems equally possible that such a position might have been intended as a form of re-birthing into a new life, since the position the bodies were found in is very similar to the foetal position. Either way, some form of belief in a life after death seems implied.

The cultures that have left us records all contain some sort of fundamental belief in survival beyond the grave. The famous pyramids of the ancient Egyptian culture were designed to serve the deceased leader entombed within in his future existence. The tombs were designed to be impenetrable; and they housed equipment, food and even living slaves to serve the King in the afterlife.

1 Origins and History of Ghosts

HISTORICAL CONTEXT

Most older cultures seem to have had some kind of shaman, or witch-doctor who was responsible for looking after the general health of the village. In these cultures there seemed to be no distinction between physical and mental welfare. In order to impress the villagers with his powers the shaman may have included in his repertoire some conjuring, and possibly some genuine paranormal techniques, including 'talking to the dead' or other more physical phenomena such as levitation or moving objects without touching them.

In China and Japan, many centuries before the birth of Christ, there was widespread belief that the spirits of dead ancestors survived on some non-physical plane, and needed to be treated with respect. This belief, despite the upheavals of the last few centuries, still continues in both countries.

In Western Europe, until the mid-nineteenth century, there seemed to be no real distinction between research into the paranormal, the practice of magic and witchcraft, and practice in areas such as medicine and science. Isaac Newton, for instance, who discovered the law of gravity and was the founder of modern mathematics and calculus, also spent a great deal of his time practising alchemy, trying to turn lead into gold.

The division came with the almost simultaneous births of spiritualism and rationalism. These forces in opposition became the driving forces in the earliest ghost and paranormal researches.

THE NINETEENTH CENTURY: THE BIRTH OF SPIRITUALISM

The year 1848 saw the birth of what must be called a new 'religion', spiritualism. The two younger daughters of a Mr Fox, a Methodist farmer in Hydesville, New York State, became plagued by rappings which seemed to be of intelligent origin – questions could be asked and the raps would give a meaningful answer. In order to protect her from the enormous publicity that was building up around the girls, the youngest of the three daughters, Kate, was sent to the neighbouring town of Rochester to stay with a Mrs Fish. Despite this move, the phenomena did not abate – the disturbances continued at the Foxes home, centring round Margaret, the middle sister, but also followed Kate. In an experiment around a table, again communicating by rapping, it seemed that there was a whole host of dead members of the Fish family ready and willing to talk.

A year later, Kate Fox was able to demonstrate further powers. At one sitting she was able to make the form of a hand visible against the light of the window, in a darkened room.

In 1850 P. T. Barnum, the entrepreneurial showman, became interested in the sisters' potential, and arranged for them to visit New York, where they gave exhibitions of their powers at Barnum's Hotel, and at his museum. From that time, the Fox sisters became the first professional mediums. By 1855, spiritualism had spread across most of the US, and then to Europe.

THE NINETEENTH CENTURY: JOHN STUART MILL'S *LOGIC* AND DARWIN'S *THE ORIGIN OF SPECIES*

Almost concurrently with the spread of spiritualism there came a new kind of philosophy based on John Stuart Mill's book *A System of Logic*. Published in 1843, it defined a way of thinking based on accepting only sources of information gained by our own senses, and advocating that 'faith' and 'intuition' be rejected.

In 1858 Darwin produced his book *The Origin of Species*, which proposed a completely new theory about how life on Earth came about. This alternative way of thinking was a foundation of the rationalist school of thought.

1 Origins and History of Ghosts

THE NINETEENTH CENTURY: HENRY SIDGWICK AND FREDERIC MYERS – THE WILDERNESS YEARS

By the end of the decade, a number of men from the universities of Oxford and Cambridge were having a crisis of faith. Henry Sidgwick, a brilliant Cambridge student, was one of them. He was finding that part of his intellect, having absorbed the theories of Mill and Darwin, was inclining him towards a mechanistic view of the world, and another part (no doubt his early religious learning) was pushing him towards faith in the Christian God. At one point Sidgwick considered himself set on a career for high office in the Church (his cousin and future brother-in-law eventually became Archbishop of Canterbury). Whilst exploring several intellectual routes to try to resolve this apparent dichotomy of ideas his academic career flourished – he was appointed College Lecturer in Moral Science and became a Fellow of Trinity College, Cambridge.

In 1869, an academic contemporary and friend of Sidgwick, also a Fellow at Trinity College, Frederic Myers, suffered a severe bout of pneumonia and realised that he had lost his faith, but was appalled at the thought of simple extinction of life at the point of physical death. Sidgwick, with the same conflict of ideas, could not help resolve the problem. In 1874 Myers began experimenting with table-tilting and table-rapping, and two years later started to visit spiritualist mediums. This led to him visiting his aunt, where he watched at first hand the physical medium Stainton Moses. (A physical medium is so-called because in their presence physical things happen, such as movement of objects. In one example, witnessed by physicist Sir Oliver Lodge, a physical medium levitated. On other occasions Lodge witnessed an accordion playing by itself.)

Ghostwatching

THE FORERUNNER OF THE SOCIETY FOR PSYCHICAL RESEARCH

Intrigued by the phenomena that seemed to be produced by physical mediums, and aware that they could, in fact, be supplying first-hand evidence of life after death, Myers persuaded Sidgwick to be a member of 'an informal association' for the investigation of the phenomena. Later, other Fellows of Trinity College joined the group: Edmund Gurney, Walter Leaf, the physicist Lord Rayleigh; Arthur Balfour (who later became Prime Minister) and his sisters Elenor and Evelyn (Lady Rayleigh). They were occasionally joined by the scientist, William Crookes.

THE EARLY INVESTIGATIONS

One of the first mediums they investigated was Mrs Annie Eva Fay, who had travelled from the USA. Her sittings usually worked to a format: musical instruments and other objects were placed near her, the lights were lowered, the musical instruments would play and objects would be thrown around. Afterwards she would sit in near darkness with others in a circle, and people would have their beards tweaked and again, the musical instruments would play. After some experiments, investigators found that the phenomena did not happen when her hands were tied to separate posts. Interest ceased in Annie Eva Fay.

Not put off by this, the 'association' decided to investigate a group of Newcastle mediums – Miss Wood, Miss Fairlamb and members of the Petty family. After a visit where it was agreed there were some interesting phenomena, the mediums were invited down to Cambridge and London to hold some controlled sittings. On the twelfth sitting in London with the Misses Fairlamb and Wood, several figures materialised. Afterwards it was deemed important to search Miss Fairlamb to eliminate the possibility of her cheating, but she refused.

1 Origins and History of Ghosts

As a consequence, their suspicions of cheating strengthened and it was decided to drop any further research into the group.

1882: THE FOUNDING OF THE SOCIETY FOR PSYCHICAL RESEARCH

The foundation of the SPR was based on the assumption, by Professor W. F. Barrett, that if a group of investigative spiritualists could work with mediums in circumstances of proper experimentation, then proof of some forms of paranormal phenomena might be found. They were particularly interested in telepathy.

A conference was convened in January 1882, and it was proposed that a society be formed. After consideration by a committee, the Society was formally created at a meeting on 20 February 1882. Sidgwick was made President, and remained so for nine years. In 1886 the Society published *Phantasms of the Living*. Edmund Gurney was the main force behind its creation. The thrust of the work, using evidence from a number of cases, was not, as is often supposed, to prove the existence of life after death, but an attempt to prove the existence of telepathy.

SPECIAL EFFECTS

One reason for thorough investigation of physical mediums was that the technology for faking was available. Indeed, the degree to which it was available, and its ability to fool observers, is often surprising.

Even around the time of the French Revolution a 'special effects' entertainment called the Phantasmagoria was passing itself off as a method of 'raising the dead'. Audiences would gather in crypts and other similarly atmospheric locations to see images appear, believing them to be spirits brought from death into this world.

Ghostwatching

The show was the brainchild of Étienne-Gaspard Robertson who developed the then existing technology of the magic lantern into a whole extravaganza. His main technique was to project images from a magic lantern on to gauze and smoke from behind the screen, leaving the audience unaware of how the images were formed. Because his lantern was on wheels – later there was one that could be focused – the images were not just static; they moved. Hand-held lanterns and slides were used so that such images as winged skulls could be seen flapping their wings. For extra effect the show used coffins from which erupted clouds of smoke, hidden projectors in the coffin creating faces in the smoke.

Given these techniques and the way in which the show was presented, there is little doubt that many of the audience would have believed they were witnessing something supernatural. And the shows became widespread around Europe and America.

There were other ways, using mirrors, of producing images. In the nineteenth century, at the time of the investigations into physical mediums, the 'Pepper's ghost' trick was being used in theatres to produce 'phantom' images in front of live audiences. Such techniques were easy for fraudulent mediums to reproduce.

Because the investigators were often dealing with what was effectively a new science, they were anxious that their evidence should be absolutely 'bomb proof'. Unfortunately, with the developing new technology to fool the observers, and the physical mediums' insistence on operating in near-darkness, the investigators felt that it was almost impossible to meet their own requirements. Having said that, there were some mediums, notably D. D. Home, who at no time had ever been caught in fraud, and who always co-operated with some incredibly restrictive demands.

1 Origins and History of Ghosts

MRS PIPER

Because of the difficulties of obtaining good evidence from physical mediums, the investigators turned to examining the claims of mental mediums. (A mental medium is one who produces no physical effects; but instead provides information 'given' to him or her by psychic means, usually whilst in a trance.) The most famous of these was Mrs Piper. She lived in the USA and began her mediumship in 1884 after visiting a blind healer, J. R. Cocke. After her second visit to him, she went into a trance and wrote a message for one of the other sitters. She then began to hold sittings at her home for family and friends. Her control was a French doctor who would offer prescriptions and suggestions to sitters requiring help, and which mostly seemed to effect a cure. (A medium's control is explained as a guide in or from the spirit world who acts as a 'master of ceremonies' between spirits and the medium.)

The philosopher and psychologist William James, of the American Society for Psychical Research (ASPR), who was a distant relation to Mrs Piper, became interested in her seemingly impressive ability to describe details of visitors' family concerns. In 1886 he wrote an account of his experiments in the *ASPR Journal*. Twenty-five colleagues had visited her under false names; fifteen of them had received, on their first visit, details of themselves which would not ordinarily have been available to her.

In 1887 Richard Hodgson, who up till then had been successful in exposing many fraudulent mediums, arrived in Boston to become the Secretary of the ASPR. Over a period of some 28 years, neither Hodgson, nor any other investigator, was able to find evidence of cheating by Mrs Piper. Their investigations were so comprehensive they included the use of private detectives to follow her to ensure that she was not using private agents of her own to ferret out information about likely sitters.

Ghostwatching

When Mrs Piper and her various spirit contacts were working well – and this was most of the time – some remarkable information was revealed at the sittings. Hodgson wrote in a paper, in 1898, that he was inclined to believe that the consistency of her powers and the remarkable nature of her successes might be evidence to suggest that she was indeed communicating with the spirits of the dead. There were still some worries – the main problem was that telepathy between the sitters and Mrs Piper could explain some of the knowledge that her communicators seemed to have about the sitters.

One example of a sitting where telepathy between the sitter and Mrs Piper was extremely unlikely is when Sir Oliver Lodge tried an experiment with a gold watch he had received from an uncle, Robert. The watch had been the property of Robert's twin brother, who had died twenty years before the experiment. Lodge took the watch to Mrs Piper, and received the message from a spirit not previously heard from: 'This is my watch, and Robert is my brother, and I am here. Uncle Jerry, my watch.' Lodge then prompted Mrs Piper's control – a Dr Phinuit – to get 'Uncle Jerry' to recall some of his life with his brother, Robert. Over several sittings, 'Uncle Jerry' recalled episodes such as swimming in a creek when they were boys, killing a cat in 'Smith's field', possession of a small rifle and of a peculiar skin, like a snakeskin.

According to Lodge, these episodes could not easily be explained away by telepathy as he himself had no knowledge of them. However, they were verified by his still-living uncle Robert as having basis in fact. In case Mrs Piper had somehow managed to find this information through 'normal' means, Lodge tried an experiment using a private agent to see how easy it was to do some 'human research'; but the agent had problems even discovering information about the existence of 'Smith's field'.

1 Origins and History of Ghosts

1900: THE DEATH OF SIDGWICK, AND THE END OF AN ERA

In 1900, Henry Sidgwick died of bowel cancer. In 1901 Myers, his long-time colleague and friend, also died. Edmund Gurney had died some years before, and Hodgson died of a heart attack in 1905. Those people, along with other colleagues and friends, had been responsible for over half of the official output of the SPR: 11,000 pages of *Proceedings* and *Journals*; 1,400 pages of *Phantasms of the Living*; and Myers' own work, *Human Personality*, some 1,300 pages.

It was the end of an era.

PUBLIC PRECEPTION OF LIFE AFTER DEATH

The beliefs of the general public in Northern Europe and America have been tested by various opinion polls in the last few decades. Over one hundred years after these first research efforts, polls indicate that just over half the populations of Northern Europe and America believe in life after death of some kind, including ghosts. In fact the opinion polls have tended to show a large-scale acceptance (at least 40 per cent of the population) of a wide range of phenomena that are generally classed as paranormal.

Whilst, then, there is widespread public perception that ghosts exist, it is difficult to define what a ghost really is. A starting point for examination is to classify ghosts according to the way they behave; the chapters in this section do this.

2 Ghosts That Ignore You

THERE IS A WHOLE category of ghost phenomena that have a common appearances though it is highly likely they are the manifestations of several different 'mechanisms'. The appearances they present are ghost-like enough to be within the realm of the ghost researcher; they are the 'ghosts that ignore you'.

The tendency to think that an image of a person in ghost form must represent survival of consciousness misses the obvious point that many such images display no intelligence, no interaction and indeed no consciousness. These images appear at certain points, go through certain motions – according to reports often exactly the same motions – and then they disappear. For this reason we should consider that these images are not evidence of life after death but perhaps of some other mechanism at work.

The following four cases demonstrate the basic qualities of this category.

> At St Albans Abbey a verger opening up the building one morning was surprised to see a procession of Benedictine monks walking towards him. He stepped aside to let them pass, and was even more surprised when they walked through the stone walls.

> Elizabeth Gadd joined the staff of the Home of Compassion, a nursing home, in Surrey, in February 1990. While working in the lower corridors, near the kitchens,

2 Ghosts That Ignore You

she saw a nun walking towards her up the corridor. Nuns had occupied and run the Home in former years, although none had been at the Home for some years prior to this sighting.

Elizabeth was frightened and found it hard to look at the apparition, consequently she is vague about the details of the description of the form.

She went into the kitchen to get the supper things. When she came out she saw the nun still in the corridor, and still coming towards her. It then walked straight through her, creating a touch of panic and the feeling of a 'clammy sensation'.

Despite her apprehensions, there is no suggestion of interaction with the form.[1]

The following case is similar in that there was no interaction with the ghost, but in the report below there is evidence of some interaction with the environment in the movement of the bed:

In November 1988 'Laura' stayed at the Cavendish Hotel in Harrogate. During the night she awoke and felt the bed dip next to her. It was as if someone had sat on it. She didn't at first open her eyes, but put out her hand and felt the dip in the bed. Then she opened her eyes. She was startled to find a man sitting on the edge of the bed facing away from her as if he had just got up. He was bending forwards as if putting shoes on his feet. Laura described him as shortish, wearing red-and-white striped winceyette pyjamas, oldish looking, balding with a curtain of grey hair around his ears and the back of his head. She never saw his face.

Believing that the person was real she was in the position of being a woman alone with a man in her bedroom and uncertain what course of action would be best. Before she had the opportunity to act the person stood up and walked towards the window.

19

Ghostwatching

> Then, as he neared the window, he disappeared. She had kept quiet up to that point, not knowing what would make the situation better or worse, but on his disappearance let out a healthy – and understandable – scream.
>
> Laura did not sleep for the rest of the night, and kept the light on.[2]

Similarly, take this report by the former leader of the Liberal Party, Jeremy Thorpe.

> During his days at university he was holidaying at Trethevy in Cornwall. Mr Thorpe left other guests at a dinner party to go to the bathroom. On leaving the bathroom and walking back along the passage to go downstairs he noticed a monk in a brown habit going into the bathroom. Mr Thorpe greeted him with a 'Good evening' but the monk ignored him.
>
> Mr Thorpe asked his hosts who the monk was and was told that it was the Prior. He had apparently been 'in residence' for several hundred years, following his murder in that building.
>
> Many people had seen the Prior but he had never been a trouble to guests.[3]

This lets us start our examination of this category with a proposition – the proposition that certain events can be 'recorded' in the surrounding geography and 'replayed' – rather like a videotape – when the appropriate replay button is 'pushed'. In these cases perhaps the Abbey monks, Elizabeth Gadd's nun, Laura's bedroom intruder, and Jeremy Thorpe's monk once did do what they were later seen doing by the witnesses. They might have slept in that bedroom, or walked in those corridors, or where those corridors are presently situated. Something perhaps embedded those events into the surroundings. We can speculate that the structures

2 Ghosts That Ignore You

of the buildings might be such as to take an impression – to record the events.

Admittedly this is only a theory, but is it so far-fetched? If, in the 1890s, someone had suggested that it would be possible to put a handful of iron rust on a strip of sticky tape and record voices and pictures, that person would probably have been thought of as rather strange; however, only about 50 years later, commercial video recorders using ferromagnetic materials (iron rust) started to make their appearance.

This theory can be only part of the answer at best. Otherwise every person who walked those corridors would become a 'recordings' ghost.

Therefore, there must be either some other component in the recording process or in the playback. We might surmise that it would be necessary for a broad range of physical data in addition to the stone structures – humidity, temperature and so on – to come together in the right combination. This would limit the numbers of recordings and playbacks.

However, while we have no information about the fate of the nun, or the bedroom visitor, we cannot ignore the allegation that the monk was murdered; this may be a factor.

What we can further postulate is that the emotional state of the person who is the 'ghost' might have played some part in the recording process. Perhaps the fact that he was contemplating the situation that led to his murder is some part of the process.

A report suggesting that the emotional quality of an event plays a part in such cases came from John Masters, who served in the Indian army in the 1930s, prior to Indian Independence.

> A friend of Masters who was serving in the Indian Cavalry was living in the old bungalows that had existed since before the Mutiny of 1857. One night the friend woke up, finding his room hot and airless. On the wall above his bed he could see the reflection of a bonfire

Ghostwatching

burning on the lawn outside; but when he got up to see it he could see no fire. Yet, on the wall he could still see the reflected flames flickering. Then they faded. This occurred for four nights; on the fourth night he went out on to the veranda to smoke. On the lawn he could see two 'strangely dressed figures'. He approached them, but suddenly discovered there was nothing there.

Research indicated that the garden of his bungalow had once contained another bungalow. In 1857 two soldiers from the Bengal Native Cavalry had murdered their adjutant and his family and destroyed the other building, burning the bodies of the victims.[4]

We can also see the possibility of a recording ghost 'embedded' by emotion in an incident reported from a small Lancashire village.

The witnesses lived in a semi-detached bungalow built on old farmland. They – and friends and visitors – several times saw the ghost of a young man in old brown trousers, grey jacket and muddy shoes walk through their garden and disappear at a certain point. He always walked the same route, never interacted or seemed affected by the witnesses or indeed any part of the surroundings. He was always dressed the same, always had the same expression.

Investigation seemed to suggest that he was the son of a farmer who had once owned the land. Apparently worried by some matter, he would often walk around the fields with his head down, deep in thought. Sadly, he had been unable to work out his troubles and had ended them by drowning himself in a pond that was once on the site of the point where he always disappeared.

Perhaps his emotional state helped lay down the recording.

The witnesses to this case also noticed that on his

2 Ghosts That Ignore You

several appearances he could seem on some occasions solid, at other times more translucent. We can speculate that the playback might have different strengths under different conditions, perhaps atmospherics. If so, then we can consider that qualities of the surroundings both at the time of recording and playback are a factor in this phenomenon. This would at least explain why recordings ghosts – widely reported though they are – are not an everyday occurrence. In the case of the farmer's son he was seen in October, and is listed as an 'anniversary' ghost; one that always appears at the same time. In fact anniversary ghosts are rarely so punctual, but perhaps the weather and atmospheric conditions of particular seasons are more likely than others for 'playback'.[5]

On the subject of emotion, it has been conjectured that the emotional, or other mental, states of the 'witnesses' to the ghost may be a factor. We cannot rule that out, and indeed in some ghost phenomena (examined later in this book) it seems almost certain. With recordings ghosts, however, it is not so certain. In the above case several different people saw the ghost at different times; we can suppose that they would not all have been in the same mental state.

We might, however, consider a case where the ghost was not even perceived by the witness, where in fact it was technology that 'saw' the ghost. Take, for example, the report of the ghost of the Tulip Staircase, sometimes known as the Greenwich ghost:

> The report amounts to a photograph taken on the Tulip Staircase at the Queen's House in Greenwich. A tourist, a Canadian clergyman on holiday, photographed the staircase and was surprised to discover, when the film was developed, that there appeared to be images of a figure climbing the staircase. Photographic analysis indicated that the photo was probably not the result of a

double exposure; the implication was that the camera had taken a photograph of somebody that was on the staircase at the time, though not visible to the witness at the time of taking the picture.[2]

Clearly we cannot speculate on the emotional state of the camera at the time, though we might ask ourselves if the witness's emotional state could allow for a change in the environment that the camera could detect, although the witness could not.

Ghosts of this nature appear to be keeping up with changes in technology.

> On a sunny afternoon in September 1993 a ghost was observed and recorded on surveillance video at the East Ardsley Conservative Club in Leeds. On the video, the 'phantom' figure appeared at the doorway of the club and stayed there for several minutes before fading away. The club's treasurer had seen the figure on the monitor and, thinking it was a friend, walked to the door to greet him. When he found no one there he returned to the monitor to find the figure still visible on it. The head and shoulders of the figure returned the following month and were again caught on video recording.[6]

The next case suggests that ghosts can make simple mistakes. As in the case of the camera in the above case, this ghost was recorded on machinery, reducing the dependence on the human factors of perception.

> In late October 1992 Tony Wells was asked by a family in south-east London to investigate some phenomena at their house. The mother, Carol, and her young boy of six were disturbed regularly *just before midnight* by the sounds of someone entering their flat and coming up the stairs. When they looked, there was no one there, a frightening experience for them both. As time went on

2 Ghosts That Ignore You

the phenomena increased to the point where others became aware of what was happening; on one occasion a visitor almost fell off her chair when she felt her hair tugged roughly from behind.

Tony set up an Environmental Monitoring Unit (EMU). Three sensors were plugged in; two were Passive Infra-red sensors, the third a temperature module, set to respond to extreme temperature changes. The main sensor of interest in this case was Sensor 2, an infra-red module, which was placed on the stairway. Tony and the family waited quietly from 10 p.m. to 2 a.m.; all were disappointed as midnight came and went with no sound of footsteps.

The interesting discovery came the next day on reviewing the output from the sensors. At just after five minutes to eleven, the sensors on the stairs were triggered, and continued to be triggered for several minutes.[1]

Contemporaneous notes showed that at the time the sensors were being triggered, everyone in the house was sitting quietly in the main room. Tony realised that a few days before there had been a change over from British Summer Time to Greenwich Mean Time. The implication was that the sensor had triggered at close to midnight, but midnight *British Summer Time*. The ghost had 'ignored' the changeover to Greenwich Mean Time.

Already our recordings ghosts are looking more complex. Consider a situation where not one, but hundreds, of ghosts are seen. When we are not dependent on one person's emotional state then we are forced to broaden the possibilities.

The battle of Edgehill, Warwickshire, was the first battle of the English Civil War, fought on 23 October 1642. Shortly after it had taken place, on four successive weekend nights, there were apparently many visitors to the battlefield who were able to see the event 'replay' itself. As described in a pamphlet published at the time, 'A great wonder in heaven shewing the late apparitions and prodigious noyse of war and battels, seen on Edge-Hill, neere Keinton, in Northamptonshire 1642'. King Charles I sent out a body of men to witness this event; they swore statements that they had done so.[2]

A similar report comes from Croatia. In August 1888 there were many witnesses to a three-day vision of infantry divisions marching through the skies. The images lasted for several hours each day.[7]

In these cases we have hundreds of men all apparently part of the replay. While they will have certain emotions in common – they were all engaged in battle, or military marching, after all – each of the men must have had different emotions as well. Some would have enjoyed the fight, others would have felt fear; some may have been optimistic, others pessimistic, and so on.

We are forced then to suppose that emotions of witnesses, if applicable to our study at all, seem not to be key factors in these cases, at least.

Consider a similar case to the battle of Edgehill, but one with the twist in that the witnesses are sure that no army could ever have been in the location where their spectral replay was seen.

On Midsummer Eve in 1735 a farmhand in the English Lake District looked up towards Souter Fell. He saw what appeared to be a huge army marching east to west, disappearing into a cleft in the mountainside. Souter Fell is some 900 feet high and its sides are precipices. It would have been inaccessible to an army.

On that first occasion, the owner of the farm, Mr Lancaster, did not see the army, nor believe the farm-

2 Ghosts That Ignore You

hand. A similar sighting was made exactly two years later and yet again on Midsummer Eve 1745; in both later cases by Lancaster himself. In 1745 there were 26 other witnesses with him. The group was so convinced of what they saw that the next day many of them climbed Souter Fell to look for the hoofmarks of the horses and the wheel tracks of the carriages they had seen. They found nothing. They swore statements before a magistrate confirming the sighting and their investigation.

If the sighting represents a replay then perhaps it had somehow 'shifted' its location. The geography of the area is not likely to have significantly changed from the time when the original army was on the move.[2]

We have to be careful, though; sightings such as the above cases could as easily not be examples of 'ghost' phenomena at all. The observers could have been witnessing some kind of mirage of a distant event.

One 'ghost army' sighting, however, seemed to produce a range of strange effects.

In November 1960 Mrs Dorothy Strong was a passenger in a taxi at Otterburn in Northumberland; the location of a fourteenth-century battle. Like others had stated before her, she reported seeing a phantom army. 'Suddenly the engine died, the fare-meter went haywire and the taxi was as if it was being forced against an invisible wall,' she said. 'The soldiers seemed to close in on us and then fade into thin air.'[8]

Electrical effects are commonly associated with the paranormal; watches stopping, recording equipment failing, and so on. In Chapter 8, Mike Lewis of the Association for the Scientific Study of Anomalous Phenomena (ASSAP) reports his own electrical effects during research.

Vehicle stoppages, and vehicle interference reports, are

commonly reported in association with UFO reports. Here was a report with similar phenomena, but within a ghost context. Did the 'presence' of the ghost army affect the taxi's electrics? Did some part of the taxi's electrics cause the 'replay' of the spectral army to appear? Or did some third 'force' cause both the electrical effects and the spectral replay?

If we are to take these reports of spectral armies as valid, then we might consider a quite different interpretation. Not an embedded recording being replayed, but a window in time (and perhaps space) where a person sees into the reality of another time or location. Once again, it is only a speculation, but there have been many reports that call for such an interpretation.

A simple example would be the following report of an artist at the Palace of Versailles.

> While post-war repair work was being carried out, the artist entered a state room which he described as most beautifully furnished and hung with tapestry. Curtains were draped with silks and one of the chairs in the room he described as gilded. He left the room and went downstairs into the grounds. He later realised that he had been in that room every night for the past week and that it had always been totally featureless, no tapestries, curtains or furniture. The implication seemed to be that he had had a vision of the past.[2]

The Swiss psychologist Carl Jung reported a similar scenery 'timeslip' in Ravenna, Italy. On a visit to the tomb of the Empress Galla Placidia who died in AD 458 he became aware of a mild blue light filling the room from no apparent source. In place of the windows that Jung had seen on an earlier visit there seemed to be four huge blue mosaic designs depicting maritime events. These reflected a promise by the Empress in life that if she was protected while at sea she would build the

2 Ghosts That Ignore You

basilica of San Giovanni as thanks to the gods, adorning it with mosaics depicting the perils of the sea. Jung's claim was apparently supported by a companion travelling with him.[9]

Reports of phantom scenery have arisen in a wide variety of circumstances.

> In October 1926 Ruth Wynne and Miss Allington walked from Roughan to the village of Bradfield St George. As they approached a road they could see an old brick wall surrounding a Georgian-style house. They saw large trees in its garden. Miss Wynne described the house as having a stucco front and Georgian-style windows.
> About four months later the pair revisited the area but could not find the wall or the house. They tried several times to find them, and never succeeded.[10]

Clearly misperception, confusion, even daydreaming may play some part in these reports.

> In June 1933 Mr and Mrs Pye were travelling by bus from Wadebridge to Boscastle, in Cornwall. Outside Boscastle the bus stopped and both Mr and Mrs Pye looked at a building, perhaps a guesthouse, beside them. They described a terrace set out with tables, and striped umbrellas.
> On arriving in Boscastle Mrs Pye walked back down the road to find the building. By bus and on foot, both Mr and Mrs Pye were not able to find it again.
> However, in 1962 a Miss Scott-Eliott examined the road and located a small private hotel surrounded by a 12-foot wall and hedge; it could be seen only from one point. At the time of the Pyes' visit the building had been a private house, but the family and guests often took tea on the drive in good weather. Miss Scott-Eliott

also located a café at the foot of the hill which had striped umbrellas at the time of the Pyes' visit. Perhaps the Pyes saw these two views and constructed the rest of their beliefs about the building.[11]

Perhaps imagery, even belief systems, play a part in the visions that are seen.

When Mr and Mrs Swain and their sons were holidaying near Beaulieu Abbey in the New Forest they saw a lake. At the centre was a boulder, embedded in it was a sword. The view must have been remarkably similar to the image in the legend of King Arthur. The Swains have been unable to find the lake since that time despite over 250 visits to the site in the years since.[12]

The cases of 'phantom scenery' described here have been 'inactive'; postcard-like imagery with no obvious movement or action reported. Many timeslips, however, include action by the 'ghosts' seen, and even interaction with the witnesses.

Psychometrist Alice Pollock was in Henry VIII's room in Leeds Castle, in Kent. She was a relative of the family living there; this room was the one her parents had used when they stayed there. At one point the room suddenly changed, losing its modern attributes and becoming cold and bare. The fireplace, now with burning logs, seemed to have changed position. A tall woman in a white dress was walking up and down, seemingly in anguish and great concentration. The history of the room suggests that it had been the prison of Queen Joan of Navarre, the stepmother of Henry V who had been accused of witchcraft by her husband.[13]

'Eleanor Ford' told us of a phantom scenery experience she had in 1988. It was very similar to Alice Pollock's experience.

2 Ghosts That Ignore You

Eleanor and her friend Sally were exploring the Australian outback, near Adelaide. They stopped in the Paxton cottages, in Burra, for an overnight stay. The cottages had originally been built in 1849 as homes for the copper miners of the area and had recently been restored and refurbished.

Eleanor and Sally took cottage number 15. Eleanor described the warmth and homeliness of the place. Perhaps of significance, the friends spent some time discussing what life must have been like for the miners nearly 150 years ago; as Eleanor said, 'We felt we had stepped back in history.'

That night they dined out, did some sightseeing, and returned late to the cottages. As they approached their cottage they saw that the lights were on; Sally confirmed that she had left them on when they had gone out. Eleanor got out of the car – Sally was still sitting in it – and went to the cottage. She looked in at the window. She could see, sitting on a couch in the room, a woman of slight build talking and smiling to someone out of her view on the other side of the room. Then the woman turned directly towards Eleanor and she smiled: Eleanor was sure that she was smiling directly at her, knowing that she was looking in the window. She felt embarrassed at being a 'Peeping Tom'.

Eleanor looked away to check that it was the right cottage. It was. She looked back. Then she realised that the curtains were drawn – she had closed them before leaving the cottage – and that it was impossible to see in. She checked for reflections, but that could not apparently account for the images she had seen.

When she and Sally entered the cottage the warmth had gone. She described 'a gently chilling sensation entered my being, my feet, my limbs, my body, completely possessing me, yet at the same time causing no fear, no apprehension, just the cold.'

Eleanor examined the incident long and hard. She

considered whether the image was one from her own youth, and was sure that it was not. Even so, she felt herself asking if she and the mysterious woman had ever met before. 'I felt humble and certainly privileged that her spirit had revealed itself to me and I had glimpsed a scene from the past.'[1]

In this case we have one of very few 'timeslips' that seem to imply interaction; the woman on the couch seemed to react to Eleanor. Yet we cannot be certain of that; even given a 'reality' for this experience, she might have been reacting to a face at the window years ago.

One of the most famous cases is the report of Charlotte Anne Elizabeth Moberly and Eleanor Frances Jourdain at the Petit Trianon.

> They were colleagues, not friends; they set out on 10 August 1901 to visit the Palace of Versailles (the location of a reported timeslip in a case described above). At 4 o'clock in the afternoon Miss Moberly suggested visiting the Petit Trianon, a small house and gardens presented to Marie Antoinette by Louis XVI in 1774.
>
> They got somewhat lost, and therefore their route to the Petit Trianon was fairly circuitous. It took them around the gardener's cottage, theatre and other areas. Both ladies experienced feelings of depression and dreariness. Whether this is related to the phenomenon of 'phantom scenery' or 'timeslip' stories is unclear but it arises in many such reports. As they passed the Temple de l'Amour they saw a man described as being of 'repulsive appearance' sitting on the balustrade. Some theorists have suggested he matched the appearance of King Louis himself.
>
> They came to the rear of the Petit Trianon building. Miss Moberly saw a lady dressed for the summer sitting on the lawn below the terrace. On reaching the terrace a young man directed them to the front of the house

2 Ghosts That Ignore You

and walked around with them until they found the entrance of Allée des deux Trianons.

In November 1901, when the two ladies were talking about their visit, it seemed curious to them that only one of them had seen the lady in a summer dress sitting on the lawn outside the building. They wrote independent accounts of their experiences to see how closely they matched.

Miss Jourdain came across a story that Marie Antoinette was often seen sitting outside the Petit Trianon on a certain day in August. In her account sent to Miss Moberly, Miss Jourdain suggested that Miss Moberly's sighting had been of Marie Antoinette.

Miss Jourdain revisited the scene on 2 January 1902. She examined the Temple de l'Amour, which she decided was not the building that they had first seen, although at the time they had believed it to have been. Miss Jourdain experienced the same depression as she had on the earlier visit. During her walk she saw two labourers loading a cart; she glanced away, glanced back, and the cart was gone. During a walk in the woods she saw no visions, but reported hearing the rustling of silk dresses.

Between 1902 and 1904 Miss Jourdain repeatedly revisited the Trianon, often in the company of her pupils. In a letter to Miss Moberly she made the comment that the topography of the area was never the same as on that earlier visit they had made together.

On 4 July 1904 the two ladies visited Petit Trianon again and Miss Moberly confirmed what Miss Jourdain's letters had told her; that the topography was different, distances seemed shorter, the grounds were less developed and some features were not visible.

Other people reported similar experiences in the area: a woman in a gold dress was seen by a Mr and Mrs Wilkinson in October 1949; a man and woman in antiquated peasant costume drawing a small cart behind them were seen in 1938 by a Mrs Elizabeth Hatton; in 1910 a Mr and Mrs Gregory told how when entering Petit Trianon they had passed a group of small houses and had seen a woman shaking a cloth from the window. When they returned, after reading Moberly and Jourdain's book of their experiences, they could not find the houses they had earlier seen.[2]

Researcher Hilary Evans in his book *Visions, Apparitions, Alien Visitors* states that there is 'good reason to think that percipients were right in believing they had somehow shared a vision of the gardens as they had been in the eighteenth century, possibly at the outbreak of the French Revolution.'

Evans asks the question 'Were they transported like time travellers back to that time or did they somehow become involved in a "replay" of events at the time which were brought forward to the 1901 and 1902 period where they were?'

Michael Coleman, however, in *The Ghosts of the Trianon*, concludes that the pair experienced nothing unusual. He suggests that 'the combined effects of the warm weather, their walking and perhaps unaccustomed wine at lunch, may have given rise to feelings of oppression after entering the grounds'. He believes that 'when we consider the authors' researches, their methods and procedures strongly suggest that they were more concerned to collect evidence to confirm their original interpretation of their experiences than to expose the story to a critical examination. It seems that the notion that they had encountered the shades of Marie Antoinette and her courtiers and staff (with the appropriate contemporary scenery) stemmed from the tale with which Mlle Ménégoz regaled Miss Jourdain and of which Miss Jourdain wrote immediately to Miss Moberly. (Mlle Ménégoz first suggested the vision of Marie Antoinette.) From this point onwards – even allowing for the fact that they had limited free time to devote to their enquiries – their activities seem as if they were calculated to avoid arriving at a normal explanation of the adventure.'

2 Ghosts That Ignore You

In October 1916 Edith Olivier was travelling from Devizes to Swindon. When she neared the famous stone circle at Avebury, she interrupted her journey and entered the area of the standing stones with the huge earth mound at the centre of the site. From that vantage point she saw that a village-like fair was under way. She described the megalith stones and surrounding cottages lit by flares and torches from booths and shows at the fair. She saw swing-boats, coconut shies, and a casual crowd of villagers wandering around the stalls and stands. Some years later she discovered that the annual fair at Avebury had been abolished over 60 years prior to her seeing it. Moreover, her vision appears to have included megaliths that had disappeared sometime prior to the turn of the nineteenth century.[14]

Here though, the witness seems to have seen many people at play, interacting with their environment into which she was either looking or, if we stretch our speculations, she was transported in some way.

We can look at this question of being transported in a different way. The traditional view of a recordings ghost, or timeslip, is that some sort of glimpse between times is achieved. However, there is an interesting possibility offered by a claim made by George Russell, a friend of the poet W. B. Yeats.

He was waiting for a friend inside the remains of a ruined chapel. Suddenly he saw the chapel in another time, when it was in use. He described a small crowd of people kneeling at the altar and an abbot or bishop standing nearby, holding a crozier. Behind the abbot was a boy carrying a vessel of some description. Russell appears to have seen the scene as if he was a part of it but there is no indication that anyone in the scene noticed anything amiss about him.[15]

Ghostwatching

Had he slipped *into* the body of someone who was there at the time? Was he a ghost in their time?

Finally, we might consider the conclusion of one witness, Lucie Butler. She had the experience of a recordings-type ghost; her comments on its 'reality' give some idea of the way in which a witness perceives such an experience.

> She saw a form in her bedroom one night. She had been asleep in bed and woke to see a figure in a white outfit, which she described as a sari, walk across the end of her bedroom to the door.
>
> She felt fear; fear because there was something in her bedroom that wasn't supposed to be there. But she also felt fairly peaceful. After all, she said, 'What was that ghost going to do to me? It was not going to violate me. It was just passing through.' She did not think that the form had an interest in her bedroom; but thought that her bedroom was just in its way to wherever it was going. It did not pay any attention to the environment it was passing through.
>
> As she put it: 'I got the impression it was no more of an intrusion than people on the TV. Real, but only to a certain degree.'[1]

In the later sections on ghostwatching we suggest that it is the vigils which offer the best opportunities of seeing 'ghosts that ignore you'. The section on developing your own psychic abilities may enhance your chances, as we believe that the mental state of the witnesses may play a part, if not in the 'replay' of a ghost, then perhaps of perceiving the replay.

Timeslips, frankly, have never been seen to order to our knowledge. Collection of as much data as possible about these events may enable future researchers to be in the right place, at the right time, when they happen. For the moment they remain spontaneous and unpredictable.

3 Ghosts That Interact with You

IN THE PREVIOUS chapter we examined ghosts that ignore you; ghosts that have visible form, but no obvious intelligent presence. In other words, they may be formed by some as yet unknown process, but offer no evidence of any form of survival of spirit or intelligence after death. In this chapter we look at a different set of ghosts; those that *do* seem to have intelligence in their action, purpose in their presence. They have many similar characteristics in appearance to the previous types of ghost, but in fact they may be a quite different phenomenon.

Take for example this simple case:

In February 1932 Mrs Edwards and her eldest daughter, Mary, watched Samuel Bull, Mrs Edwards' father, walk to her bedridden mother's bedside and place his hand on his wife's forehead. They were shocked; Samuel Bull had died eight months previously.

Sightings of Samuel Bull were made by several members of the family. One five-year-old recognised him as 'Grandpa Bull'.

On one occasion the apparition – of normal, solid appearance – was visible for a continuous half-hour.[16]

Here there is *almost* no interaction – a feature of the ghosts in Chapter 2. But the interaction we do have – the figure sought out his former wife and placed his hand on her

Ghostwatching

forehead – suggests purpose and intent, perhaps even compassion.

Samuel Bull had been dead for eight months. However, many such interactive ghosts are known as 'crisis' or 'death' apparitions, appearing at, or near, the time of the person's death. Again, they exhibit apparent awareness of the surroundings they find themselves which suggests at least a survival of consciousness or 'spirit'. The following cases are examples which show this interaction:

> Sir Charles Frank, Professor of Physics at the University of Bristol, recalled his wife's Finnish grandmother waking up to see her half-brother standing by her bed, saying: 'I have come to say goodbye'. She soon after received a letter telling her that her half-brother had committed suicide at the time that she had seen his apparition.[3]

> On 19 June 1958 Colonel D. Pritchard was in the pavilion bar at Lord's. The England–New Zealand Test cricket match was about to begin. Standing alone at the bar, just yards from Pritchard, was Douglas Jardine, a cricketer most famous for the televised 'body line' cricket tour. Pritchard knew Jardine well, and regarded him as of distinctive appearance, describing him as 'impossible to mistake'. Having caught each other's eyes they raised glasses to each other. When Pritchard had excused himself from the company he was with, he went to seek out Jardine. He could not find him.
>
> Just before the start of play it was announced that Jardine had died the previous day, in Switzerland.[3]

The writer Sabine Baring-Gould recounted the story of his mother's sighting of her brother, Henry.

> On 3 January 1840 his mother had been sitting at a table reading the Bible and looked up to see, on the

3 Ghosts That Interact with You

other side of the table, an apparition of her brother, Henry.

Henry should have been serving in the Navy in the South Atlantic at the time. Baring-Gould's mother recognised straight away that this was an apparition at death. She noted down the event in her Bible at the time.

Over a month later, the family received news that Henry had died on that date, near Ascension Island.[17]

Wilfred Owen, famous for his poetry of the Great War, was killed on 2 November 1918. His family received the news on Armistice Day, the 11th. Wilfred's brother, Harold, later had a vision of him, though at the time did not know he was dead. At that time Harold was serving aboard ship near West Africa. As he recorded in his autobiography (*Journal from Obscurity*), 'I felt horribly flat. Everything else seemed flat.' He was certain something was amiss, and even considered sending an enquiring telegram.

A few days later, Harold was in his cabin; he suddenly saw Wilfred sitting in a chair, dressed in a khaki uniform. He instantly knew, of course, that he could not really be there, but asked, 'Wilfred, how did you get here?' Whether or not Wilfred was truly an interactive ghost is debatable; he did not overtly respond – neither speaking nor moving – but Harold felt his eyes were pleading with him.

Suddenly Wilfred broke into a broad smile, and this gave Harold some sort of comfort. Harold looked away briefly; when he looked back Wilfred was gone.

Harold knew, with absolute certainty, that his brother was dead: 'What I found impossible to explain was this self-existent awareness of mine, unrelated to any facts; I did not try. I accepted his death without hope and without pretence. My awareness was so profound that knowledge could not be denied.'[18]

Ghostwatching

Although there was a time difference between death and the vision, it appears that this may be a result of Harold's preoccupation. For that interim period he felt 'flat', and had the vision when he was alone and able to contemplate his thoughts.

The writer Ngaio Marsh lived in New Zealand with her family; her father's brother, Uncle Reggie, lived in England. One night her mother woke, and told her husband, Reggie's brother, 'Reggie is about and I think he wants us.' She noted her feelings at that time.

Some weeks later a letter from England informed them that Reggie had died at exactly the same moment that Ngaio Marsh's mother had woken and made the note on the opposite side of the world.[19]

On 13 March 1928, Captain W. G. R. Hinchcliffe, together with Elsie Mackay, the daughter of Lord Inchcape of the P & O shipping empire, set out to make the first East-to-West transatlantic aeroplane flight. They never made it, and were presumed to have crashed somewhere near the Azores.

In mid-July of that year Emilie Hinchcliffe, the captain's wife, was wakened by the sound of heavy footsteps walking along the hall outside her bedroom. She assumed it was one of a number of guests that she had staying with her at the time, but they made clear it was not, and that they too had heard the footsteps.

During a visit to the famous medium, Eileen Garrett, Emilie asked whether or not Hinchcliffe had been in the house. Through Garrett her husband apparently told her, 'I am still about the house. I nearly touched the red travelling clock by your bed the other night but was afraid of frightening you.' Of the specific time she had heard the footsteps Garrett, now answering for the captain, said, 'Yes, it was 4 o'clock one morning. He wanted to give an implication he was starting on an

3 **Ghosts That Interact with You**

early morning flight as he used to do in the summer; he was trying to imply this. Don't have too much to do with the subject of the psychic. He just wants to help you while there is need.'

Apparently Hinchcliffe's ghost also helped his wife by assisting in locating lost documents.[20]

We said in the introduction that there were reports by 'famous' people whose careers would hardly be enhanced by reporting sightings of ghosts. The lack of ulterior motive, and the real possibility of adverse publicity, suggest such reports are genuine. One recent report comes from Lord Jenkins's autobiography *A Life at the Centre*.

In 1977 when he had a vivid dream about his long-time friend and colleague Tony Crosland, Lord Jenkins was aware that Crosland was very ill, having been told so by Denis Healey on Monday 17 February 1977. On Wednesday the 19th he was told by David Owen that 'he regarded Tony as morally and mentally dead'.

Crosland died on Saturday 22 February, and Lord Jenkins's account is quite clear: 'When the final news arrived its impact was not diminished, the more so because of a strange coincidence which I recorded at the time. I was then in Rome, on my inaugural visit to Italy: I awoke about 6.30, having had a vivid dream about Tony being present and his saying in an unmistakable, clear, rather calm voice, "No, I am perfectly all right, I'm going to die but I am perfectly all right." Then at about eight o'clock we had a telephone call from the BBC saying that he had died that morning, curiously enough at almost exactly the same moment that I awoke from my dream about him.'[21]

There are a number of cases that suggest clues to the cause of 'apparitions', based on reports of apparitions of people not dead. In *Phantasms of the Living* there are several such cases. The following two are typical:

> Case No 348; from a Mrs Elgee of Bedford. In November 1864 she had been detained in Cairo on her way to India.
>
> Because of travelling difficulties, Mrs Elgee and a companion had to stay overnight in what seems from her description to have been a seedy, third-rate hotel. Rather nervous about staying there, Mrs Elgee and her companion locked themselves in their room and put a chair against one half of the double doors, and a large settee against the other half. Mrs Elgee also placed a travelling bag on the chair in such a way that if the door was disturbed then the bag would fall off and alert them, and hid the door key under her pillow. Because it was rather hot, they left open the windows to a private balcony; they were not too worried about intruders from there because they were three storeys up. They then retired to bed.
>
> Suddenly Mrs Elgee woke from a sound sleep with the impression that somebody had called her. Sitting up she saw to her astonishment an old and very valued friend whom she knew to be in England. She remembered saying: 'Good gracious! How did you come here?' So clear was the figure, that she remembered every detail of his dress, even to three onyx shirt studs which he wore. He took a step and then pointed across the room to her companion who was also by now sitting up in bed – and looking at the intruder in horror.
>
> Her friend from England then seemed to shake his head and retreat further and further away until he seemed to sink through the door where the settee stood. The next thing she remembered was being woken up by sunshine coming through the window. She then began to recall her experience of the night.
>
> Not sure whether she had actually had a dream, and

3 Ghosts That Interact with You

remembering that her companion also seemed to be aware of what had happened, she resolved not to say anything, unless her companion did. She then examined her security precautions which seemed to be intact.

Her companion then awoke, and remarked that their security had not been much use. On questioning her, the companion replied, 'Why, that man who was in the room this morning must have got in somehow.' Her companion then described the night's incident in detail.

Because of the vivid nature of the incident, Mrs Elgee was sure that her friend must have died but four years later she questioned him about what might have happened on that night.

After some reflection, he remembered that he had been worrying about whether he should take a job appointment which had been offered him. It seemed that after making allowances for the different time zones, at the moment Mrs Elgee and her friend had seen his form, he had been sitting in front of the fire back in England wishing Mrs Elgee had been there to help resolve his dilemma.[22]

So the apparition had in fact wanted to see and share something with the person who 'saw' it. Yet we have evidence that a third, unconnected, person also saw the apparition. The implication is that the 'appearance' was in some way real, albeit not 'known' as such even to the person who was the 'ghost'; he had only a vague feeling of need.

Here is another case from *Phantasms of the Living*:

In August 1883 a Mr Algernon Joy wrote a letter to the SPR detailing this case. He had been walking in a country lane near Cardiff when he was attacked by two men who knocked him down.

Two days later he received a letter from a friend, 'A', asking what had been happening to him at about 4.30 p.m. two days previously. This was exactly the time that Mr Joy had been attacked. The letter went on to say that 'A' had been passing Mr Joy's club and been thinking of him when he heard footsteps and turned around to see Mr Joy lay a hand on him, saying: 'Go home, old fellow, I've been hurt. You will get a letter from me in the morning telling you all about it.' According to 'A', Mr Joy then immediately vanished.[22]

Again, then, we have one participant in the drama aware of the other. The stressful circumstances of one, and the other's thinking about him, imply some sort of communication between them as in the previous case cited.

Sometimes a case arises that forces us to consider either the motives of the 'ghost', or at least allows us to ask just how much control over its 'reappearance' the ghost has. Such a case arose following the death in March 1948 of the world-famous ghost-hunter/researcher Harry Price, founder of the National Laboratory of Psychical Research.

> At around that time a Swedish man, Erson, was in hospital undergoing treatment. He saw a figure appear beside his bed speaking English, a language Erson did not understand. The figure appeared so frequently that Erson learnt some English, and conversed a little with the spirit-vision.
>
> Erson spoke about this to one of his doctors who was interested in psychical research. It was the doctor who identified the figure as that of Harry Price.[23]

Price, who presumably had many friends and colleagues who would have welcomed his reappearance if only for their own research purposes, therefore seems to have materialised in a foreign country, to a stranger who didn't know him and who had no knowledge of his field of work and interest, and where he and his subject were divided by a language barrier.

Was this selection by choice? Did Price have some obscure reason for wanting to make that contact? Or are the con-

3 Ghosts That Interact with You

ditions of 'coming through' dependent on a number of factors, perhaps to do with both the 'ghost' and the percipient, which dictate the circumstances of reappearance?

Such contact with a stranger is fairly rare; most crisis apparitions appear to family and friends. However, there is a whole group of interactive ghosts – known as 'interactive protectors' – that seem to seek out 'strangers', but with a particular purpose in mind. They seem to want to watch over them. Even within that class, there is a sub-group with characteristics all their own – the phantom hitchhikers.

On the stretch of the A38 near Taunton in Somerset, in England, one phantom hitchhiker, a man in a long grey overcoat, has been reported several times.

In 1958, lorry driver Harry Unsworth reported meeting the hitchhiker a few times. On the first occasion Unsworth picked up the man during a heavy rainstorm at three o'clock in the morning. They travelled some four miles together, and the hitchhiker spent most of that time describing the dangers and accidents of that stretch of road.

Unsworth picked up the same passenger several times, often in the rain. That November the situation became more complex, more mysterious. Having picked up the hitchhiker Unsworth took him to a location he specified, and at his request waited while he collected some belongings. However, he waited in vain; the man did not reappear. Unsworth drove off and continued along the road. Twenty minutes and three miles later Unsworth saw the figure again. This was a mystery to Unsworth; he was certain that the man could not have got a lift – there had been no other vehicles – and it seemed unlikely that the man could have walked or run.

Somewhat peeved, Unsworth tried to drive past the hitchhiker, but the man in the grey overcoat threw himself in front of the lorry. Unsworth, believing he must have hit him, stopped, got out of the cab and looked back down the road. To his shock he saw the hitchhiker standing in the road, gesticulating wildly. Then he suddenly disappeared.

Local newspapers in more recent years have included reports of the same figure at that location: in August 1970 one woman had to swerve to avoid a collision with the figure, but found that when she stopped to shout at him he had disappeared; and a motorcyclist reported crashing as a result of the apparition.[24]

In January 1976, near Bagnères in France, two men were driving somewhat recklessly, seeing just how fast they could drive the car which one of them had just bought. They saw a woman hitchhiker, and stopped to offer her a lift.

It was a two-door car; the passenger had to get out of the car and push the back of the front seat forward so that the woman could get into the back of the car. The passenger then pushed the seat into place and sat back in the car. The woman was 'sealed' into the rear of the car, unable to leave without either of the two men being disturbed.

When they set off they resumed their fast driving. The woman warned the drivers of their folly: 'Look out, fellows, there've been a lot of accidents in the bends you are just coming to – I know all about them.' They took the hint, and slowed down.

A bit later, one of the men called back to the hitchhiker, without turning round, 'You see, Madame, other people may kill themselves here, but we got by all right.'

The woman did not reply. The two men looked round to speak to her. The rear seat was empty; the woman had disappeared. She had apparently left the back seat of a two-door car, travelling at high speed, without the front-seat occupants noticing.[24]

3 Ghosts That Interact with You

One of the most famous 'locations' of phantom hitchhiker reports is Blue Bell Hill. It was the subject of an investigation in 1993 that Tony Wells took part in, under the direction of a colleague, Dave Thomas (see also Chapter 13).

At around midnight on 13 July 1974, Maurice Goodenough was driving on Blue Bell Hill between Maidstone and Chatham when, on the road, he saw a girl, apparently about ten years old and wearing a white blouse, socks and a skirt: she had seemingly appeared from nowhere in front of the car.

Goodenough braked hard, skidded, but still hit the girl. He stopped, got out of the car, and examined the wounded, bleeding girl he found there. She was injured, but not too severely. He did not move her far, no doubt cautious of what injuries she might have. He put her to the side of the road, wrapped her in a blanket and drove to Rochester police station to report the incident and get help. The police returned with him; the blanket was there, but they could find no trace of the girl, and no bloodstains.

If the girl's injuries were not serious she could have left the scene and gone to her home, or she might have been helped by some passer-by. However, no trace or report of her was found afterwards.[2]

From the midst of the area of England with the highest number of paranormal incidents – the 'Wiltshire Triangle' it is sometimes called – come frequent reports of a famous phantom hitchhiker, seen on a small road from Frome to Nunney, some ten miles from the UFO and corn-circle 'focus' of Warminster.

'Brian' was driving on that road in August 1977. He stopped to give a hitchhiker a lift; the hitchhiker got into the back seat of the car and Brian locked the doors. During the drive there was very little chat between the two; even less when Brian discovered that – in an echo of Bagnères – the man had disappeared from the moving car.

Brian reported the incident to Frome police station and got himself breathalysed for his efforts. He was sober, if somewhat distraught and disorientated.

The police admitted of similar incidents – 'We have had people coming here in a state of virtual hysteria.'

Rather as in the case of Harry Unsworth, Brian became one of very few 'repeated' witnesses to phantom hitchhikers; in his second 'encounter' he skidded to avoid a figure standing in the road, hitting an object on the verge nearby. On examination he could find no trace of the figure.

There are many speculations about the identity of the Frome–Nunney hitchhiker: a victim of Judge Jeffreys' public hangings nearby; an American serviceman killed in a car crash, and a husband wrongly hanged for his wife's murder, to name but three.[24]

In August 1991 John Spencer discussed these reports with a policewoman at Frome police station. There had apparently been no reports in the two and half years that that WPC had been stationed there, though she knew of the legend.

These reports seem to suggest that certain ghosts have decided to take on a mission, to protect travellers on the road by using various forms of warnings. The warnings seem basically divided into two categories – the friendly hitchhiker that gets a lift, gives a lecture, and leaves; and the type that 'demonstrates' the dangers of fast driving by setting him- or herself up as an accident by way of providing a frightening example.

There are, of course, a great many problems with the logic of this speculation; and indeed with the logic of phantom hitchhikers generally. First, in the case of Unsworth and Brian, we seem to be looking more at a 'haunting' in the sense that the witnesses seem to have been picked on more than once. Unless we speculate that somehow those witnesses

3 Ghosts That Interact with You

did not learn their lesson we would have to ask why these protective ghosts expended their efforts on the same person instead of attending to a larger number of people. Secondly, if we assume that the aim of the phantom was to give warnings – and that is the classic belief about phantom hitchhikers – then the logic breaks down when the hitchhiker actually causes a crash: Brian crashed his car avoiding the figure.

Before we look at cases that complicate the subject further, we should examine the question of just how 'real' the hitchhikers seem to be.

When a person gets in a car there is almost inevitably a measurable movement as the car absorbs the weight and 'bounces' on its suspension. The fact that drivers do not immediately notice anything amiss with these reports suggests that they subconsciously register 'normal' responses to the incidents, at least until the inevitable 'disappearance' of the guest. This suggests weight – mass – on the part of the phantom, at least for part of the time of the encounter. Three cases indicate conflicting evidence about this:

In 1978, South African Army Corporal Dawie Van Jaarsveld was riding a motorbike to Louterwater on the Barrandas–Willowmore road, near Uniondale. Seeing a hitchhiker, an attractive brunette in dark trousers and a blue top, the corporal stopped to give her a lift. He gave her a spare crash helmet and an earplug so that she could listen to a radio, as he was doing.

After a few miles the corporal was alerted by a bumping feeling indicating some change in the motorbike's load; when he looked back to the pillion seat, the girl had gone. Not only was there no trace of the girl on the road behind him, but the spare crash helmet was strapped to the bike.

Cynthia Hind, a diligent and energetic investigator, verified directly with the corporal that he had gone to a café in Uniondale; the café's proprietress confirmed that the corporal had been in a distracted state of mind.[2]

In this case we therefore have the suggestion of 'real' weight and mass on the part of the hitchhiker; when she 'left' the bike skewed momentarily as the load shifted.

There had been a phantom hitchhiker report two years earlier which also suggested strange characteristics on the part of the phantom.

> In May 1976 Anton Le Grange met a woman so similarly dressed it suggests the same phantom. She also disappeared from the car during the drive, at speed. However, in this case Le Grange heard a hideous scream from inside the car and saw the right rear door of the car swing open in a manner suggesting it was being deliberately opened by the car's occupant; but no one was visible. To add even more mystery to the report, the car was being followed by a police constable who apparently also saw the door open.[2]

In the third case, however, there is some suggestion that the hitchhiker had no mass at all, but the evidence is conflicting.

> On 12 October 1979 Roy Fulton was driving home through Stanbridge in Bedfordshire. He turned from Peddar's Lane on to Station Road. The street-lights ended a hundred yards or so away from that point.
>
> Fulton saw a figure hitchhiking, and he pulled up. He could see the figure in the headlights of his mini van; dark jumper, trousers and an open, white collared shirt. The figure opened the van door, and silently got in. Fulton asked him where he was going; he did not reply except to point up the road.
>
> (*At this point Fulton has not registered any 'abnormalities'; presumably he noticed that the van 'dipped' when the hitchhiker got in.*)

3 Ghosts That Interact with You

They drove for a while at at least forty miles an hour; then Fulton turned to offer the hitchhiker a cigarette. He was gone. Fulton stopped the van, looked for the hitchhiker and couldn't find him and apparently left the scene in fear – he 'gripped the wheel and drove like hell'. He reported the incident to the Dunstable police but there was no meaningful action they could take, given they had no crime, no body, in fact nothing to investigate.[2]

Fulton was sure that the interior light of the car had not turned on, which it would have done if the door had been opened. It seemed therefore that the passenger had not opened the door to get out, as was reported in, say, the Le Grange case. There is also no suggestion that the passenger could have got into the back of the van and concealed himself; mini-vans do not allow for that degree of movement without alerting the driver.

If the hitchhiker did not open the door then he must have disappeared from within the vehicle, if Fulton's report is accurate. That would imply that, if the hitchhiker had mass – as indicated by other cases – then he took up space in the van which would otherwise have been filled with air. When he disappeared he should have left a vacuum into which the air should have rushed; Fulton should have noticed a movement of air in the vehicle, or even sounds. But as he did not the implication is that there was no mass; if so, then why did Fulton not recognise something amiss when the passenger climbed into the car?

In fact these cases probably lead no nearer to fully understanding ghosts *per se*; they might, however, go some way to helping us understand the way people perceive ghosts.

Phantom hitchhikers have many of the characteristics of urban legend. They are widely reported and their stories retold, yet the witnesses rarely come forward except in a few cases such as those above. The phantoms themselves are rarely identified, and never with certainty: in the Uniondale case the witness was held to have identified the phantom as Maria Charlotte Roux from a photograph shown to him. She was a 22-year-old who had been killed ten years prior to the encounter. In most cases there are often 'candidates' but rarely specific identifications.

We must also ask ourselves why we have such a specific form of 'protecting' ghost. Accidents happen in all sorts of places, under all sorts of circumstances, to all sorts of people. Why should drivers get their own special form of protection? Why should the victims of car accidents have any more need to return and warn others of the dangers than, say, the victims of industrial accidents, household accidents and so on?

The answer might lie in two aspects of the car: its own mythology and driving circumstances.

The Cult of the Car is an accepted, if ill-defined, phenomenon. The car represents a driver's private domain, an extension of ego. The passive and tranquil Mr Walker, becoming Mr Wheeler when he gets into the driving seat of a car, often seems to undergo a personality change that would be the envy of Jekyll and Hyde. Children are often said hardly to recognise their fathers when they see them driving, and men and women have more arguments in cars about (usually) male driving habits caused by one-upmanship, overtly macho behaviour, and so on. Because of the security offered by a locked car, it provides for some a way of striking out at the world from a position of safety. It fulfils Clausewitz's first, basic requirement of warfare: a secure base from which to operate.

Drivers see themselves as overly persecuted by the police; that the police seem to have identified the Cult of the Car and reacted with oppression. Certainly no other invention in human history seems to have generated more emotion; and that must be part of the reason for the phantom hitchhiker legend. It relates to that area of our lives that we already regard as special.

3 Ghosts That Interact with You

The mythology of the car might well be part of the way in which the hitchhiker legend works, but the circumstances of driving are probably significant as well. Drivers are subject to the monotony of driving, particularly at night. So often the apparitions are seen at a significant point; when the driver might be 'released' from the 'trance-like' altered state of consciousness that highway hypnosis is held to induce. There are similarities to coming out of the sleep state; it is at this time that hallucination and misperception are most likely.

Take for example this report of the sighting of a (fairly traditional) highwayman.

> On the night of 28 January 1967, John Watson, his mother, and a navigator were driving in a car rally at Belvoir Castle, south of Denton, when, *as the car rounded a bend*, the driver saw a dark, horse-mounted figure about to cross his path. He braked to avoid a collision. The figure was dressed in the traditional highwayman garb of tricorn hat and cloak. Only the driver saw the apparition.
>
> In September of the following year Watson was told by a colleague, Pete Shenton, that he too had seen the same figure. As in Watson's case there had been others in the car, but only the driver had seen the figure.[25]

In both cases the highwayman disappeared when the car was stopped. There have been other reports of the figure in that area — legend has probably played its part in people's perceptions.

It is possible that the drivers alone saw the apparition because of the degree of their concentration, which might have created something of an 'altered state of consciousness'. The passengers might have been more relaxed, less intense.

Alternatively, perhaps the highway hypnosis could create a state where a genuine external event can be perceived by that degree of altered state of consciousness.

Ghostwatching

It is interesting that the majority of UFO sightings from cars – where drivers suddenly see a 'flying saucer' parked on or near a road – happen (as with the highwayman sighting) *just after turning a bend in the road*. Perhaps the effect of concentration followed by the sudden change of circumstances – the bend in the road, and perhaps other random factors such as road characteristics, landmarks and so on – creates the images that are perceived.

We must also ask why people perceive the images that they do. Are the images the same, but differently seen by different people; does an individual's predisposition to a particular image – a highwayman, a UFO, something else – create that image in the witness's mind's eye?

Taken together, these aspects of phantom hitchhikers certainly suggest the possibility that legend creates many of the cases.

But there are more specific cases of 'protective ghosts', less dependent on legend.

In the Billing area of Northamptonshire is a house built on a fairly new estate. It is built on farmland which was the alleged scene of the incident that led to the arrival of a protective ghost called Harry Perkins.

The 'Barbour' family moved to the house in October 1975. Approximately a month after moving into the property they began hearing strange noises in the early hours of the morning. 'Douglas', one of the sons, who narrated the tale to John Spencer, stated that he and his family, coming from Singapore and Malaysia, had had many experiences in the past and they thought that they might be a 'psychic family'; indeed, Douglas stated that his parents were quite used to this sort of thing although the children had not yet become so accustomed. After a few months they noticed that 'Caroline', Douglas's nine-year-old sister, after waking up, was speaking to someone that was apparent to her. She could see and hear

3 Ghosts That Interact with You

him and was apparently fully interactive with him, with him able to respond to her questions.

Douglas teased his sister, frankly not believing her. When she started crying, their mother, 'Margaret', was told by Caroline that Douglas did not believe her but that the person she was speaking to proposed to prove his existence to Douglas. As Douglas explained: 'A couple of nights later I was in bed and my brother was asleep, across the room from me – I always know when he is asleep because his sheets are off and he is sweaty. I couldn't go to sleep no matter how much I was trying and eventually I was just about to doze off and I felt a whack on my head and I found out that it was a pillow from his [Douglas's brother's] bed and he was still fast alseep. I actually felt a presence in the room and from then on I believed and throughout the next occurrences we sort of accepted it. I can say he is not a poltergeist, or anything like that; he is quite friendly.'

Douglas went on to say: 'My sister found out his name, which is Harry Perkins. He said he used to fly from Sywell Airport which is the local airport here. He said he was flying over after having a fight with someone – it might have been something to do with a girlfriend or something like that and he crashed on the land near [the family home].'

In our first conversation Douglas told us that he thought Harry Perkins might have been with someone but on rechecking the information with Douglas's sister it appears that he was probably alone and seemed to have been shot down. It is possible that there is some confusion between an incident when he was shot down and a separate incident when he was killed, but this remains part of the ongoing investigation.

Harry Perkins, through Caroline, asked their father, 'Buddy', to check up the details with the local council. Buddy did this and was able to find out that a crash had taken place. Unfortunately no details of that enquiry have been retained or at least could be located at the time when we were talking with Douglas. Our own enquiries to the council have not yet borne fruit. Several departments of the council, the local library and the local newspapers have all assisted in trying to find relevant information for us, for which we are grateful.

Their mother, Margaret, has also seen Harry Perkins and described him as wearing a black polo neck; she has indicated that he appears to be about 25 years old and very good-looking. Apparently every time he sees her he is always smiling. Interestingly, Buddy apparently also sees him but usually in an RAF outfit, though for some reason he appears to be 'not too pleased' with Buddy. In a subsequent conversation it was admitted that the expression 'RAF outfit' was a description really intended to describe a uniform but the family admitted that they were not quite sure exactly what uniform it was.

Douglas offered an interesting story relating to his brother 'Nicholas'. The family believes that Harry Perkins tried to help them out. Apparently Nicholas woke up feeling somebody trying to wake him and just as he woke up his car was broken into; the family believes that Harry might have been trying to warn him.

Douglas went on: 'We have friends come in and they actually see Harry, walking across from the kitchen. You don't see through him, you see him like you would an ordinary person.'

We asked whether or not anyone else in the locality had also seen Harry, and Douglas was not sure but he believed that there was a possibility of a near neighbour having had a sighting. Apparently in 1978 a lady who lived some 50 yards away had, during a time when the local 'Neighbourhood Watch' was trying to locate a local thief, described to some of the people that she had a visitor at night who walked in the house. It could not be positively identified as the same apparition, however.

3 Ghosts That Interact with You

Harry is apparently not happy with his lot; to quote Douglas: 'He actually told Dad, and Mum, to try and get in touch with a priest. He says to pray for him.'

A priest was called to bless the house and hopefully to free Harry to move on but this was not successful. Although not seen or heard of in the months immediately prior to our conversation, he had been around as late as 1991 and there was no evidence that he was yet gone.[1]

For Harry Perkins's sake, as well as research into this case, we would like to be able to find out all about him; we have further ongoing enquiries, these with the aerodrome manager of Sywell Airport and its former manager, though neither have borne fruit to date. In addition, we have been given some follow-up suggestions by a fellow writer who is an expert on the subject of the RAF and the Second World War, John Foreman, some of which will be pursued by a local researcher in the area who is assisting us. With all of these enquiries we would hope to be able to get closer to the answer to this case in due course.

For the moment Harry Perkins remains as a possible 'interactive, protective, ghost'.

Perhaps the best known specific interactive protectors are the so-called Ghosts of Flight 401.

> On the evening of 29 December 1972 a Lockheed L-1011 wide-body aircraft crashed in the Florida Everglades resulting in many deaths and casualties in crew and passengers.
>
> The plane was just coming into land when the captain, Bob Loft, noticed that there was no light to indicate that the nose gear had locked down into place. The second officer, Don Repo, thought it was probably the warning light that was faulty. The one way to be sure was for one of them to climb into a small compartment

57

under the cockpit, known as the 'hellhole', from where the nose wheel could be visually inspected. Repo climbed down.

The autopilot was on, it had been set to 2,000 feet. The plane would maintain that altitude unless the autopilot was switched off, but unfortunately there was another mechanism that allowed for the autopilot to be switched off automatically if a certain pressure was applied to the steering column. It seems that when the two officers were moving around in the cockpit, the steering column was pushed, and the autopilot switched off. The readout still told the pilots they were flying at 2,000 feet when they were descending.

An audible warning went unnoticed; possibly because the only person now in the cockpit had headphones on. The warning was not loud enough.

While the autopilot readout still registered 2,000 feet, the plane was falling 100 feet every 4 seconds. In the hellhole Repo saw the water just below them, and then the plane tore into the water, marsh and reeds of the Everglades.

After the crash the ghosts of Captain Bob Loft and Second Officer Don Repo appeared several times; often on identical aircraft, usually ones which had utilised recycled parts from 401. On one occasion, for example, it was reported that a vice-president of Eastern Airlines who boarded an L-1011 ahead of the passengers, spoke to an Eastern Airlines captain in full uniform whom he found in the cabin. He suddenly realised it was Bob Loft he was talking to; at that moment Loft vanished. When the vice-president had the plane searched, they could not locate any sign of him.

It was alleged that Bob Loft was also seen by one flight's captain and his two flight attendants. They all apparently talked to Loft; when he disappeared they cancelled the flight.

One flight attendant said that she opened one of the

3 Ghosts That Interact with You

overhead compartments during a cabin check and found Bob Loft's face looking at her. Another flight attendant opened an oven door in the galley and saw the face of Repo looking out at her. Repo was also reported seen by staff loading the galley on another flight.

During one flight the crew heard a knocking coming from the hellhole below the cockpit, where Repo had been just prior to the crash of Flight 401. The engineer climbed down and came face to face with Repo looking at him.

A passenger on one L-1011 which was then still waiting to take off found herself sitting next to an Eastern Airlines flight officer in uniform. He apparently looked sick and pale and did not respond to the passenger's enquiries. The passenger called a stewardess. Then in front of both of them, and several other passengers, the officer simply disappeared, leaving the woman completely hysterical. Shown photographs of Eastern Flight engineers she picked out Don Repo as the officer.

Needless to say, the witnesses involved wanted to remain anonymous, and Eastern Airlines have been reticent in confirming the claims; most of the information was given to researchers by informants within the airports and airlines.

But the officers were not apparently content to just put in appearances. They seemed to have a mission that they intended to take very seriously indeed. One captain of an L-1011 who spoke to Repo's spirit said Repo had told him: 'There will never be another crash of an L-1011 . . . We will not let it happen.'

And they seem to have carried out their promise:

One flight engineer doing preflight inspection of an L-1011 saw a figure he recognised as Repo, who said to him: 'You don't need to worry about the preflight, I've already done it.'

A stewardess in the galley of an L-1011 found that

one oven indicated an overloaded circuit and saw a man in an engineer's uniform fix it. The plane's own flight engineer later insisted that he was the only one on the plane, and he had not fixed it. The flight attendant, looking at Don Repo's photograph, identified him as the repair-man.

Two stewardesses and an engineer saw Repo in the galley on another flight; he said to them: 'Watch out for fire on this airplane.' Then he disappeared. On a later leg of that flight one of the engines on the starboard wing would not start. Just after take-off another engine stalled and backfired several times, needing to be shut off immediately. The plane was brought back to the runway. No reason for the malfunction was found.

The ghostly flight crew took their self-imposed responsibilities very seriously, it would seem.[26]

There is a suggestion of 'protection' in incidents following the sinking of the *Titanic* in 1912. However, no 'human' ghost appears to be involved; indeed there is almost the suggestion of the ghost of the ship itself.

The story starts even before the *Titanic* had been built, in 1898. In that year Morgan Robertson wrote a novel called *Futility*. There were striking similarities between the ship of her novel, and the *Titanic*, for example: the ship in *Futility* was called the *Titan*; it was the largest ship afloat, as was the *Titanic*; it was the most advanced ship of its time, as was the *Titanic*; it had insufficient lifeboats for the number of passengers, as did the *Titanic*; it was regarded as unsinkable, a description the media placed on the *Titanic*; it was moving at full speed when it crashed, as it is believed the *Titanic* was doing; it struck an iceberg, as did the *Titanic*; it sank in April, as did the *Titanic*. In size, displacement, passenger capacity and design the two ships had many similarities. The similarities have been regarded as evidence of premonition, or exceptional coincidence.

However, the 'ghost-like' protection was to follow. On

3 Ghosts That Interact with You

13 April 1935, almost 23 years to the day after the loss of the *Titanic*, William Reeves was on lookout aboard the steamer *Titanian*, sailing across the north Atlantic. It was just after eleven o'clock in the evening. He had been reading *Futility*, which he had left in his cabin before coming on watch. He was aware of the fictional *Titan*'s fate and the fate of the real *Titanic* and was suddenly struck by the similarity of his own position in the north Atlantic on a ship called *Titanian*. Apparently he felt an impending sense of danger. At 11.35 in the evening, approximately the time when the *Titanic* had struck its iceberg, he became so concerned that although he could see no danger ahead he ordered: 'Stop engines quickly. Iceberg ahead!' At what is said to be the exact same time that the *Titanic* struck an iceberg, the *Titanian* came to a halt just as a huge iceberg loomed directly into its path. Ice damaged the *Titanian* and its engines, though not seriously, and she was towed into St John's in Newfoundland a week later. It appeared that certain disaster was averted by Reeves's feelings. Such an incident could itself be regarded as premonition or coincidence, but it has many of the qualities of 'protection' that are recorded in some ghost, or crisis (death) apparitions.

The presence of a spirit rather than the visible form of one, or specific communication with one, was also the centrepiece of an incident involving one Bill Corfield.

In July 1941, Bill Corfield was seventeen years old; his older brother Jimmy, a pilot officer in the RAF, and Bill's hero, was home for leave.

Bill made clear to Jimmy that he wanted to be a pilot, to follow in his brother's footsteps. Perhaps seeking to protect Bill, Jimmy advised against it. But Bill was adamant.

On 12 August 1941, Jimmy was shot down and killed over the North Sea while flying on a bombing raid to factories outside Cologne.

Far from turning Bill away from the idea, it

reinforced in him the ambition to take up the baton from his older brother. In due course, he made the grade as a pilot.

After the war had ended, in January 1947, Bill was flying an Anson 19 twin-engine aircraft to Singapore. After stops in Paris and Italy Bill was on the leg of the journey that would take him to Athens.

According to the weather forecast the flight looked promising; unfortunately after reaching the point of no return, the point at which you needed the same amount of fuel to go on or to turn back, the plane ran into a severe thunderstorm which forced it down to a very low level – just 50 feet above sea level. They were now flying low, in a sky darkened by storm clouds, and in severe buffeting weather conditions.

In the poor visibility they missed the islands off the Greek coast but suddenly all three (Bill, his navigator and wireless operator), who were up at the front in the plane, saw the coast approaching. Bill banked the plane to port and flew along the coast. All of a sudden the navigator announced that he could see the Corinth Canal; instinctively Bill dived into the jaws of its opening. He afterwards admitted that he didn't know why he did it, but he felt he was following instincts.

As they travelled along between the walls of the canal all the crew noticed an extraordinary peacefulness, and silence, that enveloped the plane. One of the crew described it as being 'in a sort of cathedral'.

Bill was sure – *absolutely and without a doubt* – that Jimmy 'was with me in the aircraft. It was as natural as I am talking to you now. There was nothing physical [to see], but he was there.' It was a highly emotional moment, never before or again did Bill feel his brother's presence so closely, and with such certainty. Bill relaxed his hands allowing his brother to 'take over' the controls; perhaps in a somewhat similar

3 Ghosts That Interact with You

manner to the way mediums receive channelling or automatic writing.

They flew for four miles within the Corinth Canal in the dark, and got safely out at the other end; then the 'presence' of Jimmy left.

The crew noticed that their plane flew *dead* straight; something no normal pilot could do in a violent storm. But, more extraordinary, they later discovered that the walls of the canal were only just wider than the wing span of the aircraft (a 17-foot clearance). Even in ideal conditions such accuracy of flying would have been improbable.[1]

Bill was sure that his brother had flown the plane, thus protecting him from a variety of ways to crash.

These types of ghosts seem to be able to interact with their witnesses. This trait offers an avenue for research – if the ghost can offer information that cannot be obtained from other sources, then that offers support for the ghost's objective reality. That said, such evidence is rare; but it is a concentration on this which will probably offer the best avenues for future research.

If the observer can find a way to be on the spot at the right time, then he or she can ask pertinent questions. Any researchers placed in this position are advised to have a somewhat better plan of action than was depicted in the film *Ghostbusters*, where the research team's total plan, when confronting a female spectre, was summed up by a cry of 'Get her!'

Such ghosts are generally useful, helpful and friendly, though, like all other ghosts, they never seem to turn up 'on cue' or when you have a camera ready!

Our next category of ghosts is generally less friendly . . .

4 Ghosts with an Attitude

THE MAJORITY OF GHOST reports relate to ghosts that not only seem to interact with the witness, but often have an emotional impact on the witness. The first of these categories includes ghosts that are 'felt' by the witness, though rarely seen. There is of course overlap here between this category and the classifications in the previous chapter; Bill Corfield's brother was clearly 'felt' as a presence by Bill as well as protecting him.

PRESENCES

The following example presents a situation where three people simultaneously experienced a presence: two saw the classic 'hooded monk' while the third had the impression of a vague and indistinct patch of darkness. The important point about this case is that two of the three are the authors of this book, and we brought it on ourselves during experimentation.

We were experimenting with a Ouija board in Charlton House, Greenwich, in 1993, to see whether we could receive telepathic messages from others who were elsewhere in the building. Of course the Ouija board is generally thought to be a means of communicating with spirits but – as discussed in Chapter 11 – there is a suspicion that messages come from within the people around the table. We were twenty minutes into the session when Tony Wells turned around to stare at

4 Ghosts with an Attitude

the far end of the Long Gallery; over the next few minutes John Spencer and Lucien Morgan did the same but all three did not discuss their experiences until afterwards.

On comparing notes afterwards both John and Lucien had seen the same size and shape apparition, Tony had seen the vague darkness in the same place, and felt slightly peculiar about the room. The thing that surprised – and mildly annoyed – John the most was that of all the things to see it had to be a 'classic' hooded monk! 'We obviously don't have much imagination,' was John's complaint.

This could easily have been classified as a 'recordings' ghost were it not for the feelings of presence associated with it.

Not all presences are visual, as the following cases demonstrate. The first is an account by 'Rohan'. She described waking up in her bedroom one October or November night when she was seventeen.

> 'I could hear somebody breathing. It sounded like there was a woman sitting on my window ledge, breathing. And it was horrible. I had a feeling that maybe if I opened my curtains I'd see a witch. So I went to my mother, woke her up; she came out of her bedroom but it had stopped. She said, "Don't be stupid. It's obviously your imagination." As soon as she went back into her bedroom it started again. The following Saturday evening I had a friend with me and I heard it again, only this time it wasn't a female, it was a male. And I thought, that's that noise again and I said to my friend, "Can you hear it?" He said, "Yes, I can hear it. I didn't say anything because I didn't want to scare you, but yes, I can hear it." And then it went.'[1]

Bad enough for a teenager, but such manifestations must be even more terrifying for a young child. The following account relates to a time when the witness, Judy, was just a little girl. (Such reports are not confined to children, however – we

Ghostwatching

know of one adult, a priest, who experienced almost exactly the same presence, and spent the night in prayer to try and dispel whatever 'it' was.)

In 1950, Judy and her mother lived with her grandparents in Southsea, Hampshire. It was an ordinary, seaside house of Edwardian origin; but to Judy it contained the worst horrors of her childhood.

'There was something very strange about that house that I was very aware of, my mother was aware of to a degree and my grandparents not at all. My mother always said that it was something that didn't like the young so the younger you were the more horror it gave you.'

Judy became conscious of something 'really awful' in the house. She would hear footsteps as the 'thing' came into her bedroom and crossed the bedroom floor, and she often heard it crossing the front-room floor towards a creaking basket chair. Judy heard breathing, confirming to her that it was some sort of 'real' presence.

Judy's family apparently did their best to help, though they perhaps did not fully accept her story. They moved her into another bedroom; unfortunately, they moved her to the very room that – Judy later became sure – was the focus of the 'presence': 'The room they moved me into was the hub of whatever was wrong with the house.'

One night Judy came awake aware of this horror in the room with her. She could see nothing, but she could sense a 'creature' pulsating in the corner of the room. She felt that as it pulsated so it was also growing; she found the whole incident 'absolutely terrifying'. She was 'rigid in the bed' and unable to move to put the lights on. When in fact she did get the lights on it made no difference; she could feel the presence of the 'thing' as powerfully as ever.

4 Ghosts with an Attitude

When she broke 'free' she ran to her mother and into her bed. She remembers that she could hear the bed rattling, so much was she still shaking from fear.[1]

When 'presences' start throwing things around the fear level can be stepped up considerably. Believed by many to be the most common form of reported 'ghost', the poltergeist not only interacts with the witness, but often does so with the threat of – and sometimes actual – violence.

POLTERGEISTS

For most people their knowledge of poltergeists is coloured by the extraordinary events depicted in movies such as Steven Spielberg's *Poltergeist*. The reality is not as dramatic; but most witnesses would argue it is dramatic enough.

An early dictionary definition spells out the traditional image, if not a modern interpretation: '*Poltergeist*. A noisy ghost or hobgoblin, the name given by modern Spiritualists to the supposed agent of certain manifestations, such as the overturning or moving of furniture, breaking of crockery, or other noisy disturbances.' (*The Universal Dictionary of the English Language* published 1958.)

Because poltergeist cases are the most commonly reported of all ghost phenomena, they have the greatest potential for the ghostwatcher. Unfortunately the characteristics of the poltergeist render it extremely difficult to observe using technology.

The word poltergeist comes from the German language, and means noisy spirit. Interestingly the Germans don't use the word poltergeist, they use the word *Spuk*!

Although the poltergeist is noisy, it can be extremely shy when ghostwatchers are around. In fact in its way of working it seems to have almost human characteristics – it is playful, annoying and sometimes dangerous, although there are few

67

reported cases of anyone actually coming to physical harm from its actions.

The 'almost human' characteristic is the main reason for belief that the spirits of the dead are behind the activity. The spiritualist movement which started in the USA in the mid-nineteenth century (see Chapter 1) began in 1848 when two sisters, Margaret and Kate Fox, found that they were kept awake at night by loud rapping noises. They discovered that when they clicked their fingers, the rapping noises would copy them. A neighbour, probably because of the seeming intelligence behind the copying action, suggested that they should ask the 'rapping' questions, with replies in 'rapping code'. It turned out that the intelligence behind the rapping identified itself as a murdered pedlar called Charles B. Rosma. Apparently he had been murdered in the east bedroom and buried in the cellar.

In fact, many years after this, in 1904, after a wall collapsed at the Foxes's house in Hydesville, the skeleton of a man was found, with a pedlar's box near it.

Back to 1848: the case soon began to take a nasty turn. The rappings became worse; sounds of a death struggle were heard, and even when the sisters were separated and moved to separate houses the phenomena followed them both to their respective domains. The family, and those living in the affected houses, began to suffer more physical attentions – such as pins pricking them while they were at prayer, and objects thrown about. One person, Charles Brown, seemed to be the subject of more attention than the others. The rapping noises had grown in volume and apparently could be heard from quite a distance.

Eventually, someone proposed a further attempt at communication. A message 'came through' which started the spiritualist movement. It began: 'Dear Friends, you must proclaim this truth to the world. This is the dawning of a new era. . . .' It marked the dawning of spiritualism.

When the Fox case is looked at in more detail, it has all the characteristics of a poltergeist haunting but, as mentioned

4 Ghosts with an Attitude

before, it has the unique feature that it was the first time that someone, noticing the possible intelligence behind the phenomena, decided to try to communicate.

The spiritualist belief is that consciousness remains in spirit form after physical death and under certain circumstances it is possible to contact this spirit form. The spiritualist explanation for the poltergeist is that occasionally spirits do not leave the earthly plane for their proper place and for several reasons may cause disruptive activity. The main reason for this is that the spirits may be irritated that the living people do not recognise them or react to their presence. In their anger they may try to attract attention or simply discharge their aggression by typical poltergeist activity such as throwing household equipment around. This belief, like that of all other religions, is based on faith rather than explicit evidence.

Over 150 years later, there is now an alternative theory to explain poltergeist activity and the possible intelligence behind it. This theory suggests that living people can create the effects by psychokinesis (from *psycho* 'mind', and *kinesis* 'movement') (PK) – moving objects with the power of their own minds. Such people might be exteriorising their own frustrations or aggressions, without conscious knowledge. Very rarely, scientists come across people of this type who, under certain circumstances, have got the power of conscious control over such activity. Studies of PK may add something to our knowledge of poltergeists. (Both issues are discussed in more detail in Chapter 10, when we discuss techniques for eradication of the poltergeist.)

Poltergeists arise in almost any and every type of location – castles, shops, private homes; there is even one report of a poltergeist in a public toilet.

Probably the most famous London poltergeist case – the Enfield Poltergeist – arose in a 'typical' suburban home. This case has been the subject of so much high-profile exposure that there is no need for us to detail it again here. We refer

Ghostwatching

interested readers to the book *This House is Haunted*[47] by Guy Lyon Playfair.

Poltergeists do, however, seem to have something of a predilection for rectories. The most famous such 'haunted' rectory is Borley Rectory. In the first half of this century there were reports of nun-like apparitions; there were sightings of various other figures; presences were perceived; items in the Borley church were disturbed; music was heard coming from a locked organ; there were noises of panting and the footsteps of a dog, and sounds of smashing crockery; writing appeared on the wall ... and so on.

Although Borley Rectory no longer exists, its former site is still the subject of a sort of 'psychic pilgrimage' by people of all ages who want to see for themselves what stands on the famous site. For those who are curious, we can save you the visit: it is now a row of houses.

Perhaps one of the reasons for the Rectory's fame was Harry Price. Price was the principal investigator of the Rectory, and he was exceptionally accomplished at using the media to gain publicity for his work. Any person seriously investigating the paranormal will at some time visit the Harry Price Library which is contained within the academic library at the University of London's Senate House. Here is contained one of the widest collections of books on the paranormal, including some large volumes containing the press clippings on Harry Price and his investigations. Although Price himself appears to some sceptics to be a controversial figure, there is no doubt that at the time he did more than any other person in England to publicise the issues surrounding the paranormal.

Like the Enfield Poltergeist, Borley has been covered so extensively in other works that we feel that it would be better to direct the reader to a good source of information, rather than repeat what has been written so many times elsewhere. Probably the best source of information on Borley is Harry Price himself; his book *The End of Borley Rectory*[50] contains

4 Ghosts with an Attitude

a description of the main events at the Rectory, and has some interesting photographs.

Other rectories that have been the site of poltergeist activity include those in the following two accounts.

In 1716, the parents of John Wesley, the Reverend Samuel Wesley and his wife Susanna, experienced poltergeist hauntings at their home, Epworth Rectory, Lincolnshire.

'One night,' wrote Samuel Wesley, 'when the noise was great in the kitchen, and on a deal partition, and on the door in the yard, the latch whereof was often lifted up, my daughter Amelia went and held it fast on the inside, but it was still lifted up, and the door pushed violently against her, though nothing was to be seen on the outside.'

They heard sounds similar to breaking glass, groaning sounds and cackling laughter. Mrs Wesley wrote in a letter 'One night it made such a noise in the room over our head as if several people were walking; then ... running up and down stairs, and was so outrageous that we thought the children would be frightened so your father and I rose and went down in the dark to light a candle. Just as we came to the bedroom at the bottom of the broad stairs, having hold of each other, on my side there seemed as if somebody had emptied a bag of money at my feet, and on his as if all the bottles under the stairs (which were many) had been dashed in a thousand pieces. We passed through the hall into the kitchen, and got a candle and went to see the children.

'The next night your father got Mr Hole to lie at our house and we all sat together till 1 or 2 o'clock in the morning and heard the knocking as usual. Sometimes it would make a noise like the winding-up of a jack, at other times as the night Mr Hole was with us, like a carpenter planing deals, but most commonly knocked thrice and stopped and then thrice again.'

The Wesley children named the poltergeist 'Old Jeffrey'. The disturbances simply faded away after a period of a few months.[2]

Shortly after moving into Polstead Rectory, Reverend Hayden Foster and his wife, Margot, asked a neighbour to help them as they were frightened by strange happenings in the building. They had heard strange noises and experienced ill-at-ease feelings. Mrs Foster believed an entity had tried to strangle her. The neighbours were able to confirm that the previous occupants had suffered a series of similar problems. The fact that the previous owners had been regarded as solid, down-to-earth types had strengthened belief that the claims they were making had validity.

The neighbour summed up the situation: 'There is something definitely very odd about the rectory and the area around it. There is a kind of presence there but it only seems to attack the wives of priests.'[2]

The Polstead Rectory haunting suggests a poltergeist that is 'attached' to the building. Although many ghost sightings – and some poltergeists – relate to places, poltergeist reportees have been called 'haunted people' as it seems that generally the poltergeist is focused on a person or persons, as in the case of the Fox sisters mentioned earlier, rather than on any specific location.

Problems with evidence and the reports given are not new. The following account, in the first volume of the *Journal of the Society for Psychical Research*, shows how even a policeman can find it difficult to describe poltergeist activity.

A daily newspaper reported that at a farm in Shrewsbury, in 1884, the servants were complaining of a number of unusual events. The list included a saucepan

4 Ghosts with an Attitude

of eggs, boiling by the fire, that jumped off the fire and smashed into items laid for tea, breaking some tea things, and a paraffin lamp with a globe was lifted off its stand and then 'thrown' across the room, presumably breaking in the process. Concerned that there would be nothing left if this continued, the farmer decided to remove all movable items from the room. As he was clearing the room, a loaf of bread hit him in the back, a book was thrown out of the window, and was followed by a sewing machine. Apparently the machine was so badly damaged, it had to be sent away for repair.

A few days later, a Saturday, a Police Constable Taylor visited the farm and stayed late to investigate the happenings. Whilst there he apparently witnessed a fire fender move from its proper place under its own volition three times.

The focus seemed to be the young servant girl, Emma Davis, and the report by Mr F. S. Hughes stated that once it seemed that she was the focus, she was dismissed from the farm. (Dismissal seems to have been a commonplace action in those days, and raises an interesting point about fraud, which we will cover later.)

The report continues that, being in a (not unsurprisingly) nervous state, Emma Davis was looked after by a Dr Cooke, and placed in the care of his housekeeper, Miss Turner. Dr Cooke reported that 'Certain manifestations took place, similar in character to the farm, although she was not detected to have committed fraud, it could have taken place in all observed situations. A few days later Miss Turner observed Emma with a brick in her hand, and seemingly unaware of being observed. Emma was with a house servant outside. She threw the brick and screamed to attract attention. The servant then saw the brick flying through the air. Emma was questioned and confessed to playing tricks, and then displayed her techniques impressively.'

Mr Hughes visited the farm next morning and

interviewed some of the witnesses. The most impressive account was that of a servant, Priscilla Evans, who had seen a cupboard door (previously locked by one of the two other women in the house) fly open, whereupon Emma Davis, who was with her, and the only other person present, became 'rooted to the spot'. Priscilla tried to pull her away; Emma shrieked but couldn't be moved. Crockery began to pour out of the cupboard two or three items at a time. All the while the crockery was falling out, Priscilla saw Emma's arms folded – but it was, according to Mr Hughes, nearly dark at the time, implying that Priscilla could have made mistakes in observation.

Hughes also questioned Police Constable Taylor who had witnessed the three-times movement of the fender. Apparently there were three people present – Taylor, Emma Davis and a third person whose name was not mentioned, but the Police Constable seemed unable to describe the movement of the fender. The conclusion Hughes came to was that although there was 'abundant trickery' on the part of the girl, the cupboard incident made it possible that there might have been more incidents of an unexplainable nature.[27]

The issue of servants being dismissed from their post if they are discovered to be the focus of poltergeist activity raises an interesting point. If, as has often been asserted, much of poltergeist activity is faked then it doesn't make sense that servants should risk losing their job. Surely the opposite is true: that servants would be tempted to try to suppress evidence of the phenomena or try to blame it on other, more natural, causes.

Farm buildings have had their fair share of poltergeists. It is thought that one of the oldest reports of a poltergeist relates to a farm.

The *Annales Fuldenses* chronicles contain a report dated 858 BC.

4 Ghosts with an Attitude

A family living at a farmhouse near Bingen on the Rhine suffered a poltergeist that threw stones, vibrated walls, caused fires and burnt crops. It also exposed the farmer's sexual relationship with the daughter of one of his foremen. The farmer seemed to be the focus and the activity apparently followed him wherever he went until other people refused to have him anywhere near their homes.[28]

Poltergeist activity has been a feature of a great number of the ghostwatches we have undertaken. Many of these are described in Chapter 8. The following account is also from our own files; the investigation into this case is still in its early days, but the account summarises the typical activities we are examining.

The case was brought to the attention of one of our colleagues, Chris Walton, in June 1993 when he was given a magazine clipping. It related to the Johns Cross Inn, at Mountfield, near Robertsbridge, in East Sussex.

The article stated that Sandie, the proprietor, was concerned about the phenomena that seemed to have started up there since they moved in a year before. The reported phenomena included a piano that seemed to play by itself, beer barrels that moved in the cellar, an ashtray which tipped its contents on to the floor, and a bottle thrown across the bar.

Chris decided that it might be worth investigating, and introduced himself and his interest in a phone call, during which Sandie revealed that the strange activities had seemed to increase after the pub had been hit by a car which had inflicted considerable damage on an outside wall. It was agreed that Chris and Tony Wells would visit in July and briefly interview Sandie. As some of the activity had involved her husband, Bob, it was decided to hold a further interview in August with both authors present to discuss the activity with the whole of the family. The main thing that interested

Ghostwatching

us was how puzzled Bob was by the whole thing. Definitely a left-hand side of the brain person (as we describe in Chapter 14) – a logical thinker – he was constantly trying to explain the events in terms of a scientific or engineering viewpoint.

A list of the highlights of the reported activities follows.

1. Exploding tonic water

Bob, whilst playing pool, saw a bottle of tonic water propel itself off the bar shelves, pause, and then smash itself against the bar. This incident was witnessed by three regulars. Bob, worried that the bottle's propulsion and explosion were caused by a glass fault, contacted the manufacturers who denied that such an incident was possible.

2. Son Peter's room messed up

The bar manager noticed glass outside the pub and saw that the glass in Peter's bedroom window was broken. Bob, on trying to enter his son's room found the door difficult to open: the TV was behind the door. The mattress was found on the floor in the middle of the room and clothes from the wardrobe were strewn about. Nobody was in the room, and it would have taken some ingenuity for someone to have put the TV behind the door on exiting.

3. Pub unlocked

Sandie, being the owner, was very strict about whom she would allow to lock up the pub. One night, for the first – and only – time she allowed Bob, with their daughter's assistance, to shut up for the night. Aware that they were under trust, they carefully locked and bolted each door, turned out the lights and put the keys in the till upstairs. In the morning, Sandie took the keys from the till, and found the pub unlocked and the lights on. It wasn't until Eve, their daughter, confirmed that they had locked up for the night, that Sandie believed that there was anything strange about the event. In addition, that morning Bob found his car unlocked – something he is always careful to avoid, for the car is left out overnight on the pub forecourt.

4 **Ghosts with an Attitude**

4. Perrier bottles lined up
One evening their son, Peter, went down to the cellar on an errand, and discovered six Perrier bottles lined up in a slightly curved line, at an angle to one of the cellar walls; all the labels were facing one way. Bob, after some investigation, found that the bottles had come from a previously full and unopened but now empty, *undamaged* cardboard pack. He found that it was impossible to remove the bottles from such a packet without tearing the cardboard; the empty box was therefore the real mystery.[1]

Although we said earlier that there have been few cases where the poltergeist has been physically dangerous, this next case description – that of 'the Bell Witch' – highlights a rare exception – the poltergeist has been blamed for the death of one of the percipients.

> John and Lucy Bell, and their nine children, lived on a farm in Robertson, Tennessee, United States of America. In 1817 one of the children, Elizabeth, became the focus of poltergeist activity.
>
> The phenomenon started with noises and scrapings, a common onset of poltergeist activity, and progressed to moving and throwing things. The disturbances went on for over two years (with a dramatic sequel), Elizabeth always the focus. She was attacked; her hair pulled. Her brother Richard suffered the same experience. (In 1846 Richard went on to write a book on the case.)
>
> When scrutinised by the Bell family and their neighbour, James Johnson, the poltergeist activity worsened. Elizabeth was struck on the face – witnesses saw her cheek reddening from the impact. She was sent to a neighbour but the disturbances followed, with strange lights outside the house, stones thrown and slapping attacks on others at the house.
>
> Elizabeth's father, John, began to suffer from an illness which was attributed to the poltergeist. He was

unable to eat and his tongue swelled. The poltergeist spoke for the first time, insisting on using foul language; it announced that John would be tormented for the rest of his life, which turned out to be correct. There was not just one voice, but five, each having a particular characteristic. One was said to be that of a witch. There was one report that when Elizabeth was given an emetic to make her sick she threw up brass pins and needles and the 'witch voice' – demonstrating something of a black humour – suggested that if she vomited again she would have enough to set up a shop.

Elizabeth was later engaged to one Joshua Gardner; this apparently did not get the poltergeist's approval. Seemingly it chose to reveal their most embarrassing personal secrets causing them eventually to break off their engagement.

Poltergeist activity targeted at John Bell worsened and on 20 December 1820 he died. The poltergeist rejoiced by singing songs of triumph. By John Bell's bed was a bottle of brown liquid; a drop of it was tested on an unlucky cat – it died almost immediately.

The activity diminished after Bell's death, finally disappearing with the words 'I . . . will be gone for seven years. . . .' Lucy Bell and the only two of her children remaining with her at the farmhouse did hear manifestations seven years later but they did not last for very long and may have been imagination resulting from the prophecy. The poltergeist promised to return in 1935 but failed so to do.[2]

There has been speculation that Elizabeth and her father had an incestuous relationship; begging the question as to exactly what the energy of the poltergeist was, and whether Bell committed suicide, was killed by human hands, or was the victim of the *Spuk*.

Sexual attentions under conditions causing stress may

4 Ghosts with an Attitude

have been a contributory factor in the case of Esther Cox in 1878.

Following unpleasant sexual advances at the point of a gun made by her boyfriend Bob MacNeal, Esther Cox became the victim of poltergeist attack.

At first she thought she heard a mouse, but none could be found. A box began moving independently. The following night Esther began to be affected by something unknown that reddened her face and swelled her body.

A couple of days later Esther suffered the bedclothes being ripped off her bed. The bedclothes also hit another member of the household, who left vowing never to return again.

Above Esther's bed writing appeared on the wall: 'Esther, you are mine to kill'. Plaster flew off the wall, landing near a doctor called in to tend Esther; this continued unabated for two hours. Eventually Esther told her family about the sexual attack. When it was suggested that this strain was the cause of the paranormal activities, the poltergeist responded with loud banging that seemed to suggest it agreed.

The poltergeist became dangerous shortly afterwards; it produced lighted matches falling around the room causing small fires. Neighbours became alarmed at the potential danger to their own property and made it clear they wanted Esther sent away. She went to stay with a neighbour, but the activity followed her there. An oven door came off its hinges and metal objects were drawn to Esther as if she were a magnet. The neighbour asked Esther to leave.

The following year, 1879, magician Walter Hubbell investigated the hauntings for a book. The poltergeist obliged him: throwing his umbrella in the air, throwing a carving knife towards him and throwing his bag away. It also hit him with a chair. Hubbell tested the poltergeist by asking details such as the dates of coins in his pockets. Through rapping noises the poltergeist apparently got the right answers.

Esther was further attacked, with pins being stuck in her hand, and more fires broke out. She eventually went to stay with some friends and the activities stopped.[2]

The number of events witnessed by other people, and the circumstances of the haunting lead to the conclusion that the case, if not every incident, was genuine.

Turning to more modern times, poltergeists do not seem to be shy of even the very latest technology. There have been many occasions when investigators into the paranormal have experienced – even in their own equipment, as we have done – spontaneous and strange effects. In the following case, which comes from Rosenheim in Germany and has been widely reported on, the *Spuk* was focused, it seems, mostly on electrical activity, albeit through one individual.

In 1967 there were many events reported at a firm of solicitors; these events were witnessed by up to forty people. Telephones would ring when no one was on the line, telephone calls seemed to be being made when no one was present, calls would be cut off, or interrupted. Light bulbs exploded, fluorescent tubes twisted in their sockets and fuses blew. Engineers from the electricity company supplying the building acknowledged that the offices were suffering large and unexplainable surges in power supply; these continued even after special regulating equipment was installed. Hans Bender, professor of parapsychology at Freiburg, concluded that the activity was centred on a teenage secretary, Anne-Marie Schneider. When she was sent away the activity stopped.

Ms Schneider experienced some poltergeist activity in her new job, but it quickly died out.[29]

4 Ghosts with an Attitude

As a child, our next subject, Stan Conway, underwent years of poltergeist activity. John Spencer and his wife Anne were the first researchers to visit and interview the Conway family. Previous accounts had been third-hand and as such often incorrect or incomplete. What follows is the story as related by the family.

The Conway family lived at 88 Newark Street, Whitechapel, London, in the 1950s. Stan, then five years old, slept in a bedroom on the second floor of the four-storey building. Stan is now a married man, with a family of his own, and provided us with a unique opportunity to discuss not just the case but the longer-term effects on a witness. We were also fortunate to be able to interview him with his parents; they had all shared the events of forty years ago.

Vera, Stan's mother, opened the account. 'This first started when Stanley was just five and my little girl, Deanna, was eight months old. Harry wanted to get a workshop at the top of the house at 88 Newark Street, he wanted it so much that I agreed. This was a fairly large house. There was a young couple living downstairs, and the woman was anxious for us to move in, to take the four upper rooms and the workshop at the top of the house. That surprised me because I had two young children and I thought, "Who would want somebody to move in over their heads?" But she wanted it and I thought, "Great, marvellous, wonderful." We put Stanley in the smaller bedroom and Harry, I and our daughter had the large bedroom. From the very beginning Stanley used to wake up and scream. He claimed that someone used to touch him, and that there was a ['ghost' or 'spirit'] cat on the bed. Also, more often than not, the bedroom door would be jammed as though someone was holding it fast on the other side. We couldn't understand why; eventually Harry broke the lock and we kept a pressing iron there to stop the door from closing.

'Things then went from bad to worse. We used to hear "sounds". I used to have quarrels with the woman next door, who would say to me, "How is it that you allow that workshop to be going all through the night?" And I used to say, "Of course it's not, they are finished at 6 o'clock or whatever and it's closed up." But she wouldn't talk to me for ages thinking that we had the workshop going all through the night. But we didn't. Eventually Stanley became so ill he was sent away to a convalescent home. He was there for about six months.

'While Stanley was away I wouldn't go into the room unless somebody was with me. There was something about the room that I just couldn't understand. Stanley came home and all this happened again.' Whether or not these things happened in Stanley's absence is uncertain because the room was not used then. 'Nobody told me anything about what had happened in the house in the past. I did know, however, that the aunt of Phyllis, the young woman living downstairs, had once been sleeping in that bedroom. I asked Phyllis: "You've got to tell me what's happened in this house." At first she didn't want to say, but eventually she told me, "My aunt always said that somebody touched her. She said that there was always a cat on the bed." Everything that Stanley, as a child of five years old, had said, this girl's aunt used to say the same – but long before. Phyllis knew when she invited us that these things would happen. That was why she was so welcoming. We didn't know that at the time of course. I didn't take the curtains off for six years in that room because I just wouldn't go in there. When Harry was away once I wanted to go in for something or other and I thought, "Well, I can't be so fearful, I must try." So I tried to open the door and it wouldn't open. At this time there was a knock at the front door and it happened to be a chap called Baxter. As I opened the door he said to me, "What's the matter? Something is

4 Ghosts with an Attitude

wrong." I said to him, "I can't open that door." "Oh, can't you?" he said, and he walked upstairs, got hold of the door and it opened immediately. It was as though whoever was on the other side realised that they could not deal with him.

'Another time Harry went in for his tools. As he took hold of the bag he received a very heavy blow on the back of his neck and he just staggered out. It was terrible. And we used to hear sounds on the staircase as though someone was running up the staircase. Nothing was seen.'

All the family had various memories of events that had affected them over those years; Harry, Stan's father, remembered tapping noises in the house, as if someone was using a walking stick. He also recalled the sounds of machinery from the workshop all night, even though the machinery was switched off. Stan remembered a time when a mirror on the wall was found cracked in half, and a coffee table was split down the middle.

Vera described a seance held in the house: 'A cat appeared on the table. And there was an old lady with something wrong with her leg. I later went to the local grocery store – the owners had been there for years and years. I asked the lady in the shop if she knew anybody who had been living in our house. She said, "Yes, years ago there used to be a largish family ... the mother used to walk around with a very large cat everywhere she went. And the woman had had a leg removed."

'We went through six years of hell in that house. We had nothing but bad luck from the moment we walked into *that house*. Everything that could go wrong went wrong; the children were always ill, we lost every penny we had in this business venture. Everything went wrong. Eventually we moved. But of course I was very concerned about what was happening, and if it could happen to anyone else who moved in there. We were then very friendly with Phyllis and Alf and her in-laws across the road. They came to see us about three months or so after we had moved out to tell us that the people who had then moved into the house were very anxious to meet Harry and I and to find out what had been happening in the house. This new family consisted of two brothers and their two wives. The two brothers were going to run a business upstairs. Having opened the workshop they had got some people to come in and work and one of the girls wanted to rent a room; so she did. They let her have the back bedroom. She only stayed there one night. She said something was going on in that place that she couldn't take.

'And evidently the two wives were not very happy. In fact they had our bedroom and they said that they felt somebody pull the blankets off the bed. Downstairs in the lounge they had a table, and at a time when they had people in to visit them it seemed as though someone pulled the table-cloth very sharply and everything flew off the table . . . I also met the woman who used to live next door when we lived there; the one that had complained we kept the workshop operating through the night. She said to me, "Vera, I beg your pardon. I am so sorry. I am so sorry that I didn't believe you. After you left the noises in the workshop kept going; it was like somebody was pressing, banging, heaving, everything that was going on during the day was going on through the night as well."'

Harry was certain that the poltergeist was an 'entity' of some sort. 'When we had the seance . . . I saw the black cat in the middle of the table. I heard it miaow. The medium saw it as well. I think the entity was an unhappy spirit that had remained there in the house. The woman from the family . . . willing her daughter to come back. She never did come back and then the mother died.'

Stan remembered that his life had been one dominated for those early years by the poltergeist. It was

4 Ghosts with an Attitude

years before he could leave even his hands outside the bedclothes for fear of something attacking him. In his early years he remembers developing 'out of body' experiences to protect himself:

'At home my greatest delight was not being in my body. I used to be out of my body looking down at everything else that was going on. I didn't want to be in the room but I was safe when I was out of my body, or so I felt. And at will I could get back into my body any time I wanted to. I remember I used to go into bed and I used to close my eyes. And if I didn't want to be in my body I could just turn myself out through my head and I could look down on my body. I could do it at will. This ability gradually stopped; I lost the ability as I lost the need to do it.'[1]

Poltergeist activity tends to fade away after about six months, though there are, as we have seen, cases that differ from this general rule. Attempts to banish or eliminate poltergeists ahead of this period of time seem to work, though it is equally possible that the effects would have worn off anyway.

5 Ghosts of the Living

THERE IS A WHOLE class of ghosts that, while having all the characteristics of ghost phenomena, most certainly do not represent the spirits of the dead. These apparitions represent people that are known to be alive at the time of the sighting. Two such instances – the cases of Mrs Elgee and of Mr Joy – have been outlined in Chapter 3, where they provided clues to mechanisms of perception; further cases are detailed here.

Typical of such cases are the following two experiences. The first involved the writer Ngaio Marsh.

> She was teaching Colin, the son of a New Zealand doctor. The boy lived in a cottage nearby, and often visited Ms Marsh in the morning, bringing flowers. As Ngaio Marsh's mother was cleaning and tidying in the house one morning she commented that Colin was coming up the garden path with a bunch of geraniums, wearing a smart new jacket. When Ngaio Marsh walked down the path to meet him, he was nowhere to be seen. She assumed she had missed him, and that he had returned home.
>
> He visited the next day. He explained to her that he had intended to visit the previous day, but had been forbidden to leave the house by his nanny as he had been naughty. 'I'd got my new coat on and I'd picked you a bunch of geraniums,' he told her.[19]

The second case relates to a hospital patient and her nurse.

5 Ghosts of the Living

In May 1936 Mrs Marion Dansie was a patient in the Middlesex Hospital. Early one morning a nurse came into her room, and smiled at Mrs Dansie, who recognised the nurse as one of the day staff. The nurse came to the side of the bed and Mrs Dansie greeted her with a 'Good morning'. She said it was nice to see her, but asked why she was on duty at that time. The figure did not respond, but just immediately vanished.

When the staff changed shift, the nurse Mrs Dansie had seen was not on duty. She enquired about her, and was told that she had reported in sick, and would not be at work that day.

But this was no death-bed or crisis apparition. The nurse was back at work some days later.[30]

Ghosts of the living are complex to analyse: Was the Colin at home aware that Ms Marsh's mother was seeing 'him'? Was the Colin that Ms Marsh's mother saw physical; did he have substance or was he an apparition of some kind? If the Colin seen on the garden path was physical, did the 'real' Colin lose something of his own substance? The same questions can be asked of Mrs Dansic's nurse. Were Colin and the nurse aware that they had 'visited' their friends? There is no evidence that they were.

Perhaps the most 'classical' ghost reports are of sightings of the long-dead kings and queens of 'Olde England' in the castles and palaces they used to inhabit. Many of these are the product of hype and wish-fulfilment. In the case cited below at least a boost to tourism cannot be suspected.

At a time when Elizabeth I was severely ill in bed with pneumonia and asleep or unconscious, one of her ladies-in-waiting left the bedchamber. She received quite a shock on seeing the Queen striding purposefully towards her down the corridor; because of this she returned immediately to the bedchamber and found the Queen still lying in bed exactly as she had left her.[31]

Ghostwatching

In this case we have one witness seeing both 'forms' of the Queen within a very short space of time; again we do not know which, or if both, had substance. Neither is there any report that the lady-in-waiting had the temerity to ask the Queen if she herself remembered walking down the corridor.

Some of the cases below provide some hints to the answers to the above questions, as there are cases where the percipients were the subjects themselves.

The first such case is a simple account by Goethe.

> In his autobiography Goethe tells of a time when, while riding a horse, he saw his own projection. He was feeling depressed at the time. Suddenly, coming towards him he saw his own double riding towards him wearing a grey suit with gold embroidery. Eight years later he was riding on that road in the opposite direction, wearing the grey suit with gold embroidery, when he remembered the first incident. He did not say that he saw himself on the second occasion.[2]

In this case the 'ghost' has seen himself and therefore we know there is knowledge of the encounter. Yet on the second occasion he does not see his other self. Whether this makes one or other of the Goethes the 'real' one is unclear, however. This case could easily represent a timeslip, as mentioned in Chapter 3, or some form of ghost of the living: a vardoger (forerunner), a doppelgänger, a bi-location, or a projection.

Amélie Saegée of Livonia is one subject who, it turned out, certainly knew of her own 'talent' for bi-location, and the circumstances of some of the accounts give some indication of the mechanisms that might have been at work, at least in her case. She was a schoolteacher in the mid-1800s; the account was given by one of her former pupils.

> At the age of thirty-two, Amélie Saegée was a teacher. She was seen, together with her double, by thirteen of her pupils; both were standing at the blackboard in

5 Ghosts of the Living

front of the class. On that occasion the double, or 'other' form, appears to have been a classic doppelgänger; the duplicate mimicking exactly the movements of the 'original'. On another occasion every pupil in her class was watching her sitting in a chair in her classroom, while every pupil in the school – including those in her class – was also watching her sitting in a chair in the garden.

Some idea of the frame of mind of the witness in this case is available: Amélie felt that she was at that time 'really' in the garden, and while there she was concerned that with the headmistress absent she ought to be in the classroom, as it was likely to be unattended. This suggests that the classroom Amélie was the projection (a mechanism similar to the visible hallucinations of Ruth mentioned below).

The projection seems to have lacked substance in every sense; to the pupils in the classroom her image there seemed somewhat ghost-like, and one pupil believed that he passed through a part of the image feeling nothing. The witnesses also thought that the figure in the garden looked tired and drowsy; possibly the effect of 'sending' some part of her into the classroom; her strength divided.

When the authorities at the school learned of this 'ability' on their teacher's part she was asked to leave; it was then that she admitted that she had lost nineteen jobs because of the same problem.[32]

Here then we have some indications: the subject of the reports is aware of the incidents, and the witnesses have identified a 'real' form and a 'ghost-like' form. In one case there is a classic doppelgänger, mimicking movements, while in another case there is a projection doing what it appears the real form is thinking she should be doing.

In the cases above we have indications of possible weakness in the 'real' person: Queen Elizabeth was in bed ill, and therefore presumably weakened; Mrs Dansie's nurse was absent from work because of illness, also therefore possibly in a weakened physical state. Is this weakness part of the mechanism, or a result of it?

Such a weakness on the part of the 'real' person was reported to us by a witness, Fleur, who saw her own projection. She described the incident as 'quite frightening'.

> 'When the children were young and we had our first house in Newbury Park, we had converted the fourth bedroom into a playroom for the kids and I was there, painting or something, at the table. I looked out of the window and what I saw really frightened me. Down in the garden I could actually see myself hanging washing out at the same time as I was here in the room. It was really quite creepy. I just couldn't understand. I did feel a bit weak and I thought, "This is creepy." I had to sit down.'[1]

The weakness could have been an effect of the shock of seeing something extraordinary, or it could have been a reflection of what Amélie's pupil's thought they saw. Clearly the 'Fleur' in the garden had some sort of physical presence if she was lifting and hanging out washing, perhaps the 'playroom Fleur' was sacrificing substance to create that physical form.

The case of Ruth offers some possible explanations for at least the second part of Amélie's situation.

> Ruth was born in 1951. Her upbringing was somewhat tortuous; her father was a forger, spent time in prison, took drugs and drank to excess, was for a time committed to a mental hospital, raped Ruth, and Ruth witnessed him sexually abusing another young girl. He attempted suicide at one point. Ruth was brought up in a variety of care institutions and children's homes.
>
> Not surprisingly, she had mental problems of her

5 Ghosts of the Living

own, and suffered from hallucinations that bothered her greatly, in particular hallucinations of her father. However, she learned how to control these hallucinations and eventually could create them or dismiss them at will. Even more extraordinarily – and this is the important aspect in comparison to Amélie – on two occasions hallucinations she had conjured up were visible to someone else.[33]

We are left with the possibility that Amélie's 'other' form might have been a hallucination shared by the pupils. If so, then it asks us to reconsider our definitions of hallucinations, which are popularly conceived of as 'internal', imaginary, creations. We might also have at our fingertips some clues to understanding doppelgängers. These may also be 'visible hallucinations' but not controlled by the witness; they seem to act like mimics, almost like reflections in the mirror. But perhaps the mechanisms are the same; the person happens to be focused on what he or she is really doing, and uses the same 'projection' mechanism to send the hallucination of that elsewhere.

This is all speculation; but it cannot be dismissed without further research as there are many who testify to such sightings. However, a simple case of a doppelgänger reported in *Fate* magazine suggests other possible mechanisms.

> In 1958 'Harold' in Chicago was eating dinner and watching – opposite him – his doppelgänger mimicking his actions. After the meal the duplicate disappeared. Harold had had other such experiences of his own doppelgänger. Harold always had a migraine when these incidents happened.[32]

We can probably dismiss any suggestion that the quality of the task creates the projection – eating is too commonplace and automatic an action to require concentration. However, offering a clue to the mechanism involved is the fact of

Ghostwatching

Harold's migraines – a migraine might make even the task of eating require effort and focus. We have to ask ourselves whether or not the migraine caused the doppelgänger, or the projection caused the migraine. As yet, we only have data, no answers.

As far as deliberate bi-locations go, the most dramatic case on record is that of a nun, Sister Mary, and the Jumano Indians, in the 1600s.

It appears to be an account of physical bi-location – being in two places at the same time – for several reasons. First, the Jumano Indians had items from her convent which suggest they were physically moved; secondly, Sister Mary appears to have been acting and re-acting with the Indians, and was not therefore a mimicking doppelgänger; thirdly, she seems to have had substance as far as is possible to tell, and taking items from the convent supports this possibility. The case is often cited as one of teleportation – that the physical Sister Mary simply moved by extraordinary means to a second location – but that is unclear as there is no evidence that Sister Mary was ever absent from her convent. Of course teleportation could have occurred during times when she might have been alone and in contemplation.

The story is as follows.

> Between 1620 and 1631 it is estimated that Sister Mary visited the Jumano Indians in New Mexico some five hundred times – apparently by paranormal means – but never left the convent in Spain where she lived.
>
> In 1622, Father Alonzo de Benavides of the Islita Mission embarked on missionary work with the Jumano Indians. He found that they had already converted to Christianity, and he asked of the King of Spain and the Pope who it was that had gone on ahead of him. They could, of course, provide no answers. The Indians informed him that they got their information from 'a lady in blue', a nun who had left with them physical objects such as crosses, rosaries and a chalice. The

5 **Ghosts of the Living**

chalice was identified as one from the Spanish convent where Sister Mary lived. When in Spain some years later Father Benavides heard of Sister Mary's claims and discovered that her accounts of the visits tallied exactly with the accounts he had heard from the Indians.

Catholic authorities tried to dissuade her from making public her claims but the testimony of missionaries to the Mexican Indians eventually forced them to admit knowledge of her experiences.[7]

An interesting perspective on just who or what causes bi-locations or projections was offered by Maurice Grosse, a leading authority on poltergeist activity, and the principal investigator of the Enfield Poltergeist.

While he was at the house that was the scene of the activity he was apparently seen in one part of the house while he was definitely in another.

As Maurice related the story to us:

'I was upstairs in a bedroom with some of the family, including the girl who was the main subject of the investigation. She was having one of her very violent turns; she went into very violent trances. We were very worried that evening; I had been with her for well over an hour. Towards the end of that hour there was a knock on the front door, downstairs. I asked the mother to go downstairs and open the door, which she did. It was her niece. She was indignant and asked, "Why didn't he open the door?" Asked who she meant, the niece said, "Mr Grosse." She was told I had been upstairs for over an hour. There was a silence, and the mother and the niece came up the stairs and into the bedroom. When she came in I could see she was white as a sheet. I even said she looked like she'd seen a ghost! She explained that she had knocked on the door, and nobody had answered; then she had knocked again. She told us, "Then the curtain was pulled aside and you

93

Ghostwatching

> [Maurice Grosse] looked out of the downstairs window. I expected you to open the door, but you didn't. I looked through the door [the glass pane and the letter box] and I could see you going up the stairs, but I could only see the lower part of you. I was surprised you hadn't opened the door. I was annoyed, and thought you didn't want me to come in; I was just about to go away but I decided to knock again." That was when we heard her.'
>
> There was no one else in the house who could have been mistaken for Maurice, and no one downstairs at the time.[1]

We asked Maurice if he had been conscious of any of this happening; he was adamant that he had no perception of it. He was concerned for the girl, and concentrating hard, but he was not aware of any annoyance towards the niece and had no reason to want to bar her from the house. He had no memory of the actions of the 'double'. We asked if he had felt weakened at the time; was he, like Fleur and perhaps Amélie Saegée, dividing his strength? Maurice had no belief that he was, but pointed out that his attention was so firmly fixed on the girl that he might not have noticed.

An interesting perspective on 'double images' is offered by T. C. Lethbridge. The case is not strictly one of ghost-like reports of the living, but the perceptions of the witnesses might offer something of interest.

> Lethbridge had apparently been 'trained' by his wife to notice interesting small details around him, and about people they were with. On this occasion they were visiting a friend he refers to as Mrs X.
>
> 'I noticed our friend's outfit when I sat opposite her at coffee. She and my wife sat side by side. I don't suppose I had seen her for over a year and never very often. After coffee we were shown various things about the house. I was often within a foot or two of Mrs X

5 Ghosts of the Living

and talking to her. There was no change in her appearance even when she came to the front door to see us into our car.'

When Lethbridge was driving home in the car he and his wife chatted about the visit. 'My wife remarked: "Poor Mrs X, how terribly strange she looked. Her hair has gone so white and she looked much older. Of course that white jumper did not help." "What?" I said. "A white jumper?" "Yes," said my wife, "with a modern silver Celtic brooch in the front of it." "That is not how I saw her," I said. "She had on a smart, silk I call it, light chocolate-coloured dress. I noticed it particularly and wondered if we ought to have come in old tweed. In the front of the dress was some openwork, round, gold brooch with some kind of yellow stone in the middle. I wondered if it was a topaz or a cairngorm. Her face appeared smooth and unlined and her hair was only slightly salted."'

Lethbridge realised that this did not seem to have been a mistake in observation. He regarded it as 'a definite slip in time of some sort. Either one of us was seeing Mrs X as she had been; or the other was seeing her as she was going to be. But to each of us she was there talking, drinking coffee, eating cakes, pointing out various things about the house and seeing us to our car ... She seemed to have been in two places in time. It was a fourth-dimensional displacement. I rather think that the displacement was mine and I had been seeing a "television" picture of Mrs X; although she was alive, well and talking to me for an hour. It was a perfectly normal phenomenon and it may happen far more frequently than anyone observes. For if only one of us had been present and there had not been two to check what we had each seen, no one would have noticed anything out of the ordinary ... It seems to be a perfect example of seeing a ghost; but the ghost was alive.'[55]

6 Other Ghost Phenomena; Associated Phenomena

IN DEALING WITH ghosts we have to consider related phenomena that implies the existence of the force we believe people perceive as a form, a presence, and so on. In this chapter we look at three such associated phenomena: balls of light, the spontaneous appearance of images, and psychic photography.

BALL-OF-LIGHT PHENOMENA

It has been suggested by investigators such as Hilary Evans and John Keel that the experiences of some UFO witnesses, when examined in terms of types of phenomena, seem to be similar to some types of ghost experiences.

The letter that follows is taken from the *Journal of the Society for Psychical Research* in October 1885. In some respects it is a model of objective reporting because it has been written in a way which describes the phenomenon as it occurred to the witness, and only at the end makes an attempt to categorise it. Even though descriptions of UFO phenomena didn't begin to occur until 60 years later, the light effect seems to bear a remarkable similarity to some types of UFO reports. (There are also many other comparisons to 'alien abduction' reports; the fear of being taken away is common to both reports.)

20 March 1885; a report by Edith N. Wilson.

'I do not know whether the following experience is

6 Other Ghost Phenomena; Associated Phenomena

of any practical value, but will relate it as being at least curious.

'I cannot be certain of the precise year, but know that it was winter – and I believe that of 1870–71. My sister and I were constant companions and slept in the same room, but in separate beds. We burnt no light at night. I was then twenty years old, and my sister eighteen. She was of very calm, placid temperament, and not in the least given to having exciting dreams. One night I was roused out of my sleep by her calling my name with a sort of scream, and on immediately starting up in bed I saw the room filled with a bright red light, which extended to the passage outside our door (which we always left open at night), so that I could distinctly see an arch that was in it, and also a blaze of red in the sky outside the window. The time was 2 a.m. Hearing my sister crying in great distress, I sprang out of bed to go to her and in that moment the impression faded, and the room became dark as usual. My sister then told me she had had a frightening dream of the devil coming to fetch her in a haze of red fire – that her only hope had been to call to me to save her, but that as usual with nightmares, she seemed to have been ages calling before she could make me hear.

'Must she not in some way, through her intense desire to communicate with me, have succeeded in impressing upon my brain what she saw in her dream, and thus produced the curious impression I received?'[36]

This letter seems to have prompted a response, for a Miss Bramston wrote the following in the next month's *Journal* (November 1885). She sent a note accompanying a letter from a friend of hers, a Miss G. Horner, and wonders whether the light effect was caused by a mine fire which she heard had happened before in Cornwall.

21 October 1885; from Gertrude Horner.
'It was about five years ago, and I think in January,

that I saw the light which you call a "mine fire". I was sitting by the window, in one of the lower rooms, when I saw a light suddenly pass, about the same height from the ground as one would generally carry a lantern. Hearing afterwards that no one had passed by I considered it very remarkable. It was about a week later when I saw it again, at least, not the light, but its reflection.

'I was in bed, and about one o'clock at night the room became suddenly lighted with a bright red light, which was, to say the least of it, rather startling. It seemed to be in the same place, but higher up and much brighter and redder than on the previous occasion. It must have been very near the window (which was about ten feet from the ground), for the marks and flaws on the glass were plainly reflected on the wall. I was very much frightened when I saw it, thinking that some burglar was about to enter my room through the window. But the light seemed to pass away as suddenly as it came, leaving the room in total darkness as before.

'The only explanation I ever heard was given me by a servant whose father was a miner in Zennor. She said that it was a kind of will-o'-the-wisp, which appeared over ground in which tin or copper were to be found. This seemed to be a natural explanation, as Zennor was full of old mines which had been worked many years ago and stopped probably on account of insufficient capital to carry them out.'[36]

Ghost light phenomena are not uncommon; there have been many reports associating balls of light with spirits of the deceased.

As a young man at the turn of the century Mr Arnold Millar often visited relatives in the village of Latheronwheel on the east coast of Caithness. One New Year's night, and for three or four successive nights, many of

6 Other Ghost Phenomena; Associated Phenomena

the local people saw a light on the highest point of the road which they thought might be the lamp of a coach or vehicle. However, no vehicle ever reached the village or was actually seen at the site. The day after the light was last seen a storm at sea sank a number of vessels from the fishing fleet from nearby Lybster, killing the crews of two of the boats. Once the storm had cleared search parties climbed the cliffs, peering down trying to locate corpses that might have been washed ashore. One body was found and brought up the cliffs and laid by the side of the road, apparently unwittingly on exactly the same spot where the light had been (though it is difficult to tell how from a distance anyone could be that sure).[37]

Thereafter the light was thought to be an omen of disaster and stories began to circulate of earlier sightings and earlier disasters, now more with the strength of legend than reality.

Light phenomena have been reported on the east coast of the island of Lewis in the Outer Hebrides, near the main town of Stornoway. We must be careful of reports from areas this close to either of the poles, because of the light effects known as the aurora borealis (also known as the Northern Lights) and the aurora australis (in the south).

One such report came from a local man, Kenneth MacDonald, who at the age of twelve had been playing with four friends when they saw a huge light flare in the ground near them. All the boys saw the light and it terrified them enough to make them run for home. The old folks of the nearby village of Sandwick declared that somebody would be found dead on that location. In 1935 a young man, worse for wear from drink, was lost and was discovered at the spot, dead from exposure.[37]

Another case from the same general area related to a man named Morrison, also a local inhabitant. He was returning from a night out in Stornoway to his farm in the company of another farmer and his son, who were heading towards Stoneyfield. Travelling in this farmer's trap, they reached the point where the road branches off to Holm and Morrison got off and walked along it on foot to his home there. As he looked back at the trap now heading off towards Stoneyfield, he could see a strange light travelling in front of it at no great distance from it.

The next day Morrison spoke to the farmer's son, asking if he too had seen the light. 'I certainly saw it, and I whipped the pony as hard as I could in an effort to overtake it. But I could not gain an inch on it,' said the farmer's son. 'Instead of turning in at Stoneyfield, I drove straight ahead, following it down as far as Holm Farm. I lost sight of it in turning the corner at the byre there.'

A day or two later the farmer, whose son had seen the light that night, was drowned in Stornoway harbour, and his body was carried to Holm Farm in the trap.[37]

The ghost of Bearnn Eile inhabits Lewis Island in the Outer Hebrides. Legend has it that in the eighteenth century an Irish pedlar was touring Lewis selling his wares when he called at a house in Doune Mor to ask for directions. One of the residents of the house offered to walk with the pedlar on his way and having got him into an isolated place murdered him with a hammer. According to local legend he carried the corpse 200 yards in order to bury it in the soft peat ground. The money he stole from the pedlar he hid in a well in the neighbourhood. The ghost of Bearnn Eile is a light which has been seen by many people, reputed to travel

6 Other Ghost Phenomena; Associated Phenomena

from the spot where the body was lying to the well said to be concealing his money.

In 1922 three witnesses saw the light and reputedly dug up the ground around the well to discover a small sealskin purse containing a number of Irish pennies from the mid-1700s.[37]

While exploring the area between the Ogowe and Rembwe Rivers Mary Kingsley (as related in her *Travels in West Africa* in 1895) was bathing and canoeing alone on the lake waters.

She saw coming through the forest on the lake bank a violet ball the size of a small orange which hovered over the beach. It was later joined by another similar ball and the two appeared to circle each other over the beach.

Although pursued by Mary Kingsley they escaped her, one going off into the bushes and the other into the lake itself. She was even able to watch it glowing as it sank down deep into the lake. Local natives explained the light as a devil's spirit.[38]

Local mythology 'explains' light phenomena in Brazil, personifying it in a similar way to the African case.

For over 150 years a glowing yellow-orange ball of light in Brazil has been known as 'Mãe de Ouro', the Mother of Gold. Local belief is that you will find your fortune in gold in the first body of water that the Mother of Gold crosses after you have seen it. The similarity to the legend of leprechauns in Ireland is obvious.

Cynthia Luce reported a sighting of the Mother of Gold in June 1980. She lives in a remote mountain village on a large area of land that she bought cheaply because locals believed it to be haunted.

She was with her daughter, two maids and a

gardener when she saw a yellow-orange ball of light pass from east to west about 30 feet away from them. It was wavering like a butterfly some five feet off the ground. The gardener tried to touch it, at which point the ball faded away, reappearing some 15 feet ahead of him. Believing that this was a sign of intelligence the farmer left it alone after that!

Cynthia Luce never saw the light again, but collected many reports from local people; she explained to them that such lights probably have a natural origin, but whether she convinced them or not is another matter.[39]

A light phenomenon more closely associated with a specific person after death was reported in the *Journal of the SPR* (1889) by Mary Helena Williams, and corroborated by her sister, Isabella.

'I was living at home with my parents at Eston-in-Cleveland. There was a working man called Long living in the village, not far from our house, whose wife was taken ill. Dr Fulton, who at that time was staying with us, came in one night between nine and ten o'clock and said Mrs Long was dying. After that we sat talking over the fire for a good while, and then my sister Isabella and I went off to bed. We slept in a back bedroom, and after we got to this bedroom I said, "Oh, I have forgotten something in the large bedroom." To this latter I proceeded by myself, and, as I approached the door, something seemed to say to me, "You'll see something of Mrs Long living or dead." But I thought no more of this, and entered the bedroom, which I had to cross to the opposite end for what I wanted. When I had got the things in my hand I noticed a lovely light hanging over my head. It was a round light – perfectly round. I had taken no light with me, but went for the things I wanted in the dark. I looked to see if there was any light coming in from the windows, but there was

6 Other Ghost Phenomena; Associated Phenomena

none: in that direction there was total darkness. I grasped one hand with the other and stood looking at the strange light to be sure that I was not deceived and was not imagining it. I walked across the room to the door and all the way the light was hanging between my head and the ceiling. It was akin to the electric light: something of a cloud, though every part of it was beaming and running over with the light. It left me at the bedroom door. On first seeing it a strange impression seized me, and after it left me I was so impressed that I could not speak of it to anyone for a day or two. I wondered at the time whether it had anything to do with Mrs Long, and on enquiry I found that she died just about the time when I saw the light. If there was any difference, I judged it would be a little before, but there would not be much in it. This was about 11 p.m. and about four years ago. It left an impression on my mind which I have never forgotten, and shall never forget. Mrs Long was not ill many days – about two or three: she died rather suddenly. I was rather interested in her. I did not see her during her illness, but had often seen her and talked to her before. I was perfectly well at the time and was in no trouble or anxiety. My age at the time was 23. I have had no experience of the kind before or since. I saw no figure, only a lovely light. Before telling my sister I made her promise she would not ridicule me nor call me superstitious.'

Miss Williams went on to add in a postscript to her letter: 'The light which I saw was a palish blue. It emitted no rays, so that all the rest of the room was in darkness. It was wider in circumference than my head, so that as I walked I could see it above me without raising my head. As I left the room it remained, and when I looked again it was gone. It was in a corner, where the darkness of the room was deepest and the least chance for illumination from the windows on the right and left, and I first saw it above my head. I had no fear, but a kind of sacred awe. The light was unlike any other that I ever saw, and I should say brighter than any other, or, at least, purer. Looking at it did not affect the eyes. It was midway between my head and the ceiling.'

Isabella confirmed: 'I recollect my sister Lily seeing the bright light. When she came back to the room where I was she was quite pale, and sat down on the floor. She was so awestruck that she did not tell us what she had seen until the next day. I remember that a woman who lived near us died about the time my sister saw the light, and that we connected the two circumstances together.'[40]

Hilary Evans in his book *Visions, Apparitions, Alien Visitors* describes a case where a ball of light turned into a human form and was a positive help at a time of crisis. It is cases such as these which link the ball-of-light 'ghost' to more 'usual' ones.

A German lady wrote to Hilary about her experience in the Bavarian Alps. She was delayed during a mountain climbing tour. Daylight was fading and, finding herself in a dangerous spot, she became quite worried. At that moment she noticed a 'sort of big ball of light, and this condensed to the shape of a tall, rather Chinese-looking gentleman'. She did not feel frightened; indeed, she felt it was all quite natural. The gentleman bowed, spoke a few words and led her to the tourists' path, disappearing again as a ball of light.

Apparently, a year later a young girl fell to her death at that very spot.[32]

Investigation into these ball-of-light phenomena is not much different from that into other 'non-interactive'-type ghosts; be there and be awake when it happens. However, it is worth

6 Other Ghost Phenomena; Associated Phenomena

noting that there are many 'normal' light phenomena to be seen, particularly at night. People should be trained to recognise these strange but normal occurrences. UFO research groups have training sessions in which they demonstrate to people these shapes and forms, and are always pleased to assist.

ANOMALOUS FACES

Perhaps the most famous case of anomalous faces is that of the so-called House of the Faces. This phenomenon occurred in the village of Bélmez de la Moraleda in Andalucía, Spain.

> On 23 August 1971 Mrs Maria Pereira, a farmer's wife, saw a mark on the floor of her kitchen which turned into a face over a period of seven days.
> The apparition frightened the family and one of Mrs Pereira's sons destroyed the image. It was soon replaced by another face. The local council cut out the stone floor containing the face; analysis showed no reason for the apparition. When the damaged floor was repaired a new face appeared; this was also destroyed.
> And so the saga went on; destroy the face and a new one would appear. At one point crosses appeared on the floor.
> The house was close to a church; when the floor was dug up human remains were found some eight to nine feet down, suggesting a cemetery there in the past. One can only speculate as to whether this is connected to the images.
> One of the faces, which appeared on 6 June 1972, even seemed, over time, to change its expression; later, other faces appeared around it.
> Researcher José Romero, who examined the case, indicated that he believed there was a connection between Maria's state of health and the images on the

floor; when she was feeling ill the images would drain in colour. Romero believed that the images were disappearing: 'And once Maria disappears the phenomena will disappear with her.'[25]

It has been suggested that Mrs Pereira was creating an equivalent of 'thoughtography' (see below). Could Mrs Pereira imprint pictures directly into the stonework of the kitchen floor?

There have been many other incidences of images of faces appearing; in 1891 the face of a recently deceased woman was found etched in glass on a window pane at her home, it could only be removed by her son; in 1923, a face believed to be Dr Liddell, the Dean of Christchurch Cathedral, who had died in 1898, was reported to have appeared on a plaster wall of the cathedral.

In December 1929 two members of the crew of the SS *Watertown* died aboard ship. They were buried at sea; but on the next day their faces were seen – and the images were photographed – imprinted on the waves. Their images were always seen from the same position on the deck. On the following two voyages of the *Watertown* the same images were seen; then never reported again.[7]

In W. H. Hudson's book *A Hind in Richmond Park*, he reports that he twice saw faces in the air in front of him. He believed the images to be the result of telepathy. In fact he took that one stage further, believing that the telepathy was enhanced if the wind was in the right direction.

While walking down a London street he became aware of the face of a girl appearing in front of him. The face seemed to be blowing in the wind. (Hence perhaps his rather adventurous conclusion.) It was

6 Other Ghost Phenomena; Associated Phenomena

fluttering and waving like a 'flag or some filmy substance agitated by the wind'.

The face was that of a girl he knew well, and who lived 80 miles away from London. As Hudson said: 'It was to me an amazing experience, as I am about the last person in the Universe to suffer from delusions and illusions, being, as someone has said, "too disgustingly sane for anything".'

Hudson wrote to the girl's mother asking if all was well. He was assured that it was, but he was unconvinced. The images had provoked a concern within him. He was sure that something was troubling the girl, something of which the mother was unaware. He visited the family – a deeply religious one – and discovered there was a lot of tension arising from the girl questioning their religion, even to the point of rejection.

Hudson's second 'face' experience was while he was walking in a strong wind in Cornwall. He was looking for gloves that he had lost. Suddenly, he saw a face fluttering in front of him, just as on the previous occasion.

Again it was the face of 'an intimate and dear friend who was at a distance of something under 400 miles from me at that moment'. Hudson apparently knew why he received the 'image' but does not discuss it in his book, presumably protecting his own or the other person's privacy.[35]

Quite why this one person – Hudson – should experience either 'ghosts' or telepathy in this unique way is unclear. Since he had a rather interesting theory about telepathy it may be that he 'chose' to perceive his impressions in that way.

Ghostwatching

PSYCHIC PHOTOGRAPHY

There have been many experiments over the years to try to capture paranormal images on photographic film. It has often been postulated that because photographic materials can be made sensitive to wavelengths of light that humans cannot perceive, it may be possible to capture images on film which would not normally be seen – even ordinary domestic photographic film is fairly sensitive to light in the infra-red spectrum.

Unfortunately, there are so many mechanical and photo-technical reasons why mysterious streaks and blobs can appear in photographic pictures, that it is very difficult to be confident that a blob here or a streak there on film can be attributed to a paranormal cause. Similarly, deliberate fraud could easily be perpetrated. The late Brian Inglis, in his book *Natural and Supernatural*, describes a well-conducted scientific experiment.

In 1893 J. Traill Taylor, a member of the Council of the Photographic Society of Great Britain, read a paper on his experiments with spirit photography to the London and Provincial Photographic Association. His objective was to get a reputable Scottish medium, David Duguid, to place images of spirits on photographic plates under conditions where mistakes and fraud could be eliminated. The experiments took place in front of reputable witnesses, and with a second, binocular camera as a control. The control had the main camera in its field of view and all photographic plates remained sealed until ready for use. Throughout the sessions, Duguid was not allowed to touch the equipment, and as an extra precaution, Taylor sometimes asked the witnesses to take the pictures.

When they were developed, some of the plates showed 'abnormal images'. Some of these images could

6 Other Ghost Phenomena; Associated Phenomena

also be seen on the plates taken by the stereo camera. The curious fact of the stereo pictures was that although both the left- and right-hand sections of the plates had captured the shapes, they had no depth-of-field, and the two images were not in the same place in their respective halves, when compared to the also-present images of the sitters. The flatness of the 'spirit' images led Taylor to conclude that the images were not taken through the lens, but were imposed directly on to the plates. The images captured were clearly of human beings, some were in focus, some were not; others seemed to cover the majority of the plate. But were they pictures of the dead? An alternative theory is that Duguid was somehow able to cause the plates' photographic emulsion to be triggered by something akin to light.

Other photographic experiments with other people have yielded all sorts of shapes, not necessarily of humans.[34]

THOUGHTOGRAPHY

In 'thoughtography', a variant of spirit photography, the experimenter will think of a subject when the shutter of the camera opens, the idea being to try and capture that thought on film.

The main claims for this phenomenon come from experiments with Ted Serios in the mid-sixties.

In 1964 in front of eyewitnesses and under the observation of researcher Dr Jule Eisenbud, Serios would point a Polaroid camera at his own face and concentrate on it. Most of the pictures were unremarkable; occasionally he got blank prints either whited-out or blacked-out, but there were some astonishing, thought-provoking, successes.

Although he was working in Denver at the time

Ghostwatching

some of the resultant images were of much more distant locations: London or Venice, for example. In May 1965 Serios produced a series of pictures of a store-front in Central City, Colorado. The name 'The Old Gold Store', with a small but curious 'misspelling', was visible on the prints; the mystery was that several years previously the store had changed its name to 'The Old Wells Fargo Express Office'. Photographs of the store with the old name could not be located. The other oddity was that in Serios's photographs the name appeared as 'The Wld Gold Store', with the 'W' positioned exactly where the 'W' of Wells appeared in the modern name.

Other photographs contained similar anomalies: a photograph of a hangar belonging to the Royal Canadian Mounted Police was easily identifiable but the name 'Canadian' was spelt 'Sainadain' and the 'O' of Mounted looks like a 'D'. A picture of the Williams Livery Stable in Colorado is accurate in general shape, but actually shows a different brick facing and even some bricked-out windows. Serios shortly afterwards claimed that he had lost his abilities; he has not produced thoughtographs since. There were inevitable claims that Serios was faking the effects. He used a device he called a 'gismo' which he kept away from the researchers, and it has been suggested that this gismo might have contained images that were in some way produced on the thoughtographs. No one has yet proved, however, that this was the case.[2]

Thoughtography offers a viewpoint about psychic photography, which includes the spontaneous appearance of images — principally spirit faces — on film, as well as elsewhere. The next chapter picks up on the technological aspects; ghosts and spirits seem to be making themselves known through very advanced equipment indeed.

7 The Ghosts in the Machine?

THERE ARE MANY TYPES of ghost phenomena that arise in modern technology. Perhaps the phenomena could always interact with forces such as electricity, and ever more sophisticated modern technology only now allows us to perceive them, or perhaps the ghost phenomena evolve along with our own developments. The ability of electronic equipment apparently to pick up and reproduce 'spirit voices' – Electronic Voice Phenomena – is a case in point.

ELECTRONIC VOICE PHENOMENA (EVP)

Among researchers who accept evidence for some types of paranormal phenomena, there is debate as to whether EVP is genuine. It is claimed by many enthusiasts that it is possible to use domestic recording technology to pick up messages from the dead. The supposed advantage of EVP is that a conventional human 'medium' is not required – the spirits of the dead are able to manipulate electronic equipment to produce audible sounds. Other EVP researchers are more wary about the source of the sounds and suggest that the equipment might be picking up telepathic waves from the human mind. We will concentrate on the theory that EVP represents a form of ghost-appearance.

The phenomenon was first discussed in public in 1959 when Friedrich Jürgensen, a Swedish singer and film producer, noticed unexpected noises on tape-recordings of

Ghostwatching

birdsong. The first recording was of a voice speaking Norwegian, discussing birdsong. He assumed that the tape-recorder was accidentally functioning as a radio receiver. A few weeks later, after another recording session, he heard a woman's voice, saying in German, 'Friedel, my little Friedel, can you hear me?' The voice sounded just like that of his mother who had died a few years earlier. His initial assumption of radio pickup seemed less likely when he discovered more messages of a personal and relevant nature.

In 1964 he published his findings in a book[42]; by then he had also experimented with alternative ways to obtain the voices. His second technique was to tune a medium-wave radio receiver to a frequency between stations and to listen there for messages. His book aroused the interest of a Dr Konstantin Raudive, who after a visit to Jürgensen, decided to try his own experiments. After three months of patient listening, he picked up a message in Latvian. Encouraged, he listened again to earlier recordings and found messages that he had missed. Dr Raudive had recorded over 70,000 messages by the time he published his own book in 1968 on the subject and in 1971 the English edition, *Breakthrough*,[43] was published. The book includes a gramophone record giving samples of EVP voices from Dr Raudive's, and others', experiments.

In the UK, public discussion and interest in the subject of EVP seemed to peak in 1972. At that time, a number of eminent sound and radio engineers in Europe, including the Chief Engineer at Pye, had declared the phenomenon worthy of further investigation. The then chairman of the SPR's Survival Joint Research Committee (SJRC), R. K. Sheargold, also found the phenomenon interesting and managed to capture his own voices on tape and wrote to the UK publishers of *Breakthrough* on 20 September 1971 to say that '... I am now in a position to assure my colleagues in the SJRC that the phenomena are real!' By 1973, however, enthusiasm had waned; many of the parties who had originally been intrigued seemed to be retracting their statements.

7 The Ghosts in the Machine?

In 1978 D. J. Ellis published his book *The Mediumship of the Tape Recorder*,[51] which cast doubt on the enthusiasts' claims, propounding the likelihood that the recordings were little more than stray noises which were being interpreted as significant messages by over-enthusiastic listeners. However, the counter-argument by enthusiasts is that groups of people have individually worked through the voices, syllable by syllable, and then compared notes; in many cases there has been a consensus view of the investigators' understanding of the word-content of phrases.

WHY THE DOUBTS?

There are two main problems with verifying that EVP is a genuine phenomenon. The first is that electronic equipment of all types can under certain circumstances pick up stray radio signals. Even under the most stringent screening it is impossible to rule out radio breakthrough, especially at low frequencies. Supporters of the phenomenon answer that the messages received are often in context for the listener, and this rules out pickup of stray radio signals. However, a further complication is that the quality of the messages is often poor, usually just above the noise of the radio or recording equipment, and the messages sometimes require repeated replaying in order to make sense of the words. Interpretation of the actual words can be highly subjective, too. It is therefore possible, say the sceptics, that the listeners are hearing a meaning which they think is relevant to them, but in reality there is no message, just electronic 'glitches' or stray radio pickup. The criticism often levelled at Dr Raudive was that he could speak many languages and was able to interpret random sounds as being messages spoken in a variety of different languages.

Ghostwatching

CURRENT RESEARCH

Although public attention waned from 1973, *Breakthrough* had aroused considerable interest in the UK, and sparked off experiments by various individuals. George Bonner began his own work in October 1972 when he recorded his first voice; as with many others he had to replay the tape three times before he could make out the details. Over the last twenty years he has undertaken over £10,000 worth of research on improving the quality of the messages received, and has spent considerable time talking to EVP enthusiasts around the world.[45] Interestingly, he has also worked with staff at GCHQ and the US Air Force. The former agency helped him determine whether the sounds recorded were, in fact, voices. His view is that if the voices could be proved to be real, then it would help counter the claims of the EVP critics that the supposed relevance of the messages was simply the imagination of the listener.

He has been persistent in proving the authenticity of his voices. When he first started obtaining his recordings he discussed the issues with a psychiatrist friend to check whether he was imagining the voices. The psychiatrist concluded that 'If I can hear it, it must be on the tape, and therefore it must be real'. After receiving reassurances he approached GCHQ, Cheltenham, where James Ellis of the Joint Speech Research Unit was able to state that a spectrographic analysis of the sounds showed that they were 'male and female voices of human or synthetic origin'. George's correspondence with the US Air Force was more enigmatic; in 1981 he was approached by Philip Paul of the US Air Force Electronic Security Command, Electronic Warfare Centre, Studies and Analysis Branch. George corresponded with Philip Paul for three years, explaining the details of his EVP techniques and experiments. Information flow seems to have been mostly one-way as the reasons why the US Air Force was interested in the techniques seem to have been marked as classified.[45]

7 The Ghosts in the Machine?

WHAT IS EVP PICKING UP?

If EVP actually works, then what is it picking up? The mainstream belief by supporters is that the experiments pick up voices 'from the other side'. An alternative explanation, worthy of further investigation, is the possibility that the electronic mechanism of the radio and tape-recorder is somehow picking up thoughts telepathically from the living. There are, however, examples of recording which fit more easily into the 'other side' category. One example comes from George Bonner. He had fallen asleep in an armchair and flopped into a very uncomfortable position whilst running an EVP recording. After waking up and replaying the tape he found a message saying 'Bonner looks ridiculous'. It is unlikely that he would have made that message himself as he was asleep. In this example telepathy from his own mind is less likely than a message 'from the other side'.

THE EVP MECHANISM

Assuming that EVP works, then the mechanism for operation seems to rely on electronics to modulate noise and so produce speech patterns. It is significant that attempts to record signals using radio equipment rely on tuning to a quiet section of a band, where there is just random hiss. Modulation of noise to produce intelligible sound is not impossible. Parapsychologists have proved under laboratory conditions that experimenters are able, by concentration of will, to cause random noise from a noise source to become non-random. Tony, with his radio and electronics background, wonders whether EVP is another aspect of micro-psychokinesis (m-PK) which has been proved to exist in laboratory tests. Both EVP and micro-PK seem to rely on noise as the medium for showing up their different effects. EVP produces speech patterns superimposed on noise, whereas m-PK produces non-random pulses in digital circuits.

Ghostwatching

EVP EXPERIMENTS

The voices heard are so different from normal speech, and so difficult to pick out of the noise, that budding experimenters are advised to listen to *Breakthrough*'s gramophone record or George Bonner's tape before starting out; otherwise it is possible that if they do obtain voices they will not recognise them as such in the noise.

Dr Raudive's *Breakthrough* and D. J. Ellis's book, *The Mediumship of the Tape Recorder*, give details of experimental set-ups which can be tried without any special equipment. The first is to go to a quiet room and connect a microphone to a tape-recorder, switch to record, and announce yourself, say that you are ready to receive messages, settle down and wait. On playback, after ignoring obvious sounds such as those generated by domestic noise, you may be able to hear faint sounds which require close examination – these may be the voices to look for. The second technique is to tune a medium-wave radio receiver to a quiet portion of the band and record the sounds either using a microphone, or directly, with a connecting lead. Again the voices may be extremely faint. Investigators have often had to resort to recording scraps of sound on a tape loop and listening to that instead as re-recordings are sometimes clearer.

EXPERIMENTATION

With EVP (and 'thoughtography') experimentation there is the problem of its being difficult to verify results; in addition, there are delays in obtaining the results of the experiments. With spirit and thought photography one has to wait for the film to be developed – unless one uses Polaroid-type film. With EVP one has to sift through many minutes of tape to find the voices. Nevertheless, it is open to all to try these experiments; to us the lure of capturing these anomalies is understandable. Please remember, however, that if images or

7 The Ghosts in the Machine?

messages do come through, they should not be, to quote Dr Alan Gauld, author of *Mediumship and Survival*,[49] afforded the status of words from the oracle. The warnings given in Chapter 11 about Ouija boards also apply here.

If any reader feels that they have obtained meaningful results from these kinds of experiments, they can contact either the SPR or ASSAP and ask for the pictures or tapes to be assessed by an expert. Membership of either organisation is not necessary for this service. The authors would also be pleased to hear from people who feel that they have obtained results.

OTHER TECHNOLOGY-BASED PHENOMENA

Some people have attempted communication with the dead by means of TV pictures, and others by computer. Claims for visual communication are not new as discussed at the beginning of this chapter – 'pictures of the dead' have been with us since the invention of modern photography. However, Tony Wells, who has designed and built radios, televisions, military communications equipment and computers, thinks that there is a world of difference between putting streaks and blobs on a piece of photographic film, and displaying a picture on a television screen. He has this to say:

'I'm afraid that my boggle factor goes into the red zone when I am told that it is possible to put readable information on media which rely on sophisticated, synchronous electronics to store or display it. In the case of a TV screen, to produce a stable image that is not too distorted, the sender will have to stimulate the TV's circuits at a speed in excess of one million cycles per second and with a high degree of timing accuracy. In order to display a reasonably clear image, the picture would have to be re-scanned and sent at 25 times a second. A colour picture would be even harder to produce – in addition to the requirements just described, the image's picture would have to be broken down into its components (red, yellow and blue) and the three separate components encoded properly. Similar problems apply when discussing putting images directly on to video tape.

'In the case of computer technology, where messages are put on the computer, and assuming that the "contactor" does not literally turn the computer on and press keys on the keyboard via some kind of PK, then the data must be put into the computer's electronics somehow, and in a way which does not cause it to 'lock up'. Some claims have been made that a computer has been left, switched off, overnight, and in the morning the data is found on the disk drive and can be recalled with ease. To be able to get data on to the disk drive, similar rules as those to TV signals apply – there must be a means of providing high-speed, highly synchronous and responsive electrical signals, or of laying magnetic information on a disk platter which can be read by the computer's operating system.

'Having said all that, I do, however, remain open to discussion of how these effects could be achieved and would be interested in discussing experiments with practitioners who feel that they can produce these kinds of phenomena.'

THE TELEPHONE AS A MEANS OF PARANORMAL COMMUNICATION

As we live with more and more technology, there becomes a wider opportunity for it to be affected by the paranormal. Poltergeists have now learned to change channels on the TV, and seem able to make sound and video recording equipment misbehave or stop working completely. To most people, the humble telephone is such a familiar instrument that it is just another piece of furniture in the home. Perhaps that is why it has become another means of paranormal communication.

The book *Phone Calls from the Dead* by D. Scott Rogo and Raymond Bayliss makes a well-researched case that the telephone can be used in just such a way. One example from

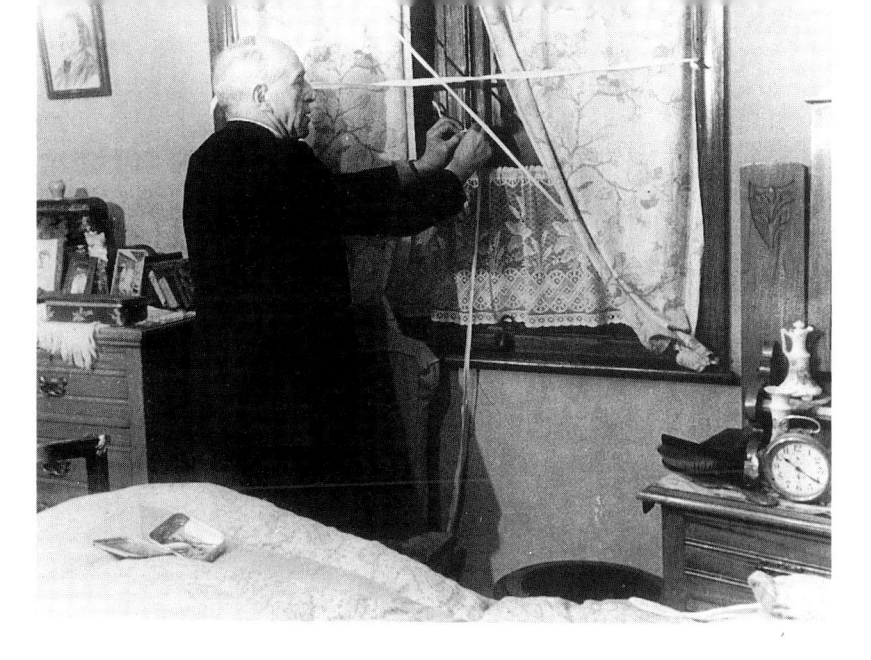

Harry Price setting up controls during the investigation of the Crawley Case, 22 December 1945. Sealing doors and windows is a common technique for investigating poltergeist phenomena (*Mary Evans/Harry Price Collection, University of London*)

The ruins of Borley Rectory before its eventual demolition. This photograph taken on 5 April 1944 shows the alleged 'flying brick' in the dark area near the centre. Borley Rectory was extensively investigated by Harry Price, one of the most famous ghost researchers of the first half of this century (*Mary Evans/Harry Price Collection, University of London*)

Charlton House in south London. Apart from several ghost reports investigated by the authors here, Charlton House has also been the site of their own group experiments and the location of their first evening classes in the Paranormal (*Tony Wells*)

A reputedly haunted staircase in Charlton House. During one vigil, Tony Wells felt particularly disturbed in this location (*Tony Wells*)

Rochester Castle in Kent, the location of a particularly uncomfortable vigil. The castle has no floors or ceiling, and during the authors' stay there, it was both cold and wet. The photograph shows the flagpole which was eventually identified as the source of the 'galloping horses' noise (*Tony Wells*)

The Environmental Monitoring Unit (EMU) module set up at the Waldorf Restaurant in Maidstone. The restaurant had been plagued by poltergeist activities which the authors' vigil team went in to investigate (*Tony Wells*)

Robin Lawrence on site in Dover Castle. Robin set up the original vigils in this location, and is an active team leader and ghost researcher in the Kent and south England area (*John Spencer*)

The interior of St John's Tower, Dover Castle, where a double bang was heard by several pairs of the vigil team. No explanation was found despite all group members converging rapidly on the location from all directions (*John Spencer*)

The Ancient Ram Inn in Gloucestershire. John Spencer and Mike Lewis, the head of ASSAP's investigations team, spent a night on vigil in a room here, which is reputedly the most haunted in England. During another vigil here, thermometers recorded an extraordinary rate of temperature fall from 18°C to below freezing (*John Spencer*)

The Bishop's Room in the Ancient Ram Inn. The vigil team set up an experiment to waken a poltergeist, which had, if nothing else, a humorous ending (*John Spencer*)

The Home of Compassion in Thames Ditton, Surrey. There have been many independent sightings of ghosts of the nuns who originally ran the home in the years since their departure (*John Spencer*)

Hampton Court, scene of many royal hauntings. Several of Henry VIII's wives have been reported here, including Catherine Howard, Anne Boleyn and Jane Seymour (*John Spencer*)

A colleague of the authors, Chris Walton, demonstrating how *not* to go ghostwatching. A large amount of equipment is often deployed, but tact and discretion are also useful tools of the ghostwatcher (*Simon Earwicker*)

The Long Gallery in Charlton House. The authors conducted experiments in table rapping on this site, with the result that three people, including both authors, simultaneously perceived the presence of a ghost in the same location (*John Spencer*)

One of the famous 'Bélmez faces' which appeared on a kitchen floor in Spain in the mountain village of Bélmez de la Moraleda in August 1971 (*Mary Evans Picture Library*)

7 The Ghosts in the Machine?

their book that struck us in particular was originally reported by Mr Don B. Owens of Toledo, Ohio, in the September 1969 issue of *Fate*.

Don had a very close friend, Leigh Epps, a bachelor who had no luck with women. Consequently he valued his few close friends, who included Don and his wife, whom he called 'Sis'. After Leigh moved to another area they drifted apart, and their meetings became rare. At 10.30 p.m. on 26 October 1968 whilst Don was out, his wife received a phone call from Leigh:

'Sis, tell Don I'm feeling real bad. Never felt this way before. Tell him to get in touch with me the minute he comes in. It's important, Sis.'

Don tried to phone Leigh back many times but with no success. He discovered later that at exactly the time of the phone call, Leigh had died in the Mercy Hospital, only six blocks away.[41]

Another case occurred in 1977, when a phantom voice desperately tried to communicate over the telephone with Mrs Elsie Pendleton of Palos Verde, California.

Her mother, Mimi, had lived some way away, in Hollywood, and they used to talk on the phone several times a week to swap gossip. Mimi became ill, and moved into Elsie's apartment block, where she finally died. At the time Elsie was beginning to be concerned about her grandson, Scott. Badly behaved at best, after his great-grandmother's death, without her moderating influence, he became uncontrollable. One evening in February 1975, about six months after Mimi's death, the family decided to send him back to his natural family in Hawaii. That evening, while Elsie was alseep, the phone rang. With her husband at sea, she was instantly awake, alert to the possibility of a problem with the ship. However, she instantly recognised the voice of her dead mother.

Ghostwatching

'Elsie, I can't find Connie,' it blurted out. (Connie was Elsie's daughter.)

At first Mrs Pendleton forgot that her mother was actually dead; she could only reply, 'Mimi, what are you calling me for at this time of night?'

'I can't find Connie. I've been trying to get in touch with Connie for two or three days and I can't get in touch with her. I can't get in touch with Connie.'

'What's the matter?' asked Elsie.

'It's Scott,' Mimi replied. 'I've got to talk to Connie. Tell Scott. *No*. Write it down so you won't forget when you see Connie. I said to tell him, to tell Scott, *No*!' The line then went dead.

It wasn't until morning that the significance of the call hit her. What really emphasised the reality of the incident was the message on the telephone pad by her bed. There were the words: 'Tell Scott, NO!' scribbled in the handwriting of her deceased mother.

There was a sad postscript. Scott's recklessness became even worse, and eventually he was killed in a senseless road accident.[41]

The past is rich with stories of ghostly church bells supposedly transmitting some kind of message. This is a twentieth-century version, with modern alarm bells. The case was reported directly to John Spencer and his wife Anne.

'Claire' was confined in Wycombe General Hospital in mid-1986, about to give birth to her second son. She was kept awake one night with the sound of a room alarm bell going off behind the nurses' station. Claire thought it rather strange that the nurses didn't respond. After about the sixth ring she was intrigued when the janitor was called to investigate and he visited not a sick room, but the patients' dining room. The next day she asked a nurse what had been happening. Apparently the room had once been the babies' nursery and the alarm

7 The Ghosts in the Machine?

used to go off in the middle of the night for no obvious reason. The wiring and equipment had been thoroughly checked out but still the alarm would be triggered. Scared that there might be some kind of ghost pressing the alarm buttons the nurses refused to visit the room at night. They were so adamant that the nursery had to be moved elsewhere. Despite this the alarm still continued to go off.[1]

COMMUNICATION BY MORSE CPDE

In *Phone Calls From the Dead*, Rogo and Bayliss discuss an early attempt at radio communication with the dead. In 1915 some extraordinary articles appeared, starting with one by David Wilson in the March issue of the psychic magazine *Light*. It is titled 'Etheric Transmission of Thought'. It is interesting for two reasons. First, he had discovered that 'something' was attempting to communicate with him by radio, using Morse code. In many respects this is an advancement of the alphabetic rapping system used in spiritualist sittings with mediums. In 1915, such communication by Morse key was probably pretty advanced stuff. Compared with today, it must be on a par, for example, with receiving paranormal messages via a computer network.

The second point of interest is that, once he had refined his methods, Wilson used a control mechanism to determine whether the messages he picked up could also be received by other stations.

His thought processes were inspired by the theory at the time that as radio waves were supposed to travel in free space by means of a medium called the ether, then it should be possible that thought, in the form of telepathy, could travel by a similar route. If this is the case, then the conjecture is that telepathy and 'wireless' are the same, or similar, systems; if so, then could radio equipment be used to pick up thought messages?

Ghostwatching

In those days, the detection of radio waves was rather primitive and insensitive; then, neither valves nor transistors, nor even the primitive crystal set using the cat's whisker, had been invented. The only detector was a tube filled with iron filings, often called a 'coherer', because the iron filings stuck together and conducted electricity in the presence of radio waves of sufficient strength.

His equipment set-up included a sensitive meter (a galvanometer), and no aerial. It seems he received nothing for a long time. Eventually he noticed a regular pattern of meter 'flicks'. There was no coincidence – it was the letter 'V' being sent.

On 10 January 1915, he again received the Morse code signal 'V' for eight minutes continuously, followed by a proper message, but in mutilated form: 'Great difficulty, await message, five days, sixth evening.'

Wilson was anxious that other people should witness the expected message, and arranged for a reputable person to be present. He also arranged for that person to learn Morse code, so as to be capable of ensuring that Wilson was not making up the message from the needle flicks.

In Wilson's own words:

'I was astonished, therefore, when at 6.04 p.m. by my watch the dial once more recorded slowly and unmistakably the Morse code signal, and continued to do so for nearly half an hour.

'At 6.31 the dial recorded the following letters by Morse, which were taken down independently both by myself and the witness to whom I have referred, and of which the following are word-for-word versions:

1. Version by witness:- TRZELIOININAMEVIVRATIMNS.
2. My version:- RYELIMINA-E-BRA-IONS---ARTK.'

Wilson stated that the two versions were taken down independently of each other and by comparing them he

7 The Ghosts in the Machine?

obtained the message: 'TRY ELIMINATE VIBRATIONS –ARTK'.

After some thought, Wilson decided that he could improve the quality of reception by interposing a Morse key in the radio circuit, and arranged for a person to press the key only when they thought that a Morse 'flick' was being received. His view was that this could work in the manner of automatic writing. The neat thing about his circuit was that it was only when both the signal was received and the key was pressed that a flick could be detected. If only one of the pair was triggered, nothing would result.

Unfortunately, the message received by Wilson was not particularly inspiring. Here is a sample quoted in his article: 'So once came the Prince of Egypt into Ptah-Mes of Memphis, saying, "How many slaves shall attend me when I go forth from Abydos to serve me on the great journey as befits my state?" "Prince," saith Ptah-Mes, "empty-handed and alone thou shalt journey through Amenti save sympathy be thy retainer."'

Over the next months Wilson added further notes on his progress. He was worried that he might be picking up telepathic messages which were not from the dead. There was little chance that the messages could have come from a radio source, as the Morse key would have prevented that. He tried a further experiment with a duplicate machine in Paris, and on 19 March 1916 he received a message in Russian: 'NYET LEEZDYES KOGONEEDBOOD KTO GOVOREET POROOSKY' – 'Is there anyone who speaks Russian here?'

The same, though greatly distorted message was picked up by his friend in Paris: 'NYET ... LEE ... (incoherent) ... KTO ... POROOSKI'.

CONCLUSION

So what does all this mean?

There is plenty of evidence to suggest that technology has

Ghostwatching

been, and is being, used to receive messages of some kind. But are they evidence of communication with the dead? Many of the messages are not particularly strong evidence of such – in many cases they are pretty boring. They do not appear to be rich in information or content, although the crises phone calls described in this chapter seem to have a specific purpose.

So where are they coming from – our own minds, from another time, from another planet or galaxy, or from the dead – or a mixture of several or all?

For the moment, all we can do is encourage those who are so inclined to keep experimenting.

We can widen the range of these questions to encompass all of the ghosts that we have described in the first section of this book. In the next sections of the book we move on to 'encourage those who are so inclined to keep experimenting' in the broadest sense of ghost research.

Part Two

GHOSTWATCHING

8 Vigils

"'Tis now the very witching time of night,
When churchyards yawn, and hell itself breathes out
Contagion into this world.'

Hamlet, III, iii

THERE ARE FEW things more exciting than watching a paranormal event which is breaking the boundaries of established science while knowing you are with colleagues whom you trust, and who are willing to confirm that such an event occurred. The purpose of this chapter is to help you plan for, and conduct, a vigil. Proper planning will help create the right conditions to observe the paranormal.

The paranormal can, of course, happen at any time; investigators may not be present, may not be prepared, and there may not be any witnesses.

A vigil has several dictionary definitions, but the one we like best is 'To maintain a purposeful watch, especially at night'. For ghostwatchers, the purpose of the vigil is to have teams and equipment on site, under controlled conditions, so that there is reliable observation of the paranormal, should it arise.

It is important to explain at this point that very few vigils actually produce observations of paranormal phenomena worthy of note. Figures vary, depending on who is consulted, and seem to range from one successful vigil in ten to none at all. One colleague, after a particularly boring vigil, pointed out the rather macabre fact that waiting for a ghost was like waiting at an airport for an aeroplane crash – it rarely happens.

But when it does happen, it can happen unexpectedly.

A few days before we wrote this chapter, Tony and two of his ghosthunting colleagues, Chris and Philip Walton,

Ghostwatching

were invited to an all-night vigil at Dover Castle (a previous vigil at this location is described below), which was conducted by the investigator Robin Lawrence. The purpose of the vigil was largely to gain publicity for the science of ghostwatching and thus to generate calls from households who wanted their ghosts investigated. A TV crew was there and we were not expecting to experience any phenomena — we were just going through the motions for the crew.

At about 2.30 a.m., Philip and Chris were walking by the castle wall towards the underground tunnels when they nearly jumped out of their skin. They heard the sound of a woman's scream coming from the top of one of the towers. They recovered their wits and separately pointed their torches at the same spot where the sound seemed to be coming from — there was nothing to be seen. There was a second scream and then a third scream which was modulated in a way which sounded as if the person had jumped off the tower. At this point Chris, who, judging by the sound, thought he was directly underneath a falling body, ran, at speed, away from the castle wall to avoid being hit. Philip, although he wanted to run, had a heavy rucksack on his back and just couldn't get moving in time. A few seconds later they realised that nothing had hit the ground. They both insist that the sound was of a woman's scream and not that of a bird of prey. Both work outdoors and are familiar with normal outdoor sounds, such as that made by animals and birds at night.

Even if nothing happens on a vigil, there are other more earthly compensations for the ghosthunter. When attending a castle for example, it is not uncommon for the group to be given a personal tour around the site, and to hear the rumours and historic details not normally given to the public.

In order to understand in detail what happens at a ghostwatch (or ghost vigil) we have chosen, first, a recent one John Spencer has undertaken. (The descriptions are taken directly from John's notes, recorded in the first person.) Being somewhat complex it supplies examples of a variety of

8 Vigils

situations. No vigil is the same, but every ghostwatcher can learn something from every vigil. Following that are notes from other vigils either or both of us have attended; showing the serious and the humorous side of the work, and the almost inevitable mistakes that we all make.

VIGIL AT DOVER CASTLE

The vigil took place on 12 October 1991 at Dover Castle, a large well-preserved castle in the south of England, run by English Heritage. We were called in to see if we could help identify and analyse some unusual visual and auditory phenomena reported in two particular locations.

The vigil was organised by Robin Lawrence, an experienced investigator who, a month before the event, briefed us on what to expect. It wasn't until we saw the aerial photographs that we realised how large the castle was. Because it was the first time we had ever worked with English Heritage we were anxious to make a good impression, so the timing of the vigil was set to precise standards. It was decided to use a watch rota, allowing the places to be investigated by eight teams working in pairs.

When we arrived, and after having our number plates and identities checked by the castle security staff we drove to the unloading point, and at that point I realised I had made my first mistake – I had brought far too much equipment. Not wanting to be ill-equipped, I thought I should bring everything that has ever been useful on a ghost vigil including: a borrowed industrial video system; cameras; two tape-recorders; and a huge box of assorted bits. To make it worse, knowing that a chair would be needed, I brought the only one I could find at the last minute – a comfortable but large reclining deckchair. The problems soon became obvious – I had to climb many flights of stairs with all this stuff. In the introduction we said that ghostwatching can be physically exhausting – perhaps now this might explain why! During

Ghostwatching

the vigil the problems presented themselves again. Our shifts had been divided into two-hour rotas, with 15 minutes allowed for changeovers and personal comfort arrangements. The carrying of all the gear absorbed a lot of this time. If any of the public had been around that night they would have seen a bizarre apparition stalking the castle carrying a huge bundle of bits and an armchair. I mentioned before that we were working in pairs: Ian, whom I was paired with, helped carry some things, but he had his own equipment to deal with.

During the first session all groups quickly realised that sound was travelling in a curiously telescoped manner. Small sounds would travel a long way, and loud sounds were attenuated quickly. Therefore for the rest of the night we had to try to work to a strict regime of silence.

Ian and I discovered our first anomaly on the first watch. We noticed a temperature difference at the end of our corridor. We set up thermometers at each end and both recorded a temperature of 55° Fahrenheit, but there was no doubt that one end *felt* significantly colder. During the first changeover we asked for the next team that would be in our location to take temperature readings – without mentioning our own findings – and they made exactly the same observation. That said, we were never able to draw any conclusion from it and certainly jumped to no paranormal explanations. It was merely a fact to be noted. Later vigils, using more sophisticated temperature monitoring and recording equipment, confirmed the observation, but still proved nothing on that point.

The rest of the first watch passed fairly peacefully during which time the only real excitement was one particularly daredevil bat that insisted on dive bombing us both for about half an hour. Neither Ian nor myself experienced any untoward feelings (either towards the vigil, or the bat).

Our next watch was in the one area of the investigation with no lights whatsoever (emergency lighting had been left on in all other areas). The problem therefore was to avoid too much sensory deprivation, bearing in mind that making any noise would have been detrimental to other parts of the investigating team. For my part, illuminated by a small night-light candle, I spent the time jotting down some notes for a quite separate research project that I was working on; I am not quite sure what Ian did since I could not see him although he was only a few feet away most of the time.

We had been asked to look out for a three-dimensional-looking figure of a seventeenth-century soldier carrying a pike, that several people had reported having seen in our location. Apparently he would walk straight through a wall, pike first, marching at right angles through the room we were in and then out through another wall. Given the description, there is the possibility that the figure was to some extent self-illuminating but that was not certain. In any case, Ian and I kept a close watch for him but he obviously wasn't on duty that night. That two-hour session up to 12.15 a.m. went by very peacefully and uneventfully and without any feeling of 'presence' on my part (but that doesn't mean anything because I'm about as psychic as a brick!).

The next problem arose on this second watch – we didn't have enough batteries for all the recording equipment and there was no mains supply. By the middle of the third watch most of the recording gear had flat batteries.

The third watch commenced at 12.30 a.m. in a rather claustrophobic area of the castle, which also turned out to be the 'hangar' of a whole squadron of noisy bats. Our earlier invader had obviously told his friends we were coming! They were making a pretty peculiar noise for some time and Ian and I spent a while trying to pinpoint exactly where they were to ensure that the noise was coming from the bats.

At a little before 2 a.m. both Ian and I listened to what seemed to be a 'chanting' sound for approximately two minutes. We thought that it was probably a radio playing somewhere on the dockside; it could have originated inside the castle but it was a very still, quiet night and we assumed that it could be sound drifting up from somewhere outside. In the debriefing at the end of the vigil one other team had heard something similar describing it as 'singing' or 'humming' but again there was nothing to suggest an extraordinary source. My diary log for the night indicates that at 2.30 a.m. there were two loud bangs when none of our recording instruments were running. They were impressive enough to be worthy of note but since they happened at the beginning of the changeover period between shifts (which is why the tape-recorders had been switched off, prior to moving), I assumed that one of the other groups in the area had caused the sounds by either closing a case loudly or dropping something. Unfortunately, it seems that no one else could recall having done so and nothing could be concluded except that, again, there was no suggestion of anything out of the ordinary.

The fourth watch started at 2.45 a.m. and was due to go on until 4.45 a.m.; this would be when most members of the team would be at their lowest ebb and most prone to suggestion. We had therefore to be careful of misinterpretation of events. So it was something of a mixed blessing when, at 3.15 a.m. the likeliest candidate for some sort of paranormal origin occurred; that said, it was not all that dramatic – a very loud bang followed by a second sound. It came from directly behind Ian and myself, and within just a second we got to the location where we were both quite convinced the sounds had come from.

At the same time another pair, Dave and Rob, were heading to the same spot from their location as they too had heard the sounds. If the sounds had a 'normal' origin then it would have had to have been something heavy being dropped on a landing where Dave and Rob were, then falling into the ground just behind where Ian and I were. Dave and Rob were quite certain that they had not even been moving at the time when the sounds had occurred just in front of them and although we all searched the area very thoroughly none of us could find anything that was likely to have caused them.

8 Vigils

Because of the strange way that sound carried in those corridors there was always the possibility that the noises had come from one of the other two groups elsewhere, but neither group had recorded any event that could have caused the sounds or could recall any when we discussed it at the changeover.

Towards the end of the vigil, at 5.27 a.m., we heard a distant bang from the direction of one of the other vigil locations, but no explanation was found. We were all keeping logs, and so at changeover times we were able to compare notes. Without the logs it would have been impossible to try and track the spread of any noises travelling through the castle.

At one point, and unfortunately without video equipment, Dave and Rob saw 'shadows' at the end of the corridor. The only people who could have caused them would have been Ian and myself and we did not enter that section of the corridor. According to the logs it appears that the shadows, apparently of moving forms, occurred at the same time as the 5.27 a.m. bang that we heard. No resolution for this was found.

The vigil ended at 6 a.m. and we returned to the assembly point for a short period of debriefing. Debriefing was not very successful or enthusiastic at that time, as might be expected; most of us were on the verge of sleep, all adrenalin had run out.

It appeared that in the other half of the watch there had been some similar sounds heard which could not be attributed to known causes. But the highlight of the evening was the capturing on video film of a large, heavy door shaking quite violently at approximately twice a second. One of the investigators had been able to touch it while it was vibrating. To the best of our knowledge there had been no wind or vibration in the castle. There was, therefore, no easy, physical explanation for the movement. Despite our tiredness we all considered the filming of the shaking door to be rather a coup – one of the rare instances of a possibly paranormal

Ghostwatching

incident captured in motion. The film has been good publicity for us, and often appears in TV programmes describing our activities.

We met some days later to debrief properly and discuss the lessons to be learnt. Sound was the biggest issue; another issue was the lack of mains electricity in some important spots. Not wishing ever to be caught again, a team member went into an ironmonger's and asked for a half-mile extension cable – and got it! We also resolved to apply a certain amount of psychology to subsequent vigils. Although a 'core' of us knew what events had occurred, we decided to keep all subsequent newcomers in the dark about what to expect. This, we hoped, would reduce the likelihood of people describing noises in terms of what they expected to hear. Future teams were, as much as possible, made up from one 'knowledgeable' team member and one 'innocent'. Lastly, on a personal note, I resolved never, never to bring every piece of equipment with me into a vigil like that again. Bring it all in the car, yes, but not deploy it all at once!

MICHAEL JACKSON AT DOVER CASTLE

Many months later another vigil at Dover Castle had amusing consequences when one of the 'innocent' team members had ignored our pre-briefings about sounds and the way they carried. A university had persuaded the team leader to allow three undergraduates to join the vigil. Sadly, we have to report that at no time did they join in our team building exercises nor did they seem to want to be part of the work we were doing. They clearly had their own agenda and were, in my view, about as much help as a chocolate teapot!

Because of the lessons learnt on the previous vigil all team members had been given strict instructions to remain silent and to note any sounds that they accidentally made in case they were picked up by other people (confirming the time and circumstances).

8 Vigils

All hell broke loose at around 3 a.m. – the time at which biorhythms are at their lowest, and suggestibility at its highest. I was in the St John's Tower with Dave and Ian; we could hear a whining electronic noise. We listened for some time and confirmed that it was fairly consistent and that we could all hear it. While these kinds of noises are often associated with psychic activity, most psychic activity has at least some personal 'element' and is rarely heard by all people at a location. When everyone can hear the same thing it usually has a more down-to-earth interpretation. Dave and I set out down the corridors to track down the source of the sound. En route to the end of the underground works (where we eventually found the source of the sound) we passed two other team groups; they confirmed (mostly in sign language) that they could hear the sounds as well.

Eventually Dave and I arrived at the completely dark, unlit underground works in the section where there are no emergency lights. We could very clearly hear this buzzing noise ahead of us. Together we rather gingerly walked into the darkness holding our torches out ahead of us; at this time they were switched off. Eventually Dave stopped (we knew we were in the last room in the works). He took my arm and tapped my torch indicating that I should turn it on on a count of three (by gently tapping the torch three times). Dave whispered the cue and we put our torches on with beams full ahead. At the end of the underground works we found one of the university students. He was lying on a camp bed, covered in blankets, eyes closed, and listening intently to Michael Jackson on his personal stereo.

FRIGHT AT FORT AMHERST

Sometimes vigils can bring unexpected frights, but with a natural cause. For some reason a vigil at Fort Amherst in 1992 collected a number of not-so-serious stories. At one point halfway through the vigil a team member came up to

Ghostwatching

John Spencer breathing fairly hard. He was laughing and said, 'I thought my time had come.' Apparently he had been staking out the grounds and casually flicking the torch over various parts of the grounds when he had suddenly lit up a huge white goat's head with curled horns looking straight at him. Everything he had ever read in a Dennis Wheatley book apparently went through his mind in a second. He needn't have worried, there *are* goats roaming around in the grounds of Fort Amherst.

Soon after this event, John became the unwitting cause of a sharp intake of breath. He describes what happened: 'It was very cold and I had taken the precaution of bringing a tartan blanket in from my car to wrap around my shoulders during the coldest parts of the night. It was a very relaxed vigil with no particular station keeping and people wandering around in the tunnels that constitute Fort Amherst at will.

'Lighting at Fort Amherst, during the vigil, consisted of low emergency lighting at ground level and so as you walk down the corridors shadows are lengthened and exaggerated in an upward direction. During one part of the night I threw the tartan blanket over my shoulder and slowly walked up the corridor towards a group of people I could hear talking quietly in another section.

'As I got closer I suddenly realised that the talking had totally stopped and I was wondering why there was such an obvious silence – you could almost feel the tension in the atmosphere. I kept on walking.

'As I got to the door I slowed down and then put my head round the door to see what was going on. Five people in the room all simultaneously breathed a sigh of relief and a couple started laughing. Apparently they had been watching this huge bat-like shape flapping its way towards them, wondering what the apparition was going to be!'

8 Vigils

VIGIL AT ROCHESTER CASTLE

We held a vigil at Rochester Castle during the summer of 1992 and that night must go into the history books for being the most physically uncomfortable vigil of all time. We had all faithfully brought the equipment we thought we would need – but forgot the umbrellas and waterproofing. Rochester Castle has no roof, and that night it poured down! For much of the night we got drenched patrolling the battlements, looking for the ghost of a lady in white reputed to walk up there. John Spencer issued the only – and admittedly flippant – instructions for the watch: 'If you see something, prod it. If your finger goes through it, take a picture.'

What was worse, there were reports of some sightings in the castle grounds, and we were persuaded to spend some time out there, exposed to the full force of the rain. At one point both of us were paired up to patrol the grounds. We were asked to pay particular attention to the burglar light-sensor on the main door, which appeared to be going on and off spontaneously. As a burglar alarm it was perfectly useless; it would come on and off when no one was there and often failed to work when someone walked right underneath it. We were satisfied that this was most probably due to radio signals from something like a local cab firm as this type of security light did not seem to be shielded from such transmissions.

We did successfully solve one mystery. We had been warned that two of the windows of the castle glowed with a flickering green light on occasions, and had aroused some interest. It took several hours of checking to be sure that it was being caused by the uplights from the castle grounds passing through the leaves and branches of trees waving in the wind, and being reflected off a perspex sheeting at the back of the windows. This may sound like a disappointment; but research is there to eliminate the spurious as well as examine the mysterious.

Ghostwatching

The castle windows were at the root of further excitement. The team that had been staking out the grounds on the far side joined us so that we could all moan about the drizzle and stamp our feet, put our hands in our pockets and watch our breath form in the air in front of us.

Suddenly Tony shouted that he thought he could see an apparition at the windows of the castle. We all looked and agreed we could all see a huge and hideous shape forming into something rather grotesque and apparently heading up the drive towards us. John ran towards it, determined to find out what it was. As he approached, the perspectives were shifting dramatically and it became apparent that the image was only on the glass panes of the windows next to the front doors. When he reached the windows he looked in and was able to see clearly that it was being caused by a rather complicated reflection of one of our own team members who had moved off station without warning anyone and was roaming about in a corridor. His shadow was being projected through the room and on to the window and as he was moving in the corridor so his image was getting larger and smaller on the window. John turned round to confirm this to the other people with him. There was nobody there!

He looked around in the darkness and could see no one, and began walking back up the drive he had come from. It was several minutes before he met the three other members of the team coming down the drive towards him. At the moment that he had run towards the castle, they had run in the opposite direction! Tony then said, 'I've never seen you run so fast – it wasn't until I saw you run like that I realised you were serious!'

It has, frankly, never occurred to us that the research we do is in any way dangerous. But we do wish people would stop putting those ideas into our minds!

8 Vigils

VIGIL AT THE ANCIENT RAM INN

John attended this vigil in the summer of 1992. They had been told that the focus of attention in the inn was the 'Bishop's Room', reputed by the owner to be the most haunted room in England. Mike Lewis, the director of investigations for ASSAP, and John spent a peaceful and unhaunted night in the room. They did, however, probably solve one mystery. The owner had told them that sometimes a green circle would mysteriously appear in the top left-hand corner of the room, facing away from the beds. At about 2 o'clock in the morning, in total darkness, John was lying awake when he suddenly became aware of a green circle above him and to his left. He checked quietly if Mike was awake, equally quietly Mike confirmed that he was. John asked him if he could see the circle of light and he said that he could not. It seemed for a moment as if there might be some paranormal phenomena occurring. However, as Mike moved closer to John he could see it too; it seemed therefore to be dependent on the angle of view. They were able to determine quite quickly that the circle was forming as a reflection in a glass panel covering a picture. Although it was quite complex they were able to trace the light source back to cracks in the ceiling and wall joints. Light coming from a nearby toilet was reflected through after someone had just entered and switched it on. The Bishop's Room was not entirely without its mysteries. Mike Lewis told us of an incident that had happened to him when he had attended a vigil there in the previous year. He had attached a light to his video camera and used it to enhance filming in the darkness of the inn's interior. When he went into the Bishop's Room the light failed; Mike assumed that it was the batteries. However, on emerging from the Bishop's Room the light came back to strength again and was working throughout the rest of the vigil.

During the vigil John attended they had the entire Ram

Ghostwatching

Inn wired up so that any intrusion around the staircase would trigger off lights and make the place look like a fireworks display. This was for a specific reason – to control any deliberate attempt to hoodwink them. (That did not mean they did not trust the proprietor, but a vigil must cover all angles.) Unfortunately, for reasons now difficult to explain, John turned off the alarm system when one member of the team was watching (at around 5 o'clock in the morning) and reset it again without telling that person. Assuming that the alarms were neutralised, she casually went downstairs to make some coffee, setting off a series of light and sound alarms that must have woken up half of Gloucestershire!

The proprietor claimed that there was a very successful way of raising the ghostly spirits. The entire team must assemble in the Bishop's Room with the entire inn shut into darkness. One member of the team should then go through to the other end of the inn and, using a wooden staff, should tap his way along the corridors holding only a candle for illumination. On reaching the door of the Bishop's Room he should use the staff to bang on the door demanding entry, and then open the door and walk in along a corridor formed by other team members. As he passed by the team members, so the rest of the team should be able to feel or even see the presence of the spirit. The spirit in question was, by the way, supposed to be extremely noisy, and poltergeist-like in following the subject.

One by one each member of the team tried this without much success. However, on one occasion they were all in the Bishop's Room listening to the sound of the person knocking his way along the corridors and gradually getting closer when suddenly it became apparent that the noise outside was tremendous and there was a feeling of expectation that the poltergeist-like banging and crashing was at last becoming real. In great anticipation they listened as the sounds approached the Bishop's Room door. There was by now a great deal of clattering and crashing and objects falling over.

The door flew open and there was total darkness outside rather than the candle-lit figure of the team member. Out of the darkness a voice wailed apologetically, 'The bloody candle blew out. I can't see a damn thing.' It took us all ages to tidy up the path of destruction he had left behind him in the darkness.

A HUNGRY GHOSTWATCHER

John was part of a team ghostwatching at a location in the South of England (the administrators have asked us not to identify it): at around two o'clock in the morning they could hear, from the castle doors, a frantic banging and screaming from the darkness down the end of the drive. It was totally dark; no lighting outside. The night was calm, no wind, and yet we could hear the iron gates rattling fiercely.

Martin and John called the team from Station 2 down to their position so that he and John could set off to investigate. When they arrived, the team from Station 2 could also hear the noises. All agreed that at least some of the noises sounded like someone shrieking and screaming and they assumed that the locals had got to hear of our stakeout and were winding them up.

Martin and John ran down the drive towards the darkened gate. John is not sure what either of them expected to see when they got there but he is quite sure that neither of them would have expected what they did see.

As they ran up to the gates they could see, stopped outside the gates, a small moped with its engine running. Standing at the gates a rather dishevelled man was peering in, looking relieved that there was someone inside after all. On the ground beside him were four large boxes of takeaway pizzas. He explained that he was delivering an order placed to the local takeaway pizza house about an hour before. John and Martin assured him that it must be for another location and explained who they were and what they were doing there.

Ghostwatching

'That's right,' he said; 'that's what they said they were doing. We all expected it to be a wind-up but I got the job of delivering the order.' He gave them the name of the person who had phoned, who was indeed one of the team, and John and Martin promised to go and get that person and bring him back to the gates. When they got back to the door of the castle the culprit (who will remain unnamed to save his embarrassment!) was talking to the people they had left on station there, confessing that the noise was probably related to him. He had used a mobile telephone to order the pizza as, he explained, 'It's bloody cold up there on the battlements.'

MAKING A VIGIL SUCCESSFUL

There are two obvious tests to decide whether a vigil was successful. The first is of course: 'Did something happen?' The second, equally valid, is: 'Did everybody feel that they all got the most out of the vigil?' Since we have been working together on vigils we have tended to concentrate on passing the second test, rather than emphasising the first. There is also a third and final test, which is: 'Will the owner allow you back again?' We feel that if vigils are organised and planned to pass the last two tests, there is a greater chance that something might happen, and so help pass the first test.

We often think of planning for a vigil as being the same as planning for a holiday, the more the preparation the more you can relax when you get there. The main piece of advice we can offer at this stage is: don't be disappointed if nothing happens on your first vigil as persistence and patience seem to bring their rewards in the end. But you have to be prepared for long periods of tedium.

Once, in the middle of a boring, long uneventful vigil John said he wondered if there was a whole army of ghostly laughing cavaliers just the other side of the door, gesticulating and making faces at us.

8 Vigils

CREATING THE RIGHT CONDITIONS

Atmosphere is important. Research seems to indicate that when the investigators know each other well, and the witnesses feel comfortable in their presence, then things are more likely to happen. As part of making everyone feel comfortable, we believe that a sympathetic attitude is more helpful than a suspicious and antagonistic one. Chapter 12 examines in detail how to create the right atmosphere. Remember, however, that being sympathetic must not stop you from being objective!

PERFORMING A SITE SURVEY

The site survey is an important part of the preparation. This need not be a formal process, and can often be performed when the owner takes you round to look at where things were witnessed. It need not involve diagrams and measurements, often a simple sketch will be sufficient. Sometimes, if the site is a public building, the owners will be able to offer you a proper plan which you can take away.

From this survey you can then identify the areas where it might be worth watching during the vigil, and get some idea of the sort of things that will be necessary to bring with you. Electrical points, lighting considerations and extremes of temperature are the sort of things to watch out for. Appendix D provides a list of things to consider, but of course only some of the things will be relevant for each site.

WORKING IN CHALLENGING CONDITIONS

Sometimes investigators will have to work in conditions which are extremely challenging. Earlier we mentioned our vigil at Rochester Castle which had no roof, and it drizzled most of the night. Because it was a summer's evening no one

Ghostwatching

had thought to bring rainwear. The list of problems which investigators may have to overcome is endless, but here is a list of typical ones. Most can be identified during initial site survey, and steps taken in advance to overcome them.

* Extremes of heat or cold (sitting in a boiler room, sitting in the open or in the dungeons of an unheated castle).
* No mains supply or not enough mains sockets for all the equipment.
* Delays in settling down to the vigil. This can often happen in establishments such as restaurants and pubs where the team has to rely on the place being vacated before starting work. If the media are present, then work will often be delayed until the media interviews are over.
* The need to bring your own chairs and food and drink.

WHO'S IN CHARGE OF THE VIGIL?

We feel that it is important for one person to be in overall charge of the vigil and where possible to have a deputy. There are several reasons for this. First, your group will have to make arrangements with the owner of the premises for access, rules of conduct and so on. It is so much easier for the owner to have one person to deal with. Secondly, some planning work needs to be done – arranging the time of arrival, co-ordinating who will be bringing what equipment, and so on.

The deputy is also useful to take on some of the workload as sometimes circumstances such as pressure of work or family commitments may make it difficult to get things organised on time. The deputy can also help during the vigil.

Tony learnt this lesson on one vigil which he had organised but where he had not arranged for a deputy. The vigil was to be carried out by some fifteen investigators, many of them not knowing each other and some with no experience of vigils. Tony spent a lot of time planning the work. Two hours into the vigil, he was feeling reasonably pleased with the night until he walked on to a landing and was suddenly taken over by the most intense feeling of cold. Every hair on his body stood on end and he was feeling so weird that he could no longer think properly. This lasted for over half an hour and overlapped with the end of a watch and well into a coffee break. After the break, people needed to be moved around to their new places and were looking to him to explain where to go and how to get there. Unfortunately, he could not help at all because he was feeling too strange, and the investigators had to sort it all out by themselves. A deputy who was fully briefed could have taken over then.

ALLOCATING YOUR RESOURCES

The reports of the types of phenomena and where they occur will help you to decide on how to organise your resources. You may be able to ask for help in obtaining more investigators from national organisations such as ASSAP and the SPR (see Appendix A).

If you have limited numbers and a lot of locations to observe (for example, in a castle) then it makes sense to focus on the locations where most of the phenomena have occurred. This is not a hard-and-fast rule; there is some anecdotal evidence to suggest that when there are investigators about, the phenomena may change location. However, you have to start somewhere.

At the Union Inn (see Chapter 10) we thought that the main phenomena could be occurring upstairs, especially as three of us had witnessed a bedroom light-switch turning itself off before we had even got our notebooks out. However, as it turned out, during the vigil itself nothing at all seemed to happen on that floor, while downstairs all present watched a door opening and closing by itself and finally slamming shut when Tony walked up to it. Two others over a period of several minutes saw shadows around the rim of

Ghostwatching

the second door, to the restaurant area. On several vigils different investigators saw laser-like flashes in the bar area. The interesting thing about the downstairs phenomena was that none of them had been reported previously by the witnesses.

While it is advisable to have some kind of strategy, you don't have to stick to it rigidly. At the Union Inn we started out with a two-hour rota, with two groups swapping between upstairs and downstairs. Once the action started downstairs at about 2.30 a.m. we radioed the other group to join us downstairs.

STILLNESS VS BEHAVING NORMALLY

We have worked on vigils where investigators sit as quietly as possible for two hours at a time – Dover Castle, for example, where a rule of silence was enforced on us by the peculiar way that sound travelled there. On other occasions we have sat in rooms lit with normal lighting and talked normally but quietly. Opinions on this matter vary, but it is our belief that unless conditions dictate otherwise, the best policy is to behave 'normally'; though we use the word with caution – there is a school of thought that believes it is not normal to sit up all night and look out for ghosts.

The table-tilting and 'Philip' experiments mentioned in Chapter 11 have been observed to work best when people are chatting and exercising their sense of humour – something that is often needed when ghostwatching.

When working in conditions of silence, sitting for several hours at a time can be exhausting, which will inevitably lead to errors of observation and, worse, leave you over-stressed from the concentration. A compromise which we often use is to alternate periods of strict silence with periods of more normal behaviour.

One problematic belief is that large amounts of alcohol reduce the barriers and leave you open to the paranormal.

The problem is that even if true it would prove nothing; no one would ever believe you.

LIGHTING THE SITE OF THE INVESTIGATION

Sometimes the lighting conditions during an investigation cannot be altered to suit the investigators. On some properties the owners will feel uncomfortable about allowing building lighting to be changed from normal. Although they may have informed the police that an investigation is under way, the act of turning lights on and off, and torches flashing, may cause unwanted attention from the local population.

When there are no restrictions on lighting we believe that the best conditions are low light levels where people can just see, but without glare. On several vigils, with different people present and at different sites we have noticed a light phenomenon that we are curious about. We have sometimes found that in a darkened room when an ill-fitting door is lit from outside the room, a 'fringing' effect around the door frame can be observed by some if not all witnesses. This has happened to us on two different vigils in the past eighteen months. The use of low light levels is an aid to seeing this kind of effect.

THE USE OF TECHNICAL EQUIPMENT

There are two main reasons for using technical equipment. The first is obvious: to record a paranormal event for posterity. The second reason is less obvious: to try to detect a paranormal event which cannot be detected by the normal senses. One example of the second type is to use a thermometer to detect temperature changes. It is not uncommon for the temperature to drop just before poltergeist-type activity. Many ghostwatchers carry some kind of air thermometer with them on ghosthunts. A maximum and minimum thermometer is handy as it records the lowest and

Ghostwatching

highest temperatures reached. Modern electronic temperature modules can be used to emit a signal when the temperature drops below a predetermined value, and so provide a possible advance warning of an event.

The scope for deployment of technical equipment is enormous but there are two prices to pay. The first is setting up the equipment – the more complicated the equipment the longer the setting-up time: This setting-up time should be taken into account when planning the start-time and shift changes during the vigil. The second problem is that paranormal phenomena are notoriously 'camera shy'. The equipment doesn't have to be a camera, it can be any type of equipment. Cynics will say that the reason why phenomena are rarely captured on sensors or cameras is because there is no such thing as the paranormal. The answer to this is to keep trying. As mentioned earlier in this chapter, at their first vigil at Dover Castle John and colleagues were rewarded with a spectacular video recording of a locked door shaking by itself at approximately twice a second.

We have set out in Appendix D a list of equipment that can be used for vigils.

For investigators starting out, there is some obvious equipment to consider: still camera, cassette recorder, and if available, a video camcorder. Citizen's Band (CB) radio is also useful to keep in touch with others, but portable CB units do not communicate far in castles with thick walls. As experience is gained and interest grows in particular phenomena, then the basic tools begin to get supplemented with extras. Our own experience with low light-level phenomena prompted Tony to purchase second-hand night vision equipment. (When not used to find ghosts, it is used to watch foxes and badgers at play.) Similarly, following a spate of phenomena occurring on almost every vigil he attended, and having only a still camera, John bought a highly portable camcorder that can operate in low-light conditions.

Another of our colleagues, Philip Walton, was inspired to build a static electricity detector after an experience he had early in 1993. He was walking along a corridor in a supposedly haunted location and felt a most powerful 'tingle', which he described as 'feeling like a massive electric shock'. Interestingly he obtained this sensation whilst walking into an area where others had experienced feelings of intense cold — no one had told him any of this prior to his own experience.

Equipment does not necessarily mean technology. One useful tool, for example, is a jar of sugar. When poltergeist activity which moves furniture is suspected, then sugar can be sprinkled around the furniture legs. Any movement of the chair (by any means, human or otherwise) will result in a crunching noise and visible movement of the sugar.

MALFUNCTIONING EQUIPMENT

Ghosthunting folklore is littered with stories of electrical equipment which 'fails' at crucial times on vigils. We have had our own share of mysterious failures which seem to be 'cured' several hours later or when re-tested at home. Some of this can be put down to over-excitement causing fumbling fingers. Other incidents have been bizarre. Even so, just because a torch stops working does not mean that paranormal events are occurring — it is prudent to bring spare bulbs and batteries.

Such failures can be all too annoying; John attended one vigil where it was important to eliminate all members of the household from 'aiding' poltergeist activity. (It's really not suspicion on our part, we assure the people concerned; it's so we can reduce pointless questions from magazine editors and other armchair critics.) John set up a concealed video lens in a room where one object was supposed to move. The members of the household had gone out and were due to arrive home at nine o'clock; the tape should have run to half-past nine. Just after nine o'clock we got a call from the family to say they had all arrived home — and the object had moved.

Ghostwatching

Whatever was going on, we thought we had it in the bag. The rest of the team members will never forget the drive to that house; John broke every rule in the book (he adamantly denies this) and frightened everyone more than any ghost could ever do. He was obsessed. On arriving, we discovered that he had loaded the wrong tape in the machine; it had run out at eight-thirty. The gremlins had struck again. John admitted that he couldn't sleep at all that night he was so annoyed. He calmed down after a conversation with Tony: John moaned, 'How could someone as experienced as me have done that?' and Tony pointed out that 'Someone as experienced as you should have known how often it happens.'

WHAT TO DO WHEN THINGS HAPPEN

Paranormal events can range from low-level phenomena, such as audible knocks or flashes of light, all the way up to furniture being moved around and visual apparitions. Sometimes people might simply 'feel weird'. Under extreme conditions things might happen thick and fast, such as in the Enfield Poltergeist investigations. Under these circumstances, all you can do is react. When things start happening it is difficult to be objective, but we try to verify what we are all seeing, and where possible to make notes. Some of our group use portable dictating machines to make verbal notes, others rely on pens and paper. To avoid group hallucination it is important not to 'lead' people with even the sketchiest description of the phenomena. One technique we try to employ is to say, 'I am experiencing something, if anyone is also experiencing something, please write down what they observe.' Afterwards, the written statements can be collected and compared. That is the ideal way of operating, but in the heat of the moment, it is quite easy to end up with the less scientific 'Wow! Did anyone see that?' while pointing to where the event happened.

8 Vigils

In the case of noise effects it is useful to note the time of the noise so as to be able to check with other groups. CB can be useful as it is possible to check immediately whether other groups have heard the same thing.

GETTING FRIGHTENED

It is worth bearing in mind that the people experiencing the phenomena, including the witnesses or, in the case of public or corporate buildings, their representatives, could become frightened by what is happening, and possibly call a halt to the vigil. Remember they may have called you in to help assess whether there are genuine phenomena and as soon as they can see for themselves that something weird is happening and others are seeing it too, then they may not want to have any more investigation. It is quite common for them to change their view and either want to be left alone or want to get rid of the phenomena. When this happens you have got to accept their view. First responsibility is to the witness.

At the Union Inn (see Chapter 10) we compromised. After our first vigil, where all present saw some kind of phenomena, the proprietor kindly agreed to allow us to continue to investigate on his premises so long as we agreed to introduce him to someone who would help banish the phenomena, and provide moral support. For us that was an ideal compromise, but that arrangement is not always possible.

From a practical point of view the fear threshold of individuals varies widely. At Dover Castle in September 1993 Tony realised how much he had insulated himself from fright, when working in the tunnels with three of the film crew. They sat in the John's Tower tunnel in near-complete darkness and he began to see what seemed to be flashes of light. After half an hour of trying to observe this more fully he wondered whether shutting the main doors at the end of the tunnel would help. So after agreeing with the others what he was going to do, he went down to the doors with one of

Ghostwatching

the crew. A few seconds later as they walked down the tunnel they became aware of ghostly footsteps behind them. Turning round they found that the two remaining members of the crew had run up behind them – they had been too frightened to stay at the other end of the tunnel on their own. Tony realised then that it is important to remember other people's feelings when proposing working in scary places.

When John rushed towards a visual effect at Rochester Castle, the rest of the team ran in the opposite direction; Tony would like to point out, however, that John's own fear level was tested at Fort Amherst when three of us (John, Jane Le Surf and Tony) were walking past a room when some very loud bangs and crashes came from our left. John and Jane jumped and ran at speed in the opposite direction. Tony also jumped, but realised, having heard it before, that it was a sound recording for the exhibition which had been set off by people in one of the other rooms!

AVOIDING ALCOHOL AND PERFUME

Avoiding alcohol might sound oppressive but it is quite practical. Seeing pink elephants as well as a headless ghost will not enhance your credibility with the site owners and witnesses. It may not be a surprise if a witness needs a stiff drink if things are getting tense, but resist temptation yourself.

It may also be wise to avoid wearing perfume of any kind, including deodorants and aftershave. This is because it is not unusual for investigators and witnesses to notice strong smells which suddenly appear, and then suddenly go. The smells can range from perfume to dirty smells like rotting garbage and drains. One example of smell reports comes from Dover Castle, where the staff have mentioned times when they have been alone and have sniffed wafts of musky perfume. Sometimes perception of the smell is selective. This

8 Vigils

happened in a restaurant we investigated in Maidstone where the proprietor suffered with a horrible smell of drains. She was very worried when the local Health and Safety inspector called on his annual visit, but she heaved a sigh of relief when she found out that he could smell nothing but the cooking.

Introducing perfume or aftershave just introduces random elements you can do without.

EXPERIMENTS

In this chapter we have of course concentrated on times when we have successfully witnessed phenomena, but there have also been many times when time has passed very slowly. Sometimes we try experiments to see if we can encourage phenomena. Mostly the ideas we try are completely unscientific, spur of the moment, and are limited only by our imagination and spare cash.

On one occasion, in a room where a chair was said to move across the floor by itself, we lit a candle and tried asking the 'spirit' to communicate to us via the candle. At one point we were rewarded by a slow gyration of the flame; but it would be wrong to make too much of it.

On an almost humorous note – during a lull in one investigation John lay face down on the floor trying to dream up what experiments we might consider. He was thinking of an article he had recently read that suggested paranormal effects were enhanced by pornographic images, but had quickly dismissed the idea of trying anything of that sort as the team was a mixed group of people not very familiar with each other (not that familiar anyway). John said nothing about his thoughts. One of the female members – sitting some way from anyone else – suddenly announced that she felt as if she was 'being touched up' (an effect that had been reported in that location by others).

Ghostwatching

LEAVING THE SITE

When leaving the premises it is important that you restore the furniture and fittings back to their proper places. Clearing up at 6 a.m. in the morning may be the last thing you want to do, but it is important to ensure that you get invited back, and that you maintain a reputation for 'professionalism'.

THE IMPORTANCE OF KEEPING CONTEMPORANEOUS NOTES

On one occasion after a vigil at Charlton House the bemused manager phoned Tony. She had stayed in her office and slept during the overnight vigil, waking up only to let the team out. After they left she returned to her office to catch up with her sleep. On the phone she said that she had heard the sound of a wind instrument playing a tune at about 5 a.m. (about an hour after the team left), but assumed it was one of the staff playing a trick on her with some kind of timed tape-recorder or radio. Where she was sleeping was almost in the centre of the building and it was not likely that someone outside could have generated enough sound to penetrate that far – and unlikely to be doing that so early on a Saturday morning. There is a postscript to the story. On a later vigil she was in her office again trying to sleep but was woken by the sound of someone singing the same tune she had heard on the wind instrument after the previous vigil. At the time she heard the music, the team was in the bar area falling asleep with boredom. This example illustrates the importance of keeping notes (no pun intended).

Because she had written down the time of the music, and the team had made notes of its own activities, they were able to rule out noises made by someone fooling around.

8 Vigils

DEBRIEFING

Discussing the vigil a day or so after the event with colleagues and with the witnesses is a good idea and can be fruitful. It provides an opportunity to learn lessons when all are wide awake; certainly more so than they would be the morning after a night sitting up in a dungeon. It also provides a teambuilding opportunity for the group – sometimes tempers can get a little frayed in the early hours.

By comparing the notes of all team members the cross-referencing eliminates noises and incidents caused by the team members themselves, or that are of known origin, and focuses on the 'real' mysteries to be examined.

THE JOB'S NOT OVER YET

Don't forget the paperwork.

If you belong to one of the national organisations (and even if you don't) they will be interested in a report of the case, and anything discovered, no matter how small or puzzling. By sifting information about your case, and all the other reported cases, it may be possible to look for connections between external, environmental effects and hauntings.

THE MEDIA ON SITE

The media can be both a help and a hindrance. They can be extremely helpful in publicising your group and its aims, but the penalty is that they may want a story. To have a newspaper reporter or TV crew with you on a vigil may be completely counter-productive – they will probably be asking lots of questions and making a lot of noise, which can be distracting. A compromise is to agree in advance that they can interview before the vigil, but when the vigil begins they must leave. That has worked well for us on several occasions.

Ghostwatching

There may be a tendency for the interviewer to be a little tongue in cheek, or to be a bit over-dramatic. The simplest antidote to that is for you and your group to restrain yourselves, not rise to the bait and treat the subject as seriously as possible – the interviewer will quickly return to normality.

On one radio show John was a guest, promoting a book he had edited with a colleague, Hilary Evans. The interviewer did all he could to make 'dubious' suggestions about 'long hours spent with Hilary' working on the book and 'what does your wife think?' John cooled that down by pointing out that Hilary Evans is a sixty-year-old man with a beard.

A FEW OTHER HINTS AND TIPS

Never work alone. If you are sitting watching a door, for example, always have at least one other person (either an investigator or a witness) near or preferably beside you. The reasons for this are twofold: first, you might get frightened if your imagination starts to run wild, or something actually happens. The second reason is that if something actually happens then nobody will be able to verify your statement and you will spend the rest of your life practising the phrase 'but it did happen, *really*'.

The body clock seems to be important. It is not uncommon for activity to fall off after 4 a.m. in the morning, when people begin to get extremely sleepy. Unless things are jumping around, plan to finish soon after that time.

If you are staying overnight then don't expect the owner to feed and water you. They might be generous on the first occasion, but don't strain the relationship by taking advantage.

9 Dealing with Witnesses

GHOSTWATCHING INVOLVES more than just sitting around in damp castles waiting for the laughing cavalier. It means taking accounts of ghosts from those who claim to have seen them – the witnesses. However, even in people's minds things are seldom what they seem. . . .

A person sees a ghost. They find a ghostwatcher to report it to. They tell you what they saw. End of story; ghost reported? Not a bit of it.

Witnesses to any event are unreliable; to a paranormal event even more so. Part of the job of the ghostwatcher or ghosthunter is to re-create the reality that inspired the report; and that is not as easy as it seems.

PROBLEMS WITH PERCEPTION

No two people see the world in the same way. If those two people come from similar backgrounds and culture, then they probably have a consensus reality (a common view of reality) and can agree on what they see. This is what makes communication effective, to the degree that it is. Where the subject strays from the concrete to the abstract, perceptions begin to differ; where it strays from the normal to the paranormal, perceptions differ even more. Ghost reports deal with an area where there is a lot of belief ('I *know* that ghosts are spirits of the dead'), a lot of conviction ('I am *certain* ghosts are real because I've seen one') but no consen-

Ghostwatching

sus reality, i.e. in truth no one can honestly say what ghosts are.

These barriers do not mean that witnesses are untruthful; only that they are unreliable because they are human.

In order to be sure we understand what they want us to understand, and to glean useful information, we have to know how people learn to perceive things, and how to unravel source from signal.

HOW WE LEARN

We learn by experience. From birth, our memory banks build up with images of everything we come across in life – apples, cars, books, flowers, people, animals, and so on, all recognised by one or more of our five senses.

When you perceive something (see, smell, touch it, etc.) you access your image bank to find out more about it and to be able to describe it. If the object is familiar then there is usually no problem; it is recognised and dealt with accordingly.

If it is not recognised then there is a sequence of events that takes place that does nothing for objectivity. First, the brain seeks to create a familiar pattern. This is because patterns are predictable, and by implication easier to deal with. Most 'optical illusion' games and tests are based on this tendency of the mind to create patterns where none really exists.

Secondly, the mind searches through the image bank to find a 'best fit'. On the basis that the unknown object can be likened to something known, then the unknown object can be 'preliminarily classified', and its parameters and potential capabilities can be judged by reference to what is known. For example, if you had never seen a pear before you might 'preliminarily classify' it as a type of apple. That would give you some idea what to do with it for one thing, i.e. eat it, not try to write with it. When you ate it you would recognise

9 Dealing with Witnesses

that it was something different, and you would begin building up a new image for the bank. But if you only had a brief glimpse of the pear, and never got to taste it, then you might be left forever thinking it was a type of apple. As ghosts are often seen for only a few seconds, the implications of this on witness perception is clear.

Thirdly, given a brief glimpse of the pear which you thought was a type of apple, you might then want to describe it to someone else. If they had never seen a pear either they might be a bit sceptical about your description of, say, its elongation. To avoid conflict you might understate that aspect of the description. More important, questioning your own perceptions might leave you doubting your own recollection about the elongation. By the time you came to describe it you might well believe yourself that it was 'rounder'; and describe it as such. In short, when we are faced with something we don't know and we have searched our image bank for a look-alike, we begin modifying our true memories of the unknown object to make it fit our expectations.

John had a personal experience of this. He saw a woman wearing clothes similar to the ones he knew his wife was wearing, and identified as walking with her one of his daughters. In fact it was not his wife, and the child with the woman was a boy, but for a while John had 'superimposed' his daughter's features on the child as he had expected to see her there with his wife. In fact, on closer observation, and once the woman had been identified as not his wife, he also realised that the boy looked nothing like his daughter.

Many ghost reports have evidence in them that the eventual description of the ghost is dependent on what the person expected to see, once they had 'decided' what they were seeing, i.e. hooded monk, cavalier, etc. This is one reason why on vigils, as described in Chapter 8, we keep certain members of the ghostwatch team 'ignorant' of the details of expected, or previously reported, ghosts.

The authors experienced a practical example of this at a

Ghostwatching

vigil at Rochester Castle. Part of the vigil team, which included John but not Tony, was told that there had been many reports after midnight of the sounds of 'hordes of galloping horses' charging through the castle. Sure enough, after midnight John and others heard the sounds and all agreed that it sounded just like the hoofs of many horses in flight. They spent a while checking for a source for the sounds; eventually we could see that it was being caused by the wind flapping the loose rope of the flag against the flagpole. Several ghostwatchers on the ground floor watched for several minutes, keeping the flagpole in the torch-beams, to ensure that it was indeed the source. This was further confirmed by our discovery that it was at midnight that the flag was lowered, creating the circumstances. However, Tony was up on the battlements, underneath the flagpole. When John went up to ask if he too had heard the 'galloping noise' he said, 'All I could hear up here was the bloody flagpole making a racket!'

The brain goes through this routine for a very simple, and sensible, reason: it is programmed to survive. Patterns it can recognise can be dealt with from experience, patterns that cannot be recognised are approached with caution.

That is why ghosts (and other paranormal experiences) bring with them an element of fear; they do not fit into controllable patterns. They are not present in our image banks. And therefore we are wary. Our adrenalin comes into play and creates a tension and a readiness for action; that blurs our understanding of what is going on. In short, even if we look calm we are probably close to (sometimes *very* close to) panic. And in a state of panic our perceptions are no longer adjusted to accuracy; they are adjusted to containment. We no longer say, 'It is five feet tall'; we say, 'It is no taller than six feet' because that gives us the worst possible parameter we may have to deal with. When we calm down later the figure in our minds is six feet, not five. And so on with a whole range of images built on containment rather than scientific scrutiny. This is a further reason why ghost-

9 Dealing with Witnesses

watchers work in groups of two or more; there is verification of what is seen or experienced.

Part of the patterning is personification. People have a tendency to personify or attribute intelligent direction to any unknown event, until it is proved otherwise. If we are walking on a moor late at night, and particularly one known to have its share of 'hooded monk' reports, we might think we are seeing a 'ghost' when we see a vague dark shape. In fact, there could be a number of natural explanations, but in the heat of the moment we must consider the most frightening possibilities in order that we can estimate the greatest potential threat to us.

RECONSTRUCTION WITHOUT CLUES

Take any solid piece of fruit, cut it in half and make an ink impression of the cut face. That is the equivalent of a report of a ghost: a partial image that remains in the mind after the object has gone.

Can anyone reconstruct the shape of the fruit from the ink stain? Could they reconstruct the texture? Could they reconstruct the taste and the smell?

Not much chance; yet often on the basis of a brief glimpse of a figure out of the corner of the eye witnesses think they have recorded extraordinary detail of a sighting. In truth, they are probably filling in the blanks from their image bank.

Researchers confronted with a witness who believes they have an accurate and unarguable knowledge of their ghost after a brief sighting in less than planned and perfect conditions are well advised to consider John Godfrey Saxe's poem 'The Blind Men and the Elephant':

> It was six men of Indostan
> To learning much inclined,
> Who went to see the Elephant
> (Though all of them were blind),

Ghostwatching

That each by observation
Might satisfy his mind.

The First approached the Elephant,
And happening to fall
Against his broad and sturdy side,
At once began to bawl:
'God bless me! but the Elephant
Is very like a wall!'

The second, feeling of the tusk,
Cried, 'Ho! what have we here
So very round and smooth and sharp?
To me 'tis mighty clear
This wonder of an Elephant
Is very like a spear!'

The third approached the animal,
And happening to take
The squirming trunk within his hands,
Thus boldly up and spake:
'I see,' quoth he, 'the Elephant
Is very like a snake!'

The fourth reached out an eager hand,
And felt about the knee.
'What most this wondrous beast is like
Is mighty plain,' quoth he;
''Tis clear enough the Elephant
Is very like a tree!'

The fifth who chanced to touch the ear,
Said: 'E'en the blindest man
Can tell what this resembles most;
Deny the fact who can,
This marvel of an Elephant
Is very like a fan!'

9 Dealing with Witnesses

The sixth no sooner had begun
About the beast to grope,
Than, seizing on the swinging tail
That fell within his scope,
'I see,' quoth he, 'the Elephant
Is very like a rope!'

And so these men of Indostan
Disputed loud and long,
Each in his own opinion
Exceeding stiff and strong,
Though each was partly in the right,
And all were in the wrong!

So oft in theologic wars,
The disputants, I ween,
Rail on in utter ignorance
Of what each other mean,
And prate about an Elephant
Not one of them has seen!

Given that the witness has settled on an acceptable description in his or her own mind then he or she now has to decide what the message is that is to be explained to the investigator. It is not just a question of 'the facts'; it is a question of personal bias.

First, witnesses will have to decide if the experience was – for them – a good or bad one, as how they felt about it will colour the way they describe it to others.

Secondly, they will have to decide what are the most important attributes they want to describe. If they think they have seen a hooded monk then they will automatically seek out and bring to the fore those details of their 'memory' that confirm and strengthen that belief. Those areas which are unsupportive of that belief will be downgraded. This is called the ratchet effect – based on the screwdriver which, when

Ghostwatching

turned in one direction tightens the screw but when turned in the other direction, simply has no effect.

EXPERIMENTAL WORK WITH WITNESSES

The witness is the only real contact with the sighting, but experimental work indicates that people are very bad at recalling what they saw. This experimental work cannot be ignored when faced with the comment 'But I know what I saw'.

Tony and John (and others) have carried out several experiments to test witness reliability.

The first related here was done on a live television programme, *Daytime Live*, by John. The subject was UFOs, but the message is equally valid for ghostwatchers.

The studio audience of about fifty people were shown, on studio monitors, a mocked-up picture of a 'classical' flying saucer for fifteen seconds. The image was then turned off. Only then were people given pencil and paper and asked to draw what they had seen. It was as near as we could get to a 'sudden' sighting where the witnesses would not know what was expected of them. The results were revealing: fifty totally different and almost entirely inaccurate images. One image was a circle with four huge wings radiating out from it.

Researchers could have been in the position of receiving fifty reports, with drawings, from fifty witnesses to one event. How would we ever have reconstructed the real image from the reports? And yet there can be no doubt that we knew they had all seen the same thing. At other times these experiments have been expanded to include time-sense. The picture is shown for ten seconds and afterwards people are asked not to draw it, but to say for how long they saw it. Estimates have regularly ranged from one second to around one minute. One estimate was three minutes!

At the time of writing the authors have started to run evening classes in the paranormal. At one of these we staged

9 Dealing with Witnesses

an experiment to see how well those attending the class could describe the guest photographer, Simon. The experiment went like this:

Philip Walton, one of the lecturers, was standing up, giving a ten-minute talk on this very subject (accuracy of observation). As he was talking, Simon walked up to the front and took a picture of Philip, then walked out. At that point, Philip explained that the incident had been staged, and asked if the class could describe Simon's appearance. (We should add that Simon had been wandering around for about an hour in full view of everybody, and had been to the previous day's class at well, so he was a familiar sight.) Of the twenty-one attending the class asked to describe the colour of Simon's eyes, only one gave the correct answer. The score on Simon's hair was slightly better – two correct replies. Nobody got his shoe style or colour correct, and only two people could describe his jumper, but no one noticed the shirt he was wearing under the jumper. To cap it all, only one person remembered to mention that he was carrying a camera!

Tony Cornell described a similar, but much more spectacular experiment in the *Journal of the Society of Psychical Research* (September 1959). The purpose of the experiment was to see how the general population would report unusual phenomena. It was run by members of the Cambridge Society for Research in Parapsychology. Whilst the tone of the report was serious, and fitting for such an august publication, we feel sure that they must have had a lot of fun. For six nights they arranged for one of their members to dress up as a typical hooded monk 'ghost'; dressed in white. The ghost's appearance and behaviour were carefully controlled, and arranged to be the same for each occasion. It would appear suddenly about 150 feet from the King's Backs Path, walk slowly for 120 feet towards an 8-foot-high mound, raise its left hand slowly in the air, lower it, raise both arms in the form of a cross – and then suddenly disappear. The whole event lasted four and a half minutes. The report does not

Ghostwatching

explain how the ghost appeared and disappeared, but we presume that it was somehow arranged.

Other members of the group were apparently scattered around the area, and their job was to observe the populace, with the intention of questioning any members of the public who observed the phenomenon, and to find out how accurate their descriptions were.

According to Cornell, over the six nights (in May 1958) a total of 70–80 members of the public were in a position to spot the 'vision' but not one of them seemed to notice the ghost! 'Not one was seen to give it a second glance, or react to it in any way,' said Cornell. A chart was provided in the report giving details for each night, and the average number of members of the public who were in a position to observe it was around 16. During Cornell's own observation four people glanced at the 'ghost' but did not seem to notice it, and on another occasion two people were actually walking towards the vision for some twenty seconds but did not show any sign of seeing it.

Apart from questions of observation, the fact that so many people ignored what they saw could mean there are a lot more ghosts walking around than we think. (On the other hand, if that one was regarded as too normal for notice, it could mean that Cambridge is a weird place to be. . . .)

Other observation experiments we carried out were the classical optical illusion tests, adapting or extending them to show people how easy it is to make mistakes in observation, and, particularly, how strong is suggestibility – if, for instance, nine people state that A is longer than B, knowing that B is longer than A, the tenth person will apparently truly believe that A is the longer line.

ASKING QUESTIONS

If anybody is asked to give the weight of an object, unless specially trained, they can only guess its actual weight. The

9 Dealing with Witnesses

only way a person can give an approximation of the weight, is to compare the unknown weight with something of which the weight is known. The person can then say, 'It is heavier than this weight, but lighter than that.'

If a researcher wants an accurate report from a witness he must take this fact into account and not 'lead' the witness improperly. Do not say 'Tell me the exact weight' or the witness will probably feel forced to make a very credible-sounding guess that will in all probability be hopelessly wrong. Do not say something like 'Was it heavier than a bag of sugar?' because you are setting the parameters for the witness to work within. Let the witness set the parameters and help only when he or she is obviously at a loss for an approach. For example, ask 'Can you compare the weight to something you know, and tell me if it's lighter or heavier?' – in other words let them set the comparison. Then you can investigate the 'known' object. If a person cannot think of anything (and under examination people can get a bit brain-dead), look around the room for something that will be familiar to the witness and suggest (don't demand) a comparison with that object.

Be as neutral as you can with the wording of your questions. There was an experiment done some years ago in which a group of people were shown the same video of two cars crashing into each other. One half of the group was asked 'At what speed would you estimate the cars crashed into each other?', while the other half was asked 'At what speed would you estimate the cars collided into each other?' One change of word was all that was different. Yet there was a consistency of around five miles per hour less in the estimates of those asked the second question; it seems that the subliminal meaning of 'collide' suggested a slower speed than 'crash'.

Ghostwatching

INVESTIGATOR TRAINING

For the budding investigator, practical training has in the past been a desirable, but difficult to obtain, commodity. ASSAP takes the subject of investigation of the paranormal very seriously, and is aware of the number of potential investigators who are keen to investigate the paranormal, but have no idea of how to go about it. ASSAP offers a way to such people by providing a training day and an accreditation system.

Tony attended one of their recent training days, in a local library in Blackpool. About twenty people, from all walks of life, were there, and it was an informal affair with a lot of subjects to cover, including:

* What is the point of investigation?
* How *not* to do an investigation
* Summary of the investigation process
* Interviewing techniques
* Submitting a Report
* The ASSAP Archives
* Practical interviewing exercises
* ASSAP code of conduct
* Dealing with press, and the ethics of authorship
* The ASSAP national investigation network

The ASSAP presenters included the National Investigations Co-ordinator, Michael Lewis, who is responsible for ensuring that investigations are undertaken properly, and passing requests from the public to the most appropriate person.

Despite the informality, the subject of proper scientific investigation was taken seriously and the reason for the lists of do's and don'ts was made quite clear.

9 Dealing with Witnesses

SUBMITTING A REPORT

Always keen on work to get us closer to the underlying mechanism of paranormal phenomena, we, the authors, were very interested in the section on report writing. By defining a standard report model, investigators can provide reports to a good level of consistency. By entering all report details into a comprehensive database, ASSAP hope to be able to use statistics to gain more information about the various types of phenomena. The authors are currently helping ASSAP set up that database.

PRACTICAL EXERCISE

The exercise on interviewing techniques was quite enjoyable. Experienced investigators set themselves up as witnesses for four historical cases, and the trainees were asked to interview them, determine the kind of phenomena reported, and recommend a suitable course of action. One of the scenarios was a classic bogus haunted pub with falling profits; no trainee was fooled by the proprietor's attempt to convince the investigators that the haunting was real.

CODE OF CONDUCT

As ASSAP's reputation requires proper behaviour from its members, the presenters were particularly keen to ensure that investigators would adhere to the ASSAP Code of Conduct: a 28-point document. We do not propose to cover the Code in detail, but it includes self-evident rules such as ensuring that at least one interviewer is a female if a witness is female, or a child; another point covers how to deal with offers of money or reward.

Ghostwatching

INSURANCE

One point that came out of one of the discussions was that ASSAP provides free third-party liability insurance for accredited members, and for those who accompany them. This type of insurance is expensive and can be essential when performing an overnight vigil in public or quasi-public buildings.

ACCREDITATION

Accreditation is not automatic after completion of the training day. Investigators are expected to work with experienced teams to 'get the feel' of conducting a proper vigil, and interviewing witnesses. The last task they are expected to complete is a small project which shows that they are able to undertake proper research and complete a report in the proper format. Surprisingly, ASSAP does not insist that the project is necessarily based on the paranormal – a report giving historical research on one's own house is acceptable; it shows that the investigator is able to search for records in the right place.

POSITIVE BENEFITS

One session in the afternoon showed how effective ASSAP's network could be. Mike Lewis showed an interesting video clip of a possible ghost, obtained by an ASSAP investigator. It is one of the few examples of possible apparitions on film. The clip was from two security cameras mounted at a pub. The owners had been out and had returned to the pub to find the front door somehow unlocked. The clip shows the proprietor entering the bar area but preceded by a wraith-like form. It seemed to be moving across the bar area at a different angle to the owner. We would not have been able

9 Dealing with Witnesses

to share this video with others were it not for the ASSAP network's efficiency.

SUMMARY

The witness problem is clear: there are witnesses who do not see what is there (Cambridge ghost); witnesses who are led to believe inaccuracies through suggestion or personal pre-disposition; and witnesses who are certain that they are accurate reporters (and who are not).

The investigator problem must be clear also; investigators also have pre-dispositions, reasons for being 'led' by peer pressure, and can be equally certain they are right about their own theories.

Put together, getting back to the 'real' facts is no simple matter.

However, sometimes the simple answer is the right one. At a recent vigil at Charlton House in Greenwich an inexperienced investigator insisted that she could smell baking bread. This was in the middle of the night in a well-preserved Jacobean mansion, in its own grounds and well away from any shops or likely source of such a smell. This investigator stuck to her guns despite the disbelief of the group.

At break time the source of the smell was discovered; a sandwich toaster had been left switched on by mistake!

A FINAL THOUGHT

The general view of witnesses is that they have seen something, that they want to report something, and that they are as keen as you are to know what it was. In many cases that is the case, but not always. Remember that there are going to be types of phenomena that are not welcomed by the witnesses who might take to calling themselves 'victims', such as poltergeist phenomena. One of John's earliest mistakes was to forget this and get very excited when a polter-

Ghostwatching

geist case was described to him, saying to the witness something like, 'That will make a very interesting subject for study.' The witness's reply was succinct: 'I don't want you to study it; I want you to get rid of the bloody thing!'

More seriously, never forget that frightened people might need more than company, they might need counselling. If you are trained, or able, to deal with that then do so. But check yourself and make sure that, if other, say medical, help is required, you take a role in suggesting or assisting in facilitating this.

The next chapter, 'Banishing Ghosts', contains more information on practical methods of eradication.

10 Banishing Ghosts

Exorcise: To expel or attempt to expel (one or more evil spirits) from (a person or place believed to be possessed or haunted) by prayers, adjurations, and religious rites.

(Collins English Dictionary)

THE DIFFERENCE between ghost*watching* and ghost*busting* is that watchers are looking for evidence of ghosts, and want to try to understand the underlying nature of the phenomena whereas ghost busters perform the task of banishing the phenomena.

The usual type of ghost that people want to be rid of is the poltergeist. Mediums and exorcists are sometimes contacted to deal with 'recording' type ghosts, but they seem to have little success. Not surprising, if our understanding of that type of ghosts is correct (see Chapter 2); probably the only way of eliminating that class of phenomenon would require piecemeal dismantlement and scattering of the surrounding environment. Not a satisfactory solution for a householder.

The symptoms of a poltergeist haunting seem to conform to a general pattern:

Stage 1. Early on the phenomena start at a relatively low level. Perhaps there are odd and unexplainable noises. Sometimes things seem to be disturbed from their usual place or are not where they were last put. This results in a general awareness by individuals that something is not quite right. Depending upon the severity or 'oddness' of the effects it is not unusual or surprising that at this stage the individual may fear for his sanity.

Stage 2. Incidents may begin to happen in front of one or more individuals; they may then compare notes, and discuss the matter with the rest of the household. Sometimes this is the first point at which different members of the household all realise that the 'funny goings-on' they had noticed and kept quiet about had in fact been noticed by others. Some members of the household may simply deny the existence of anything odd.

Stage 3. Some households may begin to look for patterns of behaviour. They may notice that the phenomena will diminish when certain people are not around, or get worse when the family is agitated. The ghost may be given a name. Names seem to vary, and are almost a 'pet' name: 'Fred' is not uncommon.

Stage 4. It is not surprising that the household may want to keep the existence of the ghost a secret, and they may develop techniques to keep the phenomena at bay. Examples include saying: 'Go away!' (or something stronger), which sometimes works – for a time. Another technique is to negotiate. For example they may ask the ghost not to throw crockery around or tip the mattress on the floor, but say it is OK to switch TV channels or play with the radio. Sometimes poltergeists leave writings around the house; the householders may start leaving messages for the poltergeist in order to 'negotiate'.

Investigators rarely get an opportunity to talk to households that have been able to negotiate with the poltergeist until long after the event. The witnesses often report that after six or so months of haunting the phenomena died away. Sometimes we hear of cases where phenomena continue for long periods – several years and more – but the witnesses are unwilling to allow investigators in for fear of upsetting 'Eric' or 'Jim' and bringing the disturbances back to their old level of severity. It can be argued that in these cases the phenomena died away a long time before, but for convenience they attribute common household problems to the ghost.

10 Banishing Ghosts

CALLING IN HELP

The vast majority of households cannot cope with the bizarre and problematic nature of the poltergeist. This is not surprising, as even our short list of poltergeist cases in Chapter 4 testifies to that type of ghost's ability to cause damage and distress. The poltergeist is therefore the usual reason for calling in an expert.

Unfortunately, there is no 'poltergeist eradication bureau' for people in this situation to contact. There are, however, four common routes for getting help: the local priest; the local spiritualist church; contacting the media; and, lastly, the national research agencies. Sometimes the 'victim' remembers the name of an organisation like the Society for Psychical Research and obtains the address and phone number from the London telephone directory.

What happens next depends on the approach used to deal with the problem. Some investigators maintain that irrespective of who is called in, the symptoms will generally diminish and disappear about six months after starting up. There is a lot of anecdotal evidence to suggest this. Certainly there have been many documented cases where no amount of attention from 'experts' of all types has resulted in the slightest difference. But there also seem to be many cases of satisfied customers who have had the poltergeist removed or their effects diminished well ahead of this 'time limit'.

THE EXORCIST

> For thirteen-year-old Douglass Deen, in 1949, poltergeist phenomena in his home started – as it so often does – with minor scratching noises. Very quickly it worsened to include dishes and fruit thrown through the air and pictures floating off the wall. Deen's bed would often vibrate when he was in it. A local priest was called in to assist.

The priest and Deen slept in a room together at the priest's house, in twin beds. Deen's bed began to vibrate and the scratching noises continued. At the suggestion of the priest, Deen moved to an armchair; but that began moving and tilting. In desperation Deen made up a bed on the floor; but even that started sliding around over the floor when he was in it.

Deen was sent to hospital, but neither medical nor psychiatric treatment helped. Eventually a Jesuit priest was asked to perform a ceremony of exorcism.

It wasn't easy to eradicate the problem; there were 30 attempts at exorcism before the effects were eliminated. During the ceremonies Deen convulsed, shouted obscenities and even spoke Latin, a language that he did not know.

This case was the inspiration for the book and film *The Exorcist*.[2]

We should make it clear that although there were clearly poltergeist effects surrounding this case, the priest regarded it as one of possession. In several other poltergeist cases the focus has occasionally gone into a trance and spoken in another voice, suggesting an overlap between the phenomena of poltergeists and possession.

Nowadays it seems that the number of exorcisms and related services is quite rare. The Church of England, which recognises a vast spectrum of opinion on this subject by its priests, has responded by setting up experts on the subject called Deliverance Ministers. For this book we interviewed Canon Dominic Walker, who is one of the Church of England's most experienced Deliverance Ministers, and has been working in this field for over eighteen years to date. It is important to note that although he has helped a considerable number of families he has only carried out six formal exorcisms in his career.

After listening to Dominic for only a few minutes, it became obvious that, in his view, care and help for the

10 Banishing Ghosts

victims was more important than just performing a ceremony.

Before an Anglican exorcism can take place, the Bishop of the diocese in which the ceremony is to be performed must be satisfied that a range of criteria has been met. Unless he is completely certain that an exorcism is required, he will not authorise the ceremony. The list of requirements includes: receiving psychiatric advice on the state of mind of the victim(s); that the family involved are prepared for what will happen, both at the ceremony, and after the ceremony; that an approved minister will perform the ceremony; and, lastly, the exorcism must be done in an environment of prayer.

These strict rules are obviously sensible, for how would the victims feel if an exorcism had no effect? Dominic Walker described to us a remarkable case where a mother was plagued by powerful poltergeist attacks. It seemed that helpers from another Church denomination had decided that the family were plagued by evil which was too powerful for them, and they accordingly washed their hands of the affair. This decision came after they had been unable to remove the demons by making the family lie on the floor and kicking them. It was at this point that the mother had no hope left of a 'cure' and, knowing she was the focus of the 'haunting', tried to kill herself in her car on a motorway. Fortunately she was stopped by the police before an accident occurred, and they were alert enough to realise this was not just a simple case of speeding.

After Dominic had visited the family it soon became obvious to him that the mother, who had had a traumatic childhood, needed counselling and psychiatric help. An interesting event occurred on their first visit to the psychiatrist. Dominic had the wrong change for the parking meter but the mother said 'Don't worry' and by concentrating with her mind, moved the mechanical dial of the meter to a position that covered the time of their visit. Although she required three years of therapy to come to terms with her childhood, the poltergeist effects began to dissipate soon after Dominic began to help and counsel her. This case demonstrates two important features. The first is that it seems that helping to reduce stress is half the battle in eliminating the poltergeist. The second is that the woman seemed to be able to control her own powers.

Dominic believes that the effectiveness of a priest in eliminating the poltergeist is based on his ability to provide pastoral care, rather than simple skill in performing an exorcism. It is important to help the whole family and the whole person – as he says, 'Jesus cured the sick and forgave them for their sins.' He prefers to use counselling techniques, and frowns on reliance on actions such as the sprinkling of holy water to eradicate the poltergeist: 'An exorcism is not a form of Christian magic,' he points out. The Church of England have published a very practical book called *Deliverance*. It explains the various types of hauntings, and sets out the Church's official position on how to eradicate them.

THE RESCUE MEDIUM GHOSTBUSTER

In the film *Ghostbusters*, the eradicators were high-tech, high-flying technicians. The spiritualist rescue medium is the reverse – low-tech and down-to-earth. They operate with just their senses and their minds.

The theory behind rescue work is that after a person dies, the consciousness or mind of that person still exists. The surviving 'entity' is often called the spirit. In the case of poltergeist activity, the idea is that the surviving spirit may want to stay with the living, and not wish to depart to its proper place. It is also thought that sometimes spirits don't realise they are dead and get very frustrated; hurling things around in anger. Sometimes, spirits move on to places that seem to be interesting. Some inns and pubs seem to collect spirits (no pun intended), leading to cases of the classic haunted inn.

The technique used by spiritualist mediums for the elimi-

10 Banishing Ghosts

nation of poltergeist activity is that of communication. A medium will try to talk with the frustrated spirits and help them realise that they are causing a problem and that they have a proper place to go to. They are called rescue mediums – they 'rescue' the soul and help it on its way.

Sometimes the medium may feel that a place is full of 'negative energy', and that beings called 'lower entities' are assisting in causing the disturbances. ('Lower entities' are generally defined as non-human or sub-human entities of a mischievous or even dangerous nature.) In this case, the medium may prefer not to deal with this kind of problem and may suggest calling in a spiritualist exorcist.

SPIRITUALIST EXORCIST

According to the dictionary definition at the beginning of this chapter, an exorcist uses prayers and religious rites. A spiritualist exorcist that we met does not use rites, but instead uses techniques to help increase the amount of positive energy around the people and the establishment.

We spoke to Philip and Sheila Scott who performed the successful exorcism at the Union Inn (the case study detailed at the end of this chapter). Philip told us, 'Whilst the manifestations seemed to appear on the landing, dowsing showed that the main source of negative energy which attracted the spirits and entities seemed to be coming from the cellar. The negative energy was very powerful and we had to use, I think, nine crystals to amplify the positive energy before we could balance everything out.'

Philip is also practical, as shown by one other case where he had successfully eliminated some poltergeist symptoms. The owner of the house complained after the event that he was suffering from bad headaches. Philip offered help in dealing with this based on the crystals and the energy but only after first ensuring the gentleman had visited his doctor to check that there was no obvious physical cause.

Ghostwatching

THE GHOSTHUNTER

Unfortunately the ghosthunter, or investigator into the paranormal, only sees a small percentage of cases. Most 'victims' are interested only in getting rid of the phenomena. The ghosthunter therefore has to be proactive in finding cases, as explained in Chapter 13.

The independent nature of the ghosthunter can also bring some positive benefits. By being able to take into account the belief system of the affected household, the investigator can help put them in touch with the type of ghostbuster which is going to be most acceptable to them. The investigator can also dispel some of the usual – and often unhelpful – myths about exorcism.

BANISHING 'FALSE' POLTERGEISTS

Whatever poltergeists are their bad effects need to be eliminated. There is an interesting case of 'defusing' the tension in the witness reported by researcher Dr Susan Blackmore. She examined a case where lights moved unexpectedly, doors opened and closed, a kettle switched on and off, the TV changed channels spontaneously and a clock moved along a mantelpiece apparently without cause.

Investigation indicated that the TV's infra-red sensor would change channels, responding to sounds such as the dog's chain rattling. The clock moved because a faulty spring made it jerk; once cleaned the clock became well-behaved.

When these two areas had been explained to the family the rest of the activity seemed to dissipate.

Canon Walker dealt with a similar problem. He had been asked for help by a woman whose husband had died some time previously, and who had since remarried. Her late husband had been a very jealous person. One night after retiring to bed the wife and her new husband read for a while, then switched the light out. A few minutes later they

10 Banishing Ghosts

were disturbed to hear a groaning noise. This continued for several weeks and, concerned that the jealous spirit of her late husband was returning to complain about her new husband, she sought help. Canon Walker visited her late one evening and asked her to go through the motions they always did before retiring to bed; he also heard the groaning noise. Because the household did not appear to be a 'household under stress' he was convinced there must be a physical cause. After repeating the bedtime ritual several times it became apparent that the groaning noise always appeared shortly after switching the bedroom light out. Sure enough, there was a problem with the lampshade; as it cooled the movements caused a friction between surfaces, and a resultant 'groaning' noise.

In these cases there was perhaps no 'real' phenomenon. In the first case, and less so the second, the belief that something real was happening caused the witnesses to 'read into' other events a more suspicious possibility. Once the 'key' events were explained the witnesses relaxed and stopped misinterpreting what they saw or heard.

Even 'genuine' poltergeist cases can have a similar pattern with apparently genuine strange occurrences leading to people misinterpreting other, 'normal', events. The researcher must identify, and deal with, the key issues.

THE PSYCHOLOGICAL METHOD OF BANISHING

This method is relatively new; and because it is so new it is not practised widely. It was adopted in 1977 by Maurice Grosse, the principal investigator for the Enfield haunting mentioned in Chapter 4.

The technique is based around reducing stress, and reducing susceptibility to misperceiving natural events. It gives the witnesses a new way of looking at their own problem by turning the household members into 'on-site investigators'. Simple methods can be used: keeping an event diary, trying

Ghostwatching

experiments to see what effect they might have, even putting domestic video cameras in rooms which are frequently affected.

The system works, we believe, because it encourages use of the left hemisphere of the brain.

For right-handed people, there is evidence to suggest that the right hemisphere is associated with artistic endeavours, creativity, perceptions and intuitions. The left-hand side of the brain seems to be associated with calculation, science and similar logical thinking-processes. There is also some evidence to suggest that a psychic operates best when the right-hand side of their brain is dominant (see Chapter 14). Philip Steff, the rescue medium who operates in the Bath area (he has eliminated over 80 poltergeists), uses music to help put himself in the correct frame of mind before visiting a client. He also uses techniques such as meditation to assist with this.

By reverse logic, it is possible to argue that by engaging the logical side of the brain, then psychic abilities might be reduced. This might explain why, when poltergeist witnesses are encouraged to become their own investigators, then the logical acts of classifying the phenomena, keeping a diary, experimenting, and so on, can help bring the haunting to a close.

In the same way, our approach to vigils may at times have seemed to the reader to be somewhat flippant, but it reflects our view that when people are relaxed, creative and having fun they are more likely to perceive, or even induce, phenomena. The opposite we feel is therefore also true; when investigators are clinical, scientific and critical they may well not perceive, or induce, anything other than boredom.

IS IT THE MIND THAT CREATES THE POLTERGEIST?

The research that leads to this question started in the early seventies with women such as the Russian psychic Nina

10 Banishing Ghosts

Kulagina. Nina was able, under scientific scrutiny, to move items such as compass needles by the force of her mind. On one occasion she not only moved a compass needle but moved across the table the whole compass, matches, a matchbox, a fountain pen cap and an apple! Determined not be outdone by the Russians, American parapsychologists managed to find their own psychic, Felicia Parise, who could perform similar psychokinetic feats. The interesting thing about Felicia was that she occasionally lost control of her abilities and found that objects would fly about when she was not concentrating specifically on psychokinesis (PK). Often this would happen at home; after a while it became too much for her and she decided to try to suppress her power, rather than continue to experiment with it.

This has led to the theory that it is the minds of people that create the phenomena, rather than third-party agencies such as spirits and 'lower entities'.

We must stress one point here. The physics of this is unknown, and there are some flaws in the theory, but certainly scientists have now shown beyond reasonable doubt that a large percentage of the population can, by concentration alone, have a statistically significant effect on random physical events, as argued by H. J. Eysenck and Carl Sargent in their book, *Explaining the Unexplained*.[53]

Here, then, is an alternative explanation as to why, when a particular individual is near, the poltergeist manifests, or why, when that person goes on holiday, say, the effect can follow him or her.

The theory isn't perfect, however. Some poltergeisted families can go on holiday and have a completely fuss-free time. One possible explanation for this, of course, could be that the change and rest brought about by the holiday can help temporarily in reducing the stress.

Ghostwatching

CONTAGIOUS POLTERGEISTS?

Another issue is that people associated with the main focus can find that the effect can spread to them. Maurice Grosse found with the Enfield Poltergeist that on more than one occasion poltergeist-like events started to happen around him while he was away from the witness's home. In fact, Maurice told us that he believes that 'genuine' poltergeist effects tend to affect the investigators as well; indeed, he believes that when he suffers no 'side effects' from an investigation he is suspicious that the case is in some way not 'genuine'.

We have great sympathy for this view. Both the authors, and many of our colleagues, have found poltergeists a little 'contagious'. In one case that we are currently examining there have been many incidents of equipment failure and interference, probably the most spectacular being the disappearance of 120 pounds' weight of radio equipment. The catalogue includes:

* a vital piece of equipment was found cut in two places preventing our EMU (Environmental Monitoring Unit) monitoring more than one floor of the house at any time
* the radio section of the EMU misbehaved whilst on site, but never before or since
* a voice-activated cassette-recorder failed to switch on, failing to pick up sounds we heard on other equipment
* faxes to two other investigators giving instructions to get to the premises both went missing from their files
* a cassette loaded itself into the car cassette player, in the car we were using to remotely monitor the EMU with; it has not done this before, since, or during attempts to try to make it do so
* battery failures on site, batteries which were tested and working once removed from site

* the loss of the 120 pounds of equipment was discovered when Tony Wells returned home from site
* at Tony's home – at the same time as the equipment went missing – two large containers of wood preservative bought especially for a woodwork job disappeared and new tins had to be purchased
* just after returning from site, John Spencer and his wife Anne both saw their oven 'hood' extractor at their home turn on while they were both several feet away from it.

Under 'other' circumstances we might well have dismissed as insignificant these individual events but they all happened over a space of two days during the investigation. We tried to see if we were falling into the trap of over-exaggerating events; on a later occasion, over a selected three-day period, we made notes of anything out of the ordinary but nothing remotely like the above catalogue happened.

WHAT TO EXPECT WHEN THE MEDIUM CALLS

The rescue medium can be someone from any walk of life, who believes that he or she has a gift. There is usually a complete lack of ceremony when the medium calls. He might bring along one or two assistants, who tend to be passive during the session, but assist with providing mental support.

Some mediums prefer to know nothing about the case before arriving, or may just want to know in general terms what the phenomenon is. On calling, he may want to sit down and chat about the experiences of the household, or he may want to walk around first, to pick up impressions and 'tingles' of a 'presence'.

After watching mediums in action, the first impression we get is that they have sympathy and empathy with the witnesses. We have also seen some sensible, objective questioning, similar to those asked by ghostwatchers. When told that banging pipes was a feature at a household, the medium asked if the central heating was on when these noises were heard. In another case, a medium was brought in to help in a shop which local residents seemed reluctant to enter for fear of the ghost. The medium did his best to get rid of the poltergeist, but on leaving made the very practical point that the shop was quite dirty, and offered the equally practical suggestion that custom would be improved if the proprietor cleaned the place up occasionally!

Sometimes mediums will make a statement about the haunting, such as: 'I think that this is a place of frequent manifestations', or 'I get the impression of pain and sorrow here'. If they do so, it is usually before being told the details of the hauntings, to test their own powers, and assuming they are right, it will help gain the confidence of the residents.

If the medium feels that there is 'a presence', and that there is benefit in trying to make contact, then he or she will ask the people present to form a circle. Mediums generally do not seem to mind where this circle is, and it is usually in some convenient place in the haunted location. He or she seems to be sensitive to the attitude of the householders. If he senses resistance or distrust, he may prefer to hold the circle without the people who feel that way: distrust or cynicism seem to make their work harder. Investigators with an open mind don't, however, seem to cause problems, and we have found that mediums have been quite happy to include both authors in their circles, providing we don't break the circle, or cause distraction by taking notes. When Tony worked with Philip Steff at the Union Inn, Philip was quite happy to have Tony sitting in; there was no need to take notes during the circle itself because it was all happening in front of a video camera.

The circle usually starts with a prayer, followed by a period of meditation where the group in the circle will sit with palms up. If the medium is successful, he will go into a trance, usually indicated by deep slow breathing. Once in the trance he will be in contact with the spirit or spirits in the location, but still be able to talk. He may give a description of what he sees, such as: 'I see a man with a red coat, trilby hat and a moustache'. He will then try to talk to the spirit and to persuade him to leave this place, and to go to its proper place, 'towards the light'.

This process may be repeated if there is more than one presence. Eventually, the medium will come out of the trance and want to talk for a minute or two about his impressions while he regains his strength. Mediums often say that this process is quite exhausting. Water may also be drunk to help return the medium and members of the circle to the 'real world'. Once rested, the circle may be closed off with a prayer.

Sometimes after the visit the witnesses may notice an increase in phenomena. Usually that diminishes after a few days, and often goes away completely within a week or so. If the effects refuse to go away, then the medium can be called back. If he feels that there is more power there than he can deal with, he may suggest a spiritualist exorcist. These people are more robust than conventional rescue mediums, and are prepared to tackle more difficult cases.

When we asked Philip Steff about his methods he explained that normally 'one visit should be sufficient. If the situation persists then the people or the place may be attracting lower entities.' In such cases, Philip refers the problem to people who can deal with these issues.

EFFECTIVENESS

Obviously the psychological and spiritualist approaches are completely different, but there is plenty of evidence to suggest that both methods work, though neither is perfect – history is littered with cases which have required repeated attempts at eradication, and visits by different types of practitioners. Unfortunately, it is not easy to derive statistics on effectiveness for either method, nor for individual practitioners. The very fact that there seem to be two diametrically opposed views on the cause and eradication of poltergeist phenomena implies that we are discussing a most inexact science. We are also dealing with people. At our present level of understanding of the subject it is impossible to speculate any further.

CASE STUDY: THE UNION INN – A MIXED BAG OF PHENOMENA

There are complexities in poltergeist cases that make eradication difficult; there seems to be no one perfect method of eradication. This is perhaps because there is more than one cause, or due to the different attitudes of different witnesses. Some cases are therefore more resistant to eradication than others; the Enfield poltergeist stayed for over two years, an ongoing case of our own has had a similar duration.

The Union Inn is an example of a complex case where more than one means of eradication had to be tried. It was fortunate for us that the proprietor allowed a number of vigils in his inn while the haunting continued.

The Union Inn case started for us in September 1992, following an article in a local newspaper about our research group, South East London Paranormal Research Group (SELPRG). The proprietor, Stephen Dartnall, phoned Tony asking if we could help stop the phenomena at the inn which had plagued them so much that no one was prepared to sleep there. This case had two significant features for us. First, experienced investigators witnessed evidential paranormal events with their own eyes (unfortunately not captured on video). Secondly, personal experiences during the investigation led Tony to wonder whether he had some psychic abilities. Thirdly, on two separate occasions, two different video cameras did not pick up loud noises from a corridor area heard by different investigators, but the cameras were sensitive enough to pick up low-volume ambient noises. Lastly, the cure for the phenomena was based on quartz crystals – unusual, but effective.

BACKGROUND

It is believed that the inn originated in the early 1400s, and used to be three separate cottages. In 1450 the cottages were joined and became the inn.

We have been told by Stephen that the local historical society has reports that, in Victorian times, the inn was owned by the local mortician, and that his daughter broke her neck falling down the cellar steps. The mummified remains of a baby were found behind the bricks of the chimney in the restaurant area by the former owner, who left the baby there, and put a glass screen in front. Since the first visit, several investigators have had a look but could not see anything like a mummified body. Stephen speculates that the daughter gave birth to an illegitimate baby, but through shame both the pregnancy and the birth were kept secret. Once the daughter had died, the mortician disposed of the baby by bricking it up in the fireplace.

THE SITE VISIT

In early November 1992 Tony Wells visited the Union Inn with his partner and colleague Jane Le Surf. The purpose of the visit was to determine whether there was any scope in holding a vigil.

THE INN

It has two levels plus a cellar. On the upstairs level are the private dwelling quarters comprising two small bedrooms, a main bedroom, a sitting room, one bathroom toilet, a toilet and a utility room with a shower unit. The floorboards are very creaky. The downstairs area comprises a bar and restaurant. These are directly underneath the upstairs rooms, while further back are toilets, utility room and a kitchen.

Ghostwatching

From the street, on the right-hand side, the inn is separated from the dental surgery next door by a passageway six feet wide. According to the proprietor, an old lady lives on the left-hand side, and does not use the top part of the house.

THE PROPRIETORS

Stephen and Anne moved in in July 1992. They have two children, at that time aged four and two and a half. Anne and the children stay mostly at their house in Dymchurch to be near the school; normally Stephen would stay at the inn, but now he returned home to Dymchurch every night – he was too disturbed by the manifestations.

Anne described herself as a sceptic, and claimed no previous paranormal experience, but said her grandmother was a clairvoyant. Stephen said he had been told that he 'had the gift' many years ago, and saw a vision of his grandfather at approximately the time he died, in the clothes that he died in.

The children seemed lively and 'normal' when observed at play for a few minutes.

ANECDOTAL REPORTS

The proprietor stated that several women in the bar area have said they have felt as if they have been touched on their backs or shoulders.

He also said that the pensioner next door had complained to the previous owner of loud noises at all hours, coming from the top half of the inn, keeping her awake. On the occasions when she complained no obvious reasons for the noise could be found. He added that several people (himself included) have seen the ghost of the mortician's daughter wandering around, and that this haunting is known by the local historical society.

He also said that both the haunting by the daughter

downstairs, and the 'thumps' from upstairs are widely known about by the locals.

INCIDENTS REPORTED TO US

1. Apparition

On a Wednesday, approximately three weeks before Tony and Jane's first site visit, the manager woke up to see a figure (male-looking) walk through the closed door of the main bedroom, and walk casually to the window. The figure turned to look at him, then walked away out through the closed door. He said nothing of this to his partner at the time. This happened at just after 4 a.m. He is short-sighted and had to scrabble for his watch and flick on his lighter to see the time. He believed his short-sightedness prevented him from making out the details of the apparition.

2. Thumping noises

The next day, just before opening time the manager and the waitress were the only occupants. They distinctly heard thumping and bumping noises from above the bar area. The manager described it as sounding like someone running along the corridor upstairs. The bar area is directly below the corridor upstairs. No radiators were on upstairs (they occasionally make loud gurgling noises).

Two days after this, they heard the noises again.

3. Tingling

About two weeks before the site visit of 8 November, at about 6.30 p.m., the waitress was in the sitting room upstairs, on the settee, brushing her hair, looking into a hand mirror, facing the sitting room door. She began to feel uncomfortable as if someone was standing behind her, and felt a tingling sensation.

Ghostwatching

4. More thumps and door open

On Friday 6 November, Stephen, his manager and two customers were alone in the bar area, when they all heard thumps coming from the sitting room above. Stephen and the manager went up to see what it was but found no explanation. They closed all the doors, and checked that the latches were firm.

They heard the thumps again shortly afterwards, and found the sitting room door open; there was a 'musty smell'. One of the customers, a girl, went upstairs and sat on the settee for a few minutes. She then complained of feeling uncomfortable, drank up and left rapidly. She was apparently on holiday from Essex, and was staying locally. She never returned.

5. Two items lost, and found in unexpected places

On that same day, Anne had left her cigarettes in the upstairs bathroom but found them in the upstairs hallway. Later she left a baby's bottle on the bar, but found it in the restaurant area.

6. Three women experience 'pleasant sexual tingling'

On Saturday 7 November after closing time, three women – Anne and two female members of staff – were sitting in the bar area, in the first booth by the door. They were discussing children. No one else was downstairs. Anne's two children were asleep in the main bedroom.

One member of the group saw a 'quick flash of light' behind the waitress, who was sitting with her back to the bar area. Anne remarked that she saw her 'go grey' when she remarked about the flash of light. All three say they then experienced a pleasant tingling sensation up their spine – a distinctly sexual feeling. One of them described the sensation as like 'being gently touched up'. They tried to ask the 'ghost'

10 Banishing Ghosts

questions. A strong tingling was felt when the question 'Did you have a tragic death?' was asked.

7. 8 November visit

On telephoning (approximately 9 p.m. on 8 November) to make arrangements for the site visit, the proprietor reported that more thumping noises had been heard upstairs that day.

COMMENTS ON THE SITE VISIT AND INITIAL IMPRESSION

1. Tony had a headache all the while he was in the inn. (Jane and Tony were in the inn during the two periods 1 p.m.–1.45 p.m., and 2.30 p.m.–4 p.m. On both occasions the headache went a few minutes after leaving the inn. It could have been the smoky atmosphere.
2. Our opinion at the time of the site visit was that either they are all very suggestible people or that one or more of these people were witnessing some unexplained events.

Accepting all reports at face value we have quite a combination:

* Visible apparition of the 'daughter'
* Audible thumps and footsteps
* Visible apparition of a 'male' figure
* Unpleasant feelings, feeling of being watched
* Women being 'touched up' by unseen hands
* Touching sensations reported by customers
* Teleportation of objects
* Door found open when last seen closed

3. In addition to the above reports, the investigators had their own experience while on the site visit. When Jane and Tony were upstairs sketching the floor layout, Jane claimed she heard someone come up the stairs from the bar and go into the upstairs toilet – after a few minutes they discovered there was nobody in the toilet. They were approximately six

Ghostwatching

feet from the stairs at the time. At the time Jane mentioned somewone coming up the stairs Tony did not hear any footsteps on the stairs, but did hear a buzzing noise in his right ear simultaneously with Jane remarking on the person on the stairs.

THE FIRST VIGIL

The investigators were Tracy Curl, Robin Lawrence, John Spencer and Tony Wells. The account of this vigil is paraphrased from John Spencer's personal notes as Tony felt extremely odd throughout the majority of the time at the inn, and was unable to concentrate enough to take notes.

Summary of principal events

11.20 p.m.   John Spencer, Robin Lawrence and Tony Wells were standing together discussing vigil stategy at the top of the stairs next to the bedroom. The door was open and the light was on. John was standing directly in the doorway and no one else could have reached the light switch without his noticing. The others were a few feet outside the doorway. Suddenly the light went off. Immediately John looked at the light switch which was in the off position but no one had heard the 'click' of the switch. Robin confirmed that the light had been on though he did not see it being switched off (he probably could not have done from where he was standing). Tony saw something like a blue flash but didn't notice the light being switched off.

At the same time from downstairs several people reported banging sounds in the corridor near the three, though we heard nothing.

2.25 a.m.   Tony reported laser-like flashes from the ceiling in the bar. At sporadic intervals other members of the group reported similar flashes.

2.35 a.m. John and Tony, then all members of the vigil, over the next few minutes, watched the bar door to the kitchen opening and closing spontaneously. Members of the vigil examined the door and there were no draughts or vibrations that could have caused the movement. All external windows and doors were shut at the time. (On a subsequent vigil it was very stormy outside but the door never moved on that occasion.) The owners of the inn confirmed that they had never seen the door move like that before. After observing this door moving back and forth, Tony decided to take his courage in both hands and walk up to the door. As he approached the door it slammed shut (dramatically) in front of him. This happened in full view of John and other witnesses. In order to see better we turned on the lights (they had been off for some time). No obvious cause for the door's behaviour could be found. We turned the lights back off again. The door remained motionless after that.

2.40 a.m. Tony and John simultaneously saw a white light flashing at the end of the bar, which both of them independently brought to the vigil's attention. There was an examination for possible causes but none could be found. There were no changes of lighting in the streets outside which could have caused the effect.

3.15 a.m. Tony found a broom leaning up against a dustbin in the kitchen which had not been there earlier. The staff confirmed that it had been moved from its normal place.

4 a.m. approximately The door to the kitchen and toilet area began opening and closing spontaneously again.

At around that time, the other door to the restaurant area was closed but light was shining through along the left-hand edge and under the door (the light being there to enable the video recorder stationed on the other side of the door to maintain recording). Anne, the proprietor's wife, and John Spencer watched for 5-10 minutes as the light changed,

Ghostwatching

seemingly affected by movement, and creating shadows within the restaurant area. However, there was nobody in the restaurant at that time. All members of the vigil were in the bar and the only access was from upstairs where Stephen was asleep. John quickly reviewed the video recording but there was no sign of anything that could have caused the shadowing effect.

CONCLUSION ON THE VIGIL

The vigil seemed to provide strong evidence for paranormal happenings at the inn. The first was the light switching itself off. The second was the door opening and closing by itself and finally slamming shut and the third was the strange light effect. Although none of the events was captured on camera, there was plenty of corroborative evidence from other investigators who were able to witness the events. The interesting thing is that none of the phenomena witnessed corresponded with the types of events described by Anne and Stephen.

VISIT NO. 3 – THE RESCUE MEDIUM

After the first vigil, the owners and staff of the inn no longer had any personal doubts – it was definitely haunted, and independent investigators had confirmed this. The emphasis was now on eradication, and we were given the name of a rescue medium who would be willing to visit and assist with this. Philip Steff and his two assistants, Rachel and Simon, arrived at the inn three weeks after the first vigil.

We do not specifically support one theory of eradication or another, and when working with practitioners in the paranormal we always try to keep an open mind, and are willing to suspend personal beliefs during sessions. We try to help in providing whatever the witness wants.

THE SITTINGS

Two sessions were attempted by the rescue team that evening. During the first sitting, both Tony and Stephen were present. Stephen left after the first sitting to eat his supper. During that sitting, Philip contacted a spirit which seemed to have grey eyes, and was wearing a sou'wester and was 'dispatched towards the light'. The sitting was then closed down. As during the other visits, throughout the evening Tony had felt weird, and was interested to note that Simon, one of Philip's assistants, was feeling similar sensations. The weirdness sensation continued after the closing of the first sitting, and so it was decided to attempt a second sitting. At the second sitting Simon tried communicating with another spirit, which seemed to have the name 'Frederick Hannaby'. Almost simultaneously with contacting 'Frederick', a crescendo of noise was heard from above; no one was on that floor at the time.

CONCLUSION ON RESCUE VISIT

The rescue medium had brought a video camera which had recorded the sittings. Several months after the event Tony was able to view a copy of the tape-recording and was surprised to find an interesting anomaly. He seemed to remember that at one easily identifiable point during the second sitting (described above) there was a lot of crashing and banging coming from upstairs but there seemed to be no corresponding sounds on the camera's recording. All that the camera had recorded on sound was the clatter of knife and fork as the proprietor ate his supper. The camera was obviously sensitive enough to pick up sounds in the next room, but seemed to be unable to pick up the cascade of noise that he remembered. He checked his contemporaneous notes – sure enough they confirmed his memory: 'As Simon stood up to communicate with the spirit there were noises

Ghostwatching

from upstairs that sounded like a team of firemen playing football.' (In Chapter 8 we pointed out the importance of contemporaneous notes. Because Tony had these notes we were able to help do further examinations of reports of sounds by others.)

FURTHER VIGILS

Although the rescue team seemed to have been able to reduce the phenomena for a few days, the proprietor reported a week later that things were back to their old levels. On advice we obtained a referral from the rescue medium on a couple who were able to deal with difficult cases. Unfortunately they were not able to come for another two months, and during this waiting period, the proprietor was kind enough to allow us to run three more vigils. The phenomena at these subsequent vigils seemed to be at a much lower level; no physical movement, such as happened with the door, was detected.

There was one item in common for each of those subsequent vigils – at approximately 5.45 each morning various different investigators reported the sound of footsteps along the corridor section above. In all three cases, the proprietor, his wife and both children were (presumably) sleeping in two separate bedrooms upstairs.

On the final vigil we had a video camera on the upstairs floor facing the corridor area. On examining the recording, nothing was visible during the time the footsteps were heard, and no unusual sounds were heard. However, the camera was sensitive enough to pick up the sounds of snoring, of the pub sign swinging outside and of church bells two hundred metres up the road.

EPILOGUE

Philip and Sheila Scott call themselves exorcists because they are often asked to deal with difficult or persistent cases. They visited the inn in mid-February 1993 to do their work but to our disappointment neither of us was able to be present during their visit, but Robin Lawrence and Tracy Curl kindly offered to observe.

The exorcists' visit completely cured the problems, and the proprietor has reported no more incidents since that time to the time of writing. We spoke to the Scotts in August 1993 and they described to me their cure for this case. After some dowsing, it seems they discovered that there were some negative ley lines which caused excessive negative energy at the inn. This, they said, attracted lower-energy 'entities' which caused disruption and uncomfortable feelings. They counterbalanced the negative energies with quartz crystals, which were placed on the positive ley lines. They went on to say that quartz amplifies energy, and the crystals (nine in all) amplified the positive energy and resulted in a proper energy balance at the inn. The crystals were placed in the cellar, and Stephen the proprietor was given instructions not to move them.

CASE CONCLUSION

There is no doubt that the witnesses at the inn were troubled by their experiences, and we are in no doubt that there were paranormal events happening there. Our view, based on the lessening phenomena over the last three vigils, was that the phenomena seemed to have reached a peak in October/November 1992, and was on its way out by mid-February 1993 when Philip and Sheila Scott visited. Nevertheless, they seemed to have done the trick with their crystals.

It is worth pointing out that when Philip and Sheila Scott called, the proprietor, although he was aware that they were spiritualists, was in his mind expecting a Roman Catholic priest with all the religious paraphernalia. For those who would argue that just simple empathy with the witness is sufficient to calm down, and eradicate, a poltergeist, it was

Ghostwatching

certainly not the case here. Because of the difference between his expectations and the reality of the people who visited Stephen was not impressed and did not expect anything to work. Yet it did. And he was entirely pleased with the result.

A FINAL CONSIDERATION...

Whilst it is relatively easy for priests such as Dominic Walker and his colleagues to aid and counsel a family (the uniform and training of their calling gives them a flying start in this area), the ordinary investigator cannot help in this way.

The ghostwatcher is restricted to the psychological method of banishment, and stress-reduction techniques. Sometimes these approaches do not work, and sometimes the families involved will not admit to stresses; in these cases the investigator should assist the witnesses in finding a suitable practitioner. The type of practitioner will depend in some part on the belief system of that witness.

11 Working at the Frontiers of Science

THERE ARE MANY EXPERIMENTS that are being undertaken by groups such as those run by the authors to try to gain further understanding of ghost phenomena by 'creating' experiences rather than just waiting around to witness them.

DIY GHOSTS

Why would anyone want to make their own ghosts? Well, one answer is quite simple – people who suffer from hauntings, especially poltergeists, 'just want rid of the damn things'. Ghosthunters, always curious about the underlying mechanism behind the phenomena, want to spend as much time as possible with instruments and probes to see if they can find some clues. Some ghosthunters therefore try to create their own phenomena. It isn't just ghosthunters who try these experiments, it is people interested in all sorts of paranormal phenomena, particularly psychokinesis.

In the West, the 1960s and 1970s saw an upsurge in research and imaginative experiments in psychokinesis or PK. The most imaginative and effective idea, however, was to invent a ghost. The ghost was invented in Canada in the 1970s; his name was Philip.

The useful thing about DIY ghosts is that you don't need to be particularly psychic, or believe in life after death. And you can work in the comfort and privacy of your own home.

Ghostwatching

THE PHILIP EXPERIMENTS

A Toronto-based research group under the leadership of Dr A. R. G. Owen undertook the Philip experiments in 1972.

They started from the assumption that before Philip could be 'brought into being' every member of the experiment would have to believe in him. To make this work, they created a totally fictitious background for him with great care and detail; interestingly it was a 'believable' background to the researchers – North Americans – which might not be so recognisable to the English, even though it was set in England. The credibility to the group was more important to the experiment than historical accuracy.

One member of the society even drew his portrait to make him all the more 'real' to the group.

Philip's story was a romantic one set in seventeenth-century England. He was an English aristocrat, married but having a romantic liaison with a gypsy girl. The girl was burned at the stake as a witch, and Philip – having failed to intervene to save her life, as he could have done – was thrown into remorse. Periodically his ghost would be seen on the battlements of his country estate, pacing in anguish.

This background gave him reason to communicate, perhaps looking for forgiveness or understanding.

After reinforcing their own belief in the existence of Philip the group of eight tried to 'manifest' him. Their first, very serious, attempts produced no results and it was not until the summer of 1973 that success began to occur – following a period of introducing a relaxed and happy atmosphere to the research. Throughout this book we have indicated that we believe atmosphere to be important in such experiments; a suggestion reinforced by other experiments in other fields, such as Professor Hasted's PK experiments. In fact, in the Philip experiments the strongest results arose when the group were having fun; another aspect of the research we have stressed.

11 Working at the Frontiers of Science

Philip communicated through rapping noises, first heard while the group was singing; he was apparently responsive to certain songs and to hearing 'his' name.

Questions were asked of him, and the answers were generally in the style of the constructed personality the team had devised for him.

Philip graduated to moving a table on which the researchers lightly placed their hands; occasionally it would shoot across the room at considerable speed.

He was even happy to 'perform' and communicate in front of the television cameras when he was taken to Toronto City Television in 1974 ('he' here being the table that represented his rapping communication). In the studio the table apparently moved independently and responded to questions by 'rapping happily'. There was an amazing twist to the story, one that we feel is an important lead for further such research; it is to do with strength of personal belief. One member of the group broke ranks and claimed to Philip, 'We only made you up, you know.' The rapping stopped; once he had been denied belief Philip ceased to exist. He was 're-born' some time later only after a period when the researchers had 're-learnt' to believe in him.

SO, WAS PHILIP A GHOST?

He exhibited the same characteristics as that form of 'ghost' generally called a spirit; interactive communication in this case through self-taught mental mediums. As such we know of course that he was not a 'natural' ghost but his construction provides for effective, comparative research into those similar cases that arise naturally.

TABLE-TILTING

Table-tilting is different from the Philip experiments in that the group does not visualise or invent a character. Table-

Ghostwatching

tilting was so common in Victorian times that it almost became a parlour game. The basic technique is quite simple: the group (often called a sitter group) simply sits around a table, and everybody rests their hands upon the table. If everyone is patient enough, and prepared to do this for several sittings, they will be rewarded with some phenomena. In the early days of the group's experiments, the table will start to rap and make knocking noises. At later sessions the table will occasionally vibrate, and eventually it will begin to move. As the number of sittings increase, the phenomena experienced by the group will increase in power, and variety.

The movement and behaviour of the table can sometimes seem extraordinarily intelligent. Once the group has begun to experience effects it is possible to ask questions, and receive raps and/or tilts in reply. When this phenomenon is experienced personally, it is easy to understand why the Victorians began to believe in spiritualism.

As well as intelligence, the table seems to have power. One researcher, Guy Lyon Playfair, in his book *If This Be Magic* describes a visit to a table-tilting group in 1983. The group's table was so powered-up that all four members of the group were actually sitting on it and it was still moving – which brings a whole new meaning to the term sitter group.[48]

The session described above was led by a senior psychologist, the late K. J. Batchelor, who in the sixties and seventies tried out many experiments with table-tilting. From his work came some simple rules of thumb that he found would improve the chances of making something happen. In addition, he came across some curious effects which may help explain some of the underlying mechanism of poltergeist phenomena. Some of these methods are very similar to those discussed in Chapter 8 on how to create the right atmosphere for a vigil.

11 Working at the Frontiers of Science

TABLE-TILTING GUIDELINES

First, especially in the early sittings, it seems to be better to avoid concentrating on moving the table. Instead the sitters should be encouraged to make jokes, talk normally and in general try and relax. This advice is similar to the ideas we discussed in Chapter 8, and possibly explains why a group of friends staying overnight in a haunted house for charity may experience more phenomena than other people who may have been watching for ghosts for years. It is conceivable that by behaving in this way they may be creating their own ghosts.

The second thing to bear in mind is the lighting. It seems to be best to work in complete or near-complete darkness. In addition, table-tilting, like most poltergeist activity, seems to be camera-shy. To the determined ghosthunter this shouldn't pose a problem, however. With infra-red-sensitive video cameras (most modern video cameras are sensitive to infra-red) it is possible to operate in conditions which to the naked eye seem like total darkness, but to the camera are almost like daylight. (See Appendix D.)

Thirdly, the group should meet regularly, once or twice a week if possible. To succeed, the group should therefore have a certain amount of dedication and be prepared to endure many sittings before any phenomena appear. The meetings should be free of interruption, and so some preparation is required to ensure this. For example the telephone should be taken off the hook, or the answerphone turned on.

Fourthly, the table should be small and fairly light, so that one person if faking movement can do so easily. More about this later.

Fifthly, stopping the proceedings to write notes can suppress the phenomena. To get around this Batchelor and others used an audio tape-recorder to record events. Such a device makes note-taking a much more natural process – people can say what is happening as it happens. For those who are using video-tape recordings, the events should be self-documenting. If technology is being used it may be worth bearing in mind that table-tilting resembles poltergeist phenomena and poltergeists seem to get up to all sorts of technological tricks.

Sixthly, it will always be tempting to experiment, but it seems that it is best to change only one thing at a time. For example if you try changing the table, don't introduce a new member at the same time. If you are changing venue, try and bring the original table with you.

Faking can actually encourage real phenomena. Batchelor experimented with this technique extensively and found that he was able to induce the table to perform after he faked rapping noises, or jerked the table. He was not observed faking this, as the sittings were held in near-darkness. Batchelor's view of why this occurs is that people have an inherent disbelief in this type of phenomena, the disbelief might be buried quite deeply, but it is always there. Faking the phenomena seems to temporarily bypass the problem and allow the mind to perform its work. In short, it seems that once other people have been led to believe something faked is true, then it really does happen, possibly because their barriers and resistances are now down.

WHY DOES TABLE-TILTING WORK?

Of course no one really understands the underlying cause, but we can hazard a guess as to why a group can achieve PK effects such as table-tilting more easily than individuals can. We think that the explanation for this lies in the way groups of people, such as committees, work together. Understandably, PK is so odd, and carries with it so much mental baggage, that the rational part of our mind spends a lot of time constantly re-evaluating what it has perceived. The authors realised the extent to which this happens during a vigil at the Union Inn. At the previous vigil together they had

11 Working at the Frontiers of Science

both witnessed a door spontaneously open and close, and finally slam shut as Tony walked up to it. At the next vigil, they each caught the other minutely examining the door, the frame and the ceiling above it. Groups of people have a tendency to carry out tasks which are more risky than an individual would dare to perform. The reason is simple – individuals in the group can blame any mistakes on the 'committee' and not themselves. Similarly by working in a sitter group, the individual can assume it is 'someone else' who is performing the phenomena.

OUIJA BOARDS

Ouija boards are controversial; they need not be avoided, but they should be approached seriously and perhaps with caution. There are many accounts of 'bad' events; and whatever the cause of these they deserve consideration.

We both feel that there is some kind of paranormal phenomenon related to these boards, but it is of course debatable what that paranormal energy is, and whether it is intelligently directed. The technique for using a Ouija board is quite straightforward. Some kind of flat surface is required on which are written or pasted in a circle the letters of the alphabet and the numbers 0–9. Answers or instructions such as YES, NO and WAIT can also be included. Some kind of free-moving object, often a wine glass, is rested on the surface and the sitters lightly rest one finger on the glass. The free-moving item is sometimes called a planchette. Ready-made boards and planchettes can be purchased in many shops which sell 'New Age', or 'occult', artefacts.

During the session, one of the sitters asks questions of the glass, such as 'Is anybody there?', or 'Is there a presence with us?', and – hopefully – the glass will move to the 'YES' position. (Sometimes it moves to the 'NO' position; nice to know the dead, if that's who they are, don't lose their sense of humour.)

Ghostwatching

Once working, the sitters can ask the glass questions. Leading questions and questions which only require a YES/NO type answer are easiest to start with.

It is quite common when starting out to receive 'junk' answers to questions. For example, a typical question might be: 'Do you have a message for anyone present?' and the glass will come back with something like: 'HZDHEM-ABCBXBE'. Not very rewarding! Persistence over several sessions can result in more meaningful messages.

Sceptics offer two main reasons for the apparent movement of the planchette. The first is that when using a glass, the heat from the fingers creates a 'cushion of air' which helps the glass slide easily around the board. The second is simply fraud – one or more people push and pull the planchette around with their finger. While both might prove true, these are less than perfect answers: experiments show that fraud is often easily detected by members of the group. When two people have their fingers on the planchette, it is easy to detect faking. Focusing on the method by which the planchette moves is, of course, only part of the research; it is important – whatever the mechanisms – also to examine the nature of the output from the Ouija, and also why subsidiary 'effects' arise; for example, in some sittings spontaneous fires have started in the houses.

Once the group has got a session where the planchette seems to be responding to questions then it is possible to try and generate phenomena. Some groups have experimented with questions like 'If anyone is there please rap three times' and been rewarded with raps. Once these effects have started to be obtained then the group can ask for more and more physical effects, such as asking for the form of the 'spirit' to show them its form – i.e. for a shape to materialise.

Once the 'system' is working, then it is possible to expand the experiment into questions that probe the telepathy and clairvoyance abilities of the sitters.

For example, questioners with fingers on the planchette can ask for messages for people who are in the group but are

11 Working at the Frontiers of Science

not directly operating the glass. Sometimes the answers can be quite revealing.

We believe that there is no *inherent* danger in using such boards, it seems simply to be a fast method of helping generate PK, and an easy way of obtaining telepathic and clairvoyant messages. There are many stories about people who have experimented with Ouija boards and then discovered that 'things begin to happen'. Typical experiences include hearing voices and finding that things move by themselves. The spiritually inclined will often say 'the person used the board whilst unprotected and so has attracted certain lower entities'. These lower entities are thought to be playing tricks (objects moving without obvious propulsion) and trying to communicate with that person (hearing voices).

Many mediums do not approve of the use of Ouija boards; perhaps part of the dislike is because the Ouija board can produce mediumship-like effects without the use of a medium.

It is possible that the board is not being used to contact spirits, but is simply an example of PK being induced in the safety of the 'committee syndrome' where the group can 'pass the buck' on to the board, and allow the board to perform, without the members feeling that they have any direct effect. To the non-spiritualists here is an alternative explanation. The board has simply helped them to exercise their PK abilities (moving objects) and improve their telepathic ability (hearing voices).

The authors' belief in the possibility that spirits might have nothing to do with the Ouija system became stronger after a session in 1993 in which both participated. After a few minutes of the glass moving it became obvious to all that one specific person was responsible for the messages. As soon as he realised he was 'in the driving seat' he started asking questions, and it turned out that he was being answered by a fictional character from a play he himself had written several years ago!

Alan Gauld also seems to feel that the minds of the sitters

Ghostwatching

play an important part in the work of the Ouija board, and in his book *Mediumship and Survival* provides the following observation:

> To the participants in such [Ouija board] seances, the mere fact that devices move often seems surprising, indeed uncanny, and should coherent sentences be written they may be accorded the respect due to the deliverance of an oracle. I have myself come across a number of cases in which a Ouija board wrote copiously and fluently and produced material which was quite alien to the conscious minds of the persons operating it. In each case, however, it appeared highly likely that the material was coming from some hidden level of the mind of a particular sitter.[49]

Gauld described a series of sittings where messages from a Nazi supporter came through. Apparently Hitler was alive and well and operating a petrol pump in Arkansas, and Martin Bormann was disguised as a priest! After several sessions it was discovered that one of the sitters was himself a former Nazi supporter. Despite his having renounced these beliefs, somehow the messages were coming from his subconscious.

To be fair to those who believe that there can be something more to the Ouija board, Alan continues with: 'I have also come across a number of instances of Ouija and planchette writings in which correct information was given which was prima facie unknown to any person present.'

MORE EXPERIMENTS

At this point in the chapter we hope that the reader has noticed a common thread in the techniques described above. 'Philip ghosts', table-tilting and Ouija boards are all able to produce the same kind of phenomena, and many of these

11 Working at the Frontiers of Science

phenomena can be produced by people who would not call themselves psychic. Earlier we mentioned the 'committee effect' as a possible explanation of why sitter groups can induce PK and other phenomena. To support the hypothesis further there is some documented experimental evidence to show that, under hypnotism, subjects can improve the reliability of their paranormal abilities. This is covered in notes of our own, and other, experiments in Chapter 14.

The chapters in this section have presented our very practical experience of ghostwatching, and experimentation. The following, last, section of the book sets out the practical ways in which you, the reader, can become a ghostwatcher, or improve your own ghostwatching techniques.

Part Three

SO YOU WANT TO BE A GHOSTWATCHER?

12 Getting the Team Together

'Raising team spirits helps to raise the spirits . . .'

GETTING THE MEMBERS

As mentioned elsewhere, there is little point in a ghostwatcher spending a night in a haunted house alone. If something exciting did happen, then a) he may have a heart attack, b) go grey overnight, and c) no one will believe him. (Admittedly it may be easier to convince people that something happened if the ghostwatcher had both a heart attack and went grey overnight.)

Getting members to turn up for one or two meetings or vigils is relatively easy, but, like many other things in life, keeping them and melding them into a team is a lot harder.

Friends and family are an obvious starting point. But they may not have the same interest in the subject, nor the dedication. Early in 1993 Tony needed a lot of cover to run a vigil at Charlton House in Greenwich. To help make up the numbers he drafted in some friends who were quite excited about 'ghosthunting in a haunted house'. Unfortunately, it was probably the quietest vigil ever held in the history of ghosthunting. None of those friends ever mentioned the ghosthunt again, and have never expressed an interest in attending another vigil.

Tony started his group, the South East London Paranormal Research Group, by contacting his local newspaper and asking for an interview. The publicity from the article generated both members and cases. Time, of course, will tell whether people are willing to stick with it.

Ghostwatching

Both authors believe that most is achieved where there is the minimum of paperwork and the maximum fun; members are likely to stay if that is the case. Of course, no one can guarantee that a vigil is going to be successful, but as we have pointed out elsewhere, having a good team attitude may be a factor in helping create the right conditions to encourage ghosts to come out of their shell.

John has been ghosthunting for over twenty years and has all too often been appalled by the disagreements and arguments that arise. Of course there will always be different views over tactics and strategy, but it helps considerably if everyone is briefed in advance and is therefore aware of the issues for that particular site. Have your 'robust' discussions well in advance of the vigil and at a time when everyone is in good humour – not at 2 a.m. in the morning.

This section of the book will, we hope, assist you in creating a good team atmosphere that will help you survive the low points that arise when you have been up all night in less than perfect conditions.

SETTING OBJECTIVES

Setting objectives, and ensuring that all members are happy with how to achieve them, is probably the single most important factor in making an effective team. We know of no group which is over-resourced, and so having objectives in mind will help ensure that scant resources (time, money, people . . .) are utilised as effectively as possible. If you are a member of a group with too many people best of luck . . . On the other hand if you're a member of a group with too much time or money, can we join please?

An obvious objective is finding a ghost. But what does one actually mean by that? Goals often change with time and it is important that members realise that. Once you have found a ghost the next objective is to prove to others that you have found it.

12 Getting the Team Together

You might then move on to how to make that ghost appear again in front of others.

TEAM ORGANISATION

Different groups seem to employ different methods of working. Some seem to act like a loose collective where decisions are taken by discussion and broad consensus. Others seem to be strict democracies with a structure and roles assigned (publicity officer, vigil organiser, librarian, and so on). Others seem to be based around one or two individuals who do most of the work, and ask people to join them on specific projects such as a vigil.

Empowerment is a fancy management consultancy term. In the case of making a good ghosthunting team, it means allowing members to take responsibility for their own work. They must own the work, and the eventual outcomes. If a member of a group reads a report of a haunted inn, and wants to follow it up, then he or she should be encouraged to become the 'team leader' on that case and be assisted by the others. The right man or woman to lead the team is often dependent on the circumstances, and should not depend on the hierarchy.

Some people enjoy organising events – encourage them to have a go. Other members may be keen on delving into public libraries and looking at historical records – encourage them. Others may want to create fancy letter-headings to improve the group's public image. Always encourage those with energy and enthusiasm.

INTERVIEWING

Consider the witness's situation. We recommend that when interviewing a woman or children, you have a woman as part of your interviewing team.

Interviewing witnesses takes practice. If a member of the

Ghostwatching

group has little or no experience then the only way to get it is to do the job. Provide back-up with a more experienced member of the group, even do some 'practice' sessions. But never discourage anyone, and never, never appoint a single individual to do this job. Again, it is the right person for the individual task at any given time. It can sometimes be quite surprising who builds rapport with particular witnesses.

In any case, it is wise for members to watch others interviewing; we all have something to learn from others. The only person on any team who is probably useless is the person who is sure they have nothing left to learn.

TECHNIQUES OF TEAMBUILDING

It is worth looking at the teambuilding techniques used by the biggest and most successful companies in the world. There is a widespread belief that less time spent 'playing' leaves more time for 'doing'; and companies all too often allow very little time for play – or what we prefer to call rehearsal – time. This has never proved effective in the most dynamic of companies. Every evidence we have accumulated over the years indicates that by increasing the time spent developing the team, the team becomes more effective in its real work. It may, arguably, have less time for action, but it will produce more results in the time it does have.

Rehearsal is the basis of putting together any Quick Response Team that needs to get an effective job done quickly. The mistake often made is to underrate the value of rehearsal.

For ghostwatching the most effective teams seem to be those that devote some effort and time to rehearsal, and teambuilding. As ghostwatching is always a voluntary effort it is hard to demand time of others; but it must be made clear that if they want results, if they want value from their research, and – we don't underrate this either – if they want fun, then they have to work at it.

12 Getting the Team Together

Management trainers have long recognised that an important part of the relationship between team members relies on building trust. To some extent this has often been allowed to develop in its own right because there seemed to be time to allow it to happen 'naturally'. Where a team has a long-term life of many years then this may be appropriate. However, in ghostwatching as in other activities, there are always going to be newcomers or people who leave. It may or may not be ideal to have a ghostwatch team of the same people for five years; but in any case it just doesn't happen. People come and go. So ghostwatchers have to acknowledge that they are in a position of creating what the business world calls Quick Response Teams or Corrective Action Teams. They have to form quickly, gel together, and get out and do the work.

The skills required to generate trust come mainly from the performing arts and some of these techniques are described below. They may seem strange for teambuilding, or for ghostwatching, but from practical experience both authors can be certain that long ghostwatch vigils are enhanced, and enjoyed more, when the teams involved have gone through these techniques.

1. Establish the ground rules of the teambuilding techniques

In any teambuilding session where trust between individuals is an essential element there must be clear ground rules.

First, there will, from time to time, be intimate disclosures from individuals and it must be made clear from the outset that information gleaned will be strictly confidential. At the end of the day all the participants will have put something of themselves into the teambuilding and therefore all will be equally vulnerable; as a consequence this trust is almost always respected.

Secondly, there must be no criticism – overt or covert. People will be asked to disclose very personal information which may possibly be something that breaks certain social

Ghostwatching

conventions. The ground rules must state that no one will attack or question such disclosure directly or, as importantly, by gesture or expression. Again, this is usually accepted by participants provided the team leader is skilled at putting people at ease.

2. Eye contact

Many people in a group, and particularly when first brought together, set up a barrier by avoiding eye contact with each other. To break any barriers the group should stand, or sit, in a circle and each person should make direct eye contact with every other person in the circle, one at a time, and at their own random choice. Eye contact should last for perhaps one minute after which the person should say aloud, 'Thank you' and then move on to the next person.

The contacts must be mutual; this should be easily achieved as all members of the circle are seeking eye contact with the others. It will take some minutes before everyone has made eye contact with everyone else. This is the beginning of a warming to each other which is essential for this kind of session.

3. The most traumatic or upsetting moment

Each individual in turn, team leader first, is asked to describe to the group, in detail, the most traumatic and upsetting event of their lives. It may seem, in cold black and white, that it will be difficult to get people to disclose such personal information. In fact experience indicates that this is not the case. On the occasions we have employed this technique we find that many people are almost seeking an audience; people want to open up to others if they know they can trust them.

Fairly run-of-the-mill disclosures include accidents that have resulted in significant fear which the person then feels ashamed of. In some cases the disclosure is extraordinary; you must be ready for some very intimate details.

The material being discussed is not, of course, important.

12 Getting the Team Together

What matters is sharing it with others, and feeling safe in doing so. It is the vulnerability of allowing others to share a secret part of yourself which begins a process of bonding. The first step towards real friendship is to exchange and share vulnerabilities. As a by-product of our teambuilding sessions we can confirm that even when people leave teams to go off to other interests they often stay in touch, or remain friends, with members of the team; significantly more so than in paranormal research teams where no teambuilding takes place.

The process is not designed to show weakness which others can sympathise with; it is to share a vulnerability that others can empathise with.

The honesty with which someone gives a part of themselves to others is very apparent and it creates in people a willingness to respond in like manner. It is what the person gives which is important, not what they receive. In fact they give away their barriers to friendship and inevitably find that they lose a part of their fear. Most such barriers are created by fearing the disapproval of others, yet when brought down in an atmosphere of honesty, and with the right team leader, others do not want or try to take advantage.

4. *Your best moment*

Just as above, each participant is asked to disclose the best or most exciting moment or achievement in their life.

Again, it is the person's own feelings towards their disclosure which is important rather than the feelings of the others. It is actually very difficult to describe a good moment without a certain pride or boasting; we do that to 'nip in the bud' any potential criticism.

Part of the session is to encourage using the trust – which is already building up from earlier sessions – to encourage people to disclose their greatest moments without the need for boasting and bragging. As a general rule, during such sessions there is a great deal of camaraderie with much humour between participants; this becomes one of the first drivers towards friendship.

5. *The magic chair*

Each member of the team sits in 'the magic chair', facing all the other members who are arranged in a semi-circle around the front of it. The team members are then told to give whatever praise they can to the person in the magic chair. They cannot be critical, only praising. They can comment on how good-looking a person is, how intelligent they have found him or her to be, how well dressed he or she is, or indeed on any other positive aspect of the person which they believe to be true. The rule is that the praise must be honest.

Following this session, the person in the magic chair is asked to say how he or she felt about the praise received. The results of this are revealing; people are so often on the receiving end of false praise they find genuine praise hard to accept. In the magic chair they have to face praise which they know is genuine and it is remarkable how barriers break down as a person begins to lose the fear of being falsely praised and accepts the pleasure of praise for its own sake. We must stress that this is not an ego-reinforcement exercise; the value is the interaction between the group.

6. *Tongue twisters*

Each person is given a sheet of three of four tongue twisters which they have to say out loud to the other members of the group. This usually creates considerable humour and camaraderie; an essential part of breaking down barriers between people. As an added refinement, the team leader can ask the individual to deliver a particular tongue twister in a variety of strange voices just to add to the humour. Learning to laugh *with* one another rather than *at* one another is a basic trust-building exercise and very easily achievable through this method.

12 Getting the Team Together

7. Leading someone around blindfold

The subject is blindfolded and led through a building, up stairs, down stairs, from room to room, and so on. He or she depends entirely on the others. Done with humour, this is a significant team-builder.

For the brave the variation is to be led around at very high speed – but remember to wear shin pads!

8. Falling backwards

As in 7 above, the subject surrenders himself to others here. This exercise is one of the standard training techniques used, not only in business training, but in scouting movements, outward bound-type courses and the like.

One member of the team stands on a chair or table with his back to the group; the other members of the team stand in two lines behind him or her, with their arms outstretched and locked together, forming a 'cradle' into which the standing person will fall. All the subject has to do is to discard any doubts, trust the group, and fall backwards into the cradle.

Having done this exercise, we can confirm that it is a very significant trust-builder. If it sounds easy we can assure you that the hardest part of the job is to be relaxed enough with others to be able to make that drop into the unknown. But once everyone has done it, the confidence the team members have in each other is magnified greatly.

9. Building bricks together

Children generally learn to play with each other without the fuss of introduction and 'testing' that adults seem to need. Go into any of these 'Eater' restaurants where they have a table and a few chairs and a mass of Lego bricks and watch children who are total strangers start playing and sharing very quickly. Part of this, the psychiatrists tell us, is that they

Ghostwatching

are literally building something; as they build their temporary friendships, they build with the bricks.

All ghostwatch teams need some equipment, or some adapted equipment (just sticking red filters in the torches, for example); do not give this job to someone to do in his backroom alone. Do it as a team. Literally build your ghostwatch equipment together so that you all own, if not the physical objects, the use of them.

THE RIGHT TEAM LEADER

Someone has to be the team leader, and it is useful if he or she also has a deputy with similar qualities. The sort of leadership ghostwatching requires is empowering leadership, leading by the trust and respect of colleagues.

We do not believe that the type of team leader needed is a 'war leader' type: 'When I say "Jump!" you just ask how high!'

Particular characteristics in those who make good leaders for this type of research are:

* morale builder
* communicator within and outside the team
* spokesperson for the team
* negotiator within and on behalf of the team
* proactive rather than reactive
* demonstrates interest in people
* is flexible and willing to learn

Few people are born this way; like everything else it takes effort and practice.

THESE TECHNIQUES WORK

If a few of these sessions are well led then they create a team of people who feel easy with each other. Conflicts of opinion

12 Getting the Team Together

are reduced, a willingness to try new experiments or techniques is increased, there is more fun.

Following these 'games' team members have often demanded more such teambuilding sessions. For one thing they can be fun. Mainly, we recognise, it is that people have forged friendships and they seek to keep the atmosphere we created.

Such people are usually much more confident in forming teams with other people, and acting in groups with others. They are more keen to share ideas with others, and become proactive – looking for work for the team, rather than passively waiting for someone else to suggest something.

ONE LAST WARNING

The old cliché about avoiding sex, religion and politics as topics of disclosure is valid here; they are topics where discussion of the subject matter will often replace the process. They are also the three subjects where avoiding overt or covert criticism is often difficult; opinions on these subjects are usually driven by conviction rather than reason.

13 Finding People and Places to Research

THERE ARE SO MANY reports of ghosts nowadays that it hardly seems necessary to go out looking for them. However, there are some good reasons for doing so. First, for the sake of sheer convenience it is useful if you can examine the ghosts nearer your doorstep than travel halfway up the country for the purpose. That said, an investment in time and effort to travel round the country and abroad in the search for answers to these mysteries is very broadening for the mind.

Secondly, getting to a case as early as possible means you can 'control' the amount of witness-contamination the case suffers. Once a person has seen a ghost they are often driven to seek out information about it in libraries and so on. The more he or she reads, the less 'pure' the information given at interview afterwards.

Thirdly, there is nothing quite so pleasurable (in this field of research, at least) as finding and investigating your own cases rather than trailing around behind others.

FINDING CASES

There are three main routes for finding new cases.

The first is by joining one or both of the national groups, and asking to be put on their register of investigators. ASSAP have a policy of making attendance at a training day a compulsory part of being a registered investigator. We

13 Finding People and Places to Research

believe that the SPR are thinking of doing this as well. Don't worry if once on the register you hear nothing for a while – ghosts are a bit like buses, nothing comes along for ages and then everything happens all at once. They also seem to be somewhat seasonal; spring and summer are often quiet, but autumn and winter can be busy. ASSAP are currently researching why this should be.

The second are ghosthunts organised by ASSAP. These require ten to twenty people and the Association invites ghosthunters from all parts of the country. Robin Lawrence brilliantly organised the 1992 Rochester Castle vigil with ASSAP as the umbrella organisation. That night could have done with a real umbrella; the constant drizzle in the roofless castle probably broke the record for the most miserable vigil in history. We all forgave Robin for he had also organised the Dover Castle vigils on behalf of ASSAP in the same year; as discussed in Chapter 8, most people regarded the results from that as a spectacular success.

The third route for obtaining leads is by reading the newspapers. Occasionally the national press, and more often the local press, will publicise a case where someone is plagued by a haunting. In the likely event of the name and address of the haunted person being withheld from the article you can try approaching the newspaper and ask to talk to the journalist who wrote the piece. If you ask nicely, and send him a letter of introduction, then he will probably be willing to pass your details on to the people involved. If they respond to your overture then the rest, of course, is up to you.

The local media will also help with drumming up publicity for members and cases. The media, when given a free rein, tend to try and play up the subject, but they will usually take the lead from you. If you represent yourself and your group as serious and responsible then they will usually report in the same way.

But beware! The Fourth Estate are a divided lot. The local media usually have a vested interest in not making local people look foolish, and they will give you the respect you

Ghostwatching

command. They like local eccentrics of course, and there are plenty of people who like to *be* local eccentrics; make sure the media know you are not one of them.

The national media are another breed altogether. They have so large a catchment area and circulation that they fear no one and no action. They are also blessed by virtually no effective controlling legislation, and reporters' scruples are surgically extracted on admission to the 'club'.

Generally speaking, reporters for the national media tend to make up their own mind about the subject, report it as such, and use you to 'explain' their theory – often no matter what you may actually say to the contrary. Of course there are good and responsible people in the national media also, but beware – 'here be dragons'.

ACCURACY AND PRESS REPORTS

While it is not uncommon for press reports to be useful as a source of information about ghosts and hauntings, there is a strong tendency for the press to sensationalise the subject and distort the reality behind the reports. As soon as a reporter's search for sensation takes precedence over relating facts, then accuracy flies out of the window. Anyone compiling a list of hauntings from press reports has to take great care to ensure that the original story has not transmuted into something completely different.

Accuracy is important for several reasons. For those trying to understand a bit more about the underlying nature of the subject, if one is to attempt a statistical analysis of a large number of reports, then one cannot rely solely on a newspaper report. Inaccuracy and mendacity can also cause investigators to waste time, and money; if one is looking for an anniversary ghost for example, then there is no point in setting up an expensive vigil, with twenty people and half a ton of recording equipment if the anniversary date obtained from a newspaper report is wrong.

13 Finding People and Places to Research

One should, then, be cautious about newspaper reports of the paranormal, and they should only be used as an indicator of a possible haunting. A proper investigation into the case is required before one can even think about committing time and resources to a vigil.

A colleague of ours, David Thomas, has been researching the reported phenomena at Blue Bell Hill, in Maidstone. David has been amazed at how much time he has spent separating fact from fiction. He was kind enough to send us some examples of how newspapers are able to change a story. Here is what he sent us:

> Blue Bell Hill is set between the M2 and the M20 and is one of the highest points in Kent, overlooking a rural scene of Kent's Medway Valley. Despite the new dual carriageway which cuts through its chalk and tree-lined slopes there are many quiet and beautiful paths that cross a landscape where legends were made. It is believed that where Kits Coty House now stands, ancient battles were fought, and the Countless Stones (just down the road), and the White Horse Stone are said to be 'as old as the hills'. Legend also has it that this area is the domain of many ghosts, some from long ago, and some of this age.
>
> The current legend began on the evening of 19 November 1965. Four girls were travelling by car towards Maidstone down the old Blue Bell Hill, when they had an accident with another vehicle which resulted in three deaths. One died instantly, the other later in hospital. The third, due to be married only hours after the crash, died five days later. It was a sad fact that some of the wedding guests only found out about the disaster when arriving for the wedding service. The incident was widely reported in the press, and a photographer was on the scene soon after the crash. Just four days later the catalogue of inaccuracy started. Numerous media reports were conflicting and inaccur-

Ghostwatching

ate. They confused dates, names, details of deaths, and circumstances. The next reported incident on Blue Bell Hill was in the *Kent Messenger* of 9 September 1968; this was the first reference to 'the phantom hitch-hike girl'. This 'ghost' was reported to have hitched a lift near the bottom of the hill and asked to go to Maidstone; she promptly disappeared from the car. No witnesses came forward to be interviewed and this story was added to local legend.

Six years later, in 1974, a Rochester bricklayer was the next to report an incident. He apparently hit a 'very young girl of about 10', just after midnight on a Saturday. He stopped, carried her to the roadside, wrapped her in a blanket and then rushed to call the police. On returning he and the police discovered the blanket empty. Newspaper reports of this accident seem to diverge sharply from reality. The *News of the World* of 14 July of that year reported the incident and made a reference to the crash of 1965, but said that two girls were killed, and gave the date incorrectly as being 1967. A second newspaper made things even muddier, reporting the bricklayer's story, but adding that the 1968 phantom hitchhiker was one of the three girls who died in the 1965 crash. The article reported the bricklayer's story but for some reason left out the small but significant detail about the girl's age. Readers were therefore left with the impression that the bricklayer had met Judith Lingham's ghost. To cap this, the article also got the day of the 1965 crash wrong.

On Sunday 8 November 1992, Ian Sharpe, a coach driver from Maidstone, according to the *Kent Today* of 10 November believed that he ran over a girl on Blue Bell Hill who looked him straight in the eye before falling under his car bonnet. A similar incident happened to a second person, Christopher Dawkins, who was reported in the *Kent Messenger* of 27 November. Emma Cooper covered the earlier of the two incidents

13 Finding People and Places to Research

in *Kent Today* on 10 November and stated that the ghost was believed to be one of the dead girls from the crash. A national newspaper also got it wrong in an article which discussed the case. It reported that the girls were returning from Maidstone, whereas all contemporary reports had them heading towards Maidstone. It also got the details of two of the girls' deaths wrong. It probably even got the weather wrong; it stated that on the night of the 1965 crash, the conditions were foggy. In fact contemporary reports mention it was cold and wet but not foggy; the press photograph taken shortly after the crash does not show any fog.

[David adds:]

Apart from the irritation of the inaccuracies, which can result in a lot of time-wasting for serious investigators, there is also the impact of the sensationalism on the witnesses, and the families involved. I know for a fact that many people have had peculiar encounters on the Hill but are reluctant to come forward to tell their stories for fear that the local press (and the national press) will re-publicise the deaths in 1965, reopening old wounds. Another witness became a virtual recluse after being hounded by the press. I'm sure that the families of the dead girls would like to see the whole matter rest in peace.

IMAGE

If you want people to allow you to investigate ghosts on their premises you need to win their trust. There are no magic answers; you need to look and sound credible. Once you have done several cases you can mention people and organisations that you have worked with, and that will add to your credibility and help win the trust of witnesses.

Remember, of course, to respect confidences when mentioning previous cases. We often refer merely to 'a pub in

Ghostwatching

Worthing' or 'a castle in Kent' when talking about cases. If you reveal too much about other cases then they may wonder if you will talk about their details to others.

When starting out, it might help to belong to one of the two national organisations, the SPR or ASSAP (see Appendix A). When introducing yourself, you can then say, 'I'm so-and-so from – '. When you do use an organisation's name in this way, bear in mind that you are acting as a representative of that organisation, and they will not take kindly to unprofessional behaviour, which can bring them into disrepute. It is also polite to let the organisation know that you intend to use their name before you contact the witnesses, and to ensure that they do not object, and to find out if there are any requirements they have of you in those circumstances.

FORMAL PRESENTATION

If you have access to a word processor, or can get some letter-headed paper, then you are much more likely to get a response when writing to people or organisations. A low-cost way of creating letter-headings and business cards is to use the printing machines that have recently sprung up in motorway service stations. You don't have to have an organisation name on your letter heading, you can simply put your own name, but it can help having an organisation name that people can remember.

Do not, however, let the tail wag the dog. In some fields of paranormal research some organisations are now so bureaucratic it is all they can do to run their administration; they ceased doing any useful research years ago.

DRESS CODE

This may appear to be stating the obvious, but it is important to dress properly when visiting and interviewing witnesses or

13 Finding People and Places to Research

the media. They often have no other information to work from, and will be looking at you and your colleagues to try and pick up clues about what you are up to. You don't have to wear a suit, but dress in a way that will help inspire confidence. Also – the actor's trick – dressing the part will help give *you* confidence. Obviously, when staying overnight on a vigil, then the dress code is considerably relaxed. For this occasion, comfort and convenience are more important. There is no conflict here; you probably won't be invited to stay on their premises for the night until they've formed some positive opinions about you anyway.

AWKWARD QUESTIONS

Don't feel embarrassed when someone asks you questions and you don't know the answer. This is not an exact science and we believe that certainty is suspicious. It can actually add to your credibility when someone asks you 'Have you seen a ghost?' and you reply in truth 'Not yet, but I'm working on it.' If you don't know the answers to questions admit it – never bluff. You can lose all the respect of the witness if you are caught out on even one bluff.

14 Are You Psychic?

We believe that ghosts are perceived by psychic means, and, as this chapter shows, we believe that psychic abilities are inherent in us all. Those who have random, one-off, ghost sightings, or other one-off perceptions, we believe might be 'accessing' those abilities only for those brief moments. Others claim more control over these abilities, and claim to see ghosts 'all the time' or at least more frequently. Some evidence, noted in this chapter, suggests that the psychic abilities are 'stored' in the right (artistic and intuitive) side of the brain.

It is our view that these abilities are trainable, and that the training is an aid – and certainly no barrier – to seeing a ghost for yourself.

Belief about the varying psychic abilities of people is itself a subject of some controversy. There is, almost inevitably, the highly sceptical school of thought that believes there is no such thing as psychic ability; that it is a self-delusion created by fantasy-prone people. Neither of the authors would agree with that extreme view, and it is worth remembering that the people who hold that extreme a view are themselves slaves to a belief system – as are we all, whatever we believe. In some cases this belief is a knee-jerk reaction to a vested interest: scientists whose self-image or credibility needs reassurance, magazine editors with an ego to salve. . . .

It would be unreasonable not to accept the possibility of mistake, fraud and self-delusion; but we are not dealing with these here; this chapter will examine psychic abilities on the basis that we believe them to be 'real' (whatever that 'real' means).

There are more people in the world who are open to the possibility that there are such things as psychic abilities than are not; but within that large group is a great diversity of interpretation.

DOES EVERYONE HAVE IT?

There are many people who will admit to believing in psychic abilities without believing themselves to have any. They may believe a relative is psychic, or perhaps they know someone who seems to exhibit such abilities; this convinces them of 'something' even if they do not feel they have it themselves. The question therefore is: do they (and everyone) have such abilities, or is it just a chosen few? The answer is that no one knows for sure. Certainly there are those who seem to have such abilities, and those who seem not to.

For an answer we would suggest turning to the theory of evolution and, perhaps, logic.

As far as we know, all human (and animal) attributes have a purpose in survival either of the individual or the species. Physical attributes can usually be related to sexual reproduction or day-to-day maintenance such as eating. Higher-level attributes, such as intelligence, seem to relate to longer-term survival (though some may argue that there are exceptions).

There are, arguably, exceptions; lemmings migrating towards the sea — into which they often fall — hardly seems survivalistic and the H-bomb might well be little to be proud of, but perhaps even lemmings have a self-culling process that is good for the species as a whole. (What does that suggest for humans and the H-bomb?)

On the basis that all attributes are there for a purpose, probably to do with survival, it is reasonable to assume that psychic abilities are complex methods of perceiving, developed for survival. One day they will probably be understood as quite natural abilities, on the same basis as the five senses; at the moment their mechanisms elude our studies. If this is the case, then almost certainly everyone has the same potential, though – as with so many things in life – there will be those who use their potentials and those who do not.

Even that need not be a question of ability; it may be needs-driven. All abilities, like muscles, atrophy without use and perhaps many people do not exhibit psychic abilities because they have no use for them. Certainly in the technological West we rely on instrumentation far more than on instinct.

Perhaps the modern interest in the psychic relates to the fact that we feel our world is getting a little out of our control. As we feel threatened, so we may reach deeper into ourselves for defence abilities; and certainly the best starting point for defending yourself is to switch on every external perception you have. (If you ever find yourself in a limited space with a wild animal like a tiger, just see how sharp your hearing becomes.) These talents therefore might also not be constant; their appearance might vary according to need.

We might therefore conclude that everyone has the potential for psychic talents.

WHAT ABOUT PEOPLE WHO SEEM TO HAVE FULL, NATURAL PSYCHIC ABILITY?

Few people play a piano at concert-level but for those who do it is a natural and easy process. Many people claim that they have known of and used their psychic abilities all their life; for them it is not a matter of turning them on, it is just there for them when needed as sight and hearing are for the majority of people.

One psychic we spoke to pointed out that her first surprise as a child was not finding out that she could see figures other children could not, but that other children could not see the figures she could easily see, and always had.

ARE CHILDREN MORE PSYCHIC THAN ADULTS?

'Sally' told us of an incident which indicates a possible special perception in children:

> 'A very close friend of mine died. He had been an acquaintance for ten years and after my husband passed away we became very close for about six weeks until his death in a car crash. He was a good friend to my daughter, who was two and a half at the time, and she got very attached to him. Within a couple of days of his death she started saying unusual things. To begin with I didn't take a lot of notice of it but I had to go over to his house to see his daughters and his son after the funeral and when we got there my sister-in-law took my little girl out to the garden. A few minutes later she came back in, very distressed; she said, "I think you ought to hear what your daughter is saying." I asked what the problem was and she said, "She's saying that there's a man in the garden." So I went out with her and I said, "Where is the man?" My daughter kept pointing in the direction of where my friend used to do all his gardening. He was a keen gardener. She insisted he was there. And I said, "Where is he? I can't see him", and she said, "He is there, Mummy, he is there." And at two and a half years old, she was not really going to make these sorts of thing up.
>
> 'It wasn't the only incident. When we were at my house we were all sitting round the dining table in the kitchen and she kept looking through the doorway into the living-room. She was smiling and she kept moving her head back and forwards, smiling all the time. I said, "What are you doing?" And she said, "I am just

watching the man." And she kept insisting there was somebody there. So I asked, "Where is the man now?" and she pointed to the doorway. Then she got down from the table and came round and gave me a hug right out of the blue; then she looked across to my sister-in-law and said, "You've got to give Mummy a hug." My sister-in-law asked why and my daughter said, "Because the man said you have to. Mummy needs a hug." Then she got back up to the table and sat there for a few moments. Then I said to her, "Where is the man now?" and her eyes were literally watching as though somebody was walking round the table towards me. She said, "There's the man" and she pointed directly at me as though he was standing next to me. I asked her if it was my friend and she said it was. I asked her a couple of minutes later, "Is the man still here, darling?" and she said, "No, he has gone now, Mummy."'[1]

Nearly all of the many psychics we have spoken to have said that they were encouraged, or at least not discouraged, in their early years when talking about their psychic perceptions, because their mother, father, or other close relative had 'the gift'. We have yet to find one psychic – who has had these abilities since childhood – to tell us that he or she was constantly told off and smacked for talking about them. It seems, by implication, that the abilities are inherent and that they can be developed or 'turned off'.

A negative attitude effectively teaches children to stop using their abilities. Perhaps they do just that; perhaps psychic muscles, like any muscles, atrophy with lack of use.

ADULTS BECOMING PSYCHIC

There are many cases of adults developing psychic abilities late in life (or reawakening them). This often happens under 'forced' conditions; several UFO close-encounter witnesses develop measurable abilities after their encounters which we believe encourage or force them to use the right-hand, creative, side of their brains. Elsie Oakensen is one who, following a UFO encounter, became a successful healer, and medium.

The Dutch psychic Peter Hurkos was an exceptionally talented psychic who helped several police forces with their murder investigations. He had no psychic abilities until late in life when he fell off a ladder, hit his head, spent three days in a coma, and woke up in hospital immediately able to warn his doctor of impending danger (the doctor ignored him, and was killed shortly afterwards).[54]

DIFFERENCE BETWEEN PSYCHICS AND 'NORMAL' PEOPLE

As mentioned earlier, the sitter group technique works and allows 'unpsychic' people to achieve things that are normally the province only of the psychic or medium. It is tempting to suggest that the difference between psychics and 'unpsychic' people is that psychics don't need the support system offered by the group techniques. Perhaps the main difference is due to the fact that the psychic knows he has abilities, and is comfortable with the knowledge. In the case of an experimental sitter group with little-known psychic abilities then there seems to be the need to overcome initial disbelief. This is not unsurprising. It was easier to overcome disbelief in Victorian times when table-tilting and Ouija boards became a popular pastime; an initiate could go and sit with a group, experience the phenomena, and, with disbelief overcome, try out his or her own experiments. In the modern, technological world there is a lot of inherent disbelief in the paranormal and so it takes a long time before phenomena can appear. As pointed out by Colin Brookes Smith and D. Hunt in 1973, in an article in the *Journal of the Society for Psychical Research*, once disbelief is overcome, then phenomena can snowball.

Ghostwatching

BUT WHAT DOES PSYCHIC ABILITY DO?

Assuming that people have psychic abilities, and that some people are using them, what do they do in relation to seeing ghosts? There are two possibilities:

* One possibility is that ghosts are an 'imaginary' thing generated by certain types of minds. Those who claim psychic ability might also be the type to 'invent' ghosts. Such a theory cannot be ruled out, but we would argue that there are enough cases of ghosts and mediumship to suggest a more 'external' reality.
* The second possibility, and one which we more strongly favour, is that psychic abilities allow you to perceive that which is there but which is not within the range of the 'normal' senses. On that basis, ghosts are around a lot more than we might know, but we only perceive them at certain times, or under certain conditions. (Unless you are one of those people permanently 'switched on' to them.)

SO WHERE ARE THESE ABILITIES?

Almost certainly these reside in the right brain rather than the left. They are not the product of logic, scientific scrutiny or analysis. One day they might be, but for the moment they have characteristics that suggest they reside in the side of the brain that deals with artistic expression, spatial awareness, emotion and passions.

There is evidence for this in work John has been doing with close-encounter (UFO) witnesses. One of the elements that arose from research into large groups of these people was that there were a great many such people who had – following their perceived extraordinary encounters (with aliens, flying saucers, etc) – found they seemed to have acquired previously unsuspected artistic talent. They felt compelled to draw, or make music, or in some way express themselves through art. They became more ecologically aware, more passionate about the quality of life around them, and so on.

For many it represented so powerful a transformation that they changed their careers to do something totally different, or, if younger at the time of the incident, embarked on careers that reflected their new-found passions.

And almost every case carried with it some hint of heightened psychic ability — extra-sensory perception, clairvoyance, PK, and so on.

Whatever is behind such experiences — and we believe them to be essentially natural if still not understood — then part of the effect seems to be to 'switch on' dormant abilities in the right brain, including psychic abilities.

ENHANCING PSYCHIC ABILITIES

We believe that it is possible for people to 'learn' how to be psychic; at the very least we believe there are certain conditions which allow people to be more psychic than they normally are.

Both of us have had some personal experience of that. John is a management trainer working in profit-geared corporations, and is professionally qualified as an accountant. As such, his day-to-day work is very left-brain; very scientific, very logical and very analytical. And by his own admission he is 'psychic as a brick'. Normally, at least.

But John has had one or two experiences that suggest at least a perception of the psychic; and Tony and John together have shared incidents, noted in Chapter 8. On each of those occasions John noted that he had been away from his day-to-day work for a time and had spent some days focused on 'the paranormal' (experimenting, reading research material, talking to witnesses, etc.). The suggestion is that if the right brain was in use, then other talents hidden there could come to the fore.

Similarly, Tony is a technical consultant who has worked for many large corporations (such as the London Stock Exchange), and spends most of his time solving problems on complex computer systems. About as left-brain as you can get. Yet, as described later in this chapter, with a little help from hypnosis he had an even greater exposure to the paranormal.

ENHANCING PSYCHIC POWERS USING HYPNOTISM

The forerunner of hypnotism, mesmerism, seemed to be quite capable of inducing all sorts of paranormal effects. Indeed, it was difficult for investigators to separate the tool from the phenomena it induced. Nowadays, the use of hypnotism is widespread, it has gained popular acceptance by the general public; psychologists and psychiatrists use it in both research and clinical work. Parapsychologists have also found that hypnotism can be a useful tool in research into the paranormal, particularly in assisting in the production of PK effects, and helping improve results in telepathy.

Mesmerism began in 1766 when Franz Mesmer wrote in his dissertation at the University of Vienna that the cosmos was linked by invisible fields which permeated a type of subtle fluid. Copying some healers, he discovered that magnets when pointed at certain subjects could influence their physiological behaviour. As he experimented further he discovered that a magnet was not required – fingers or hands could be used to get the same effect, and this led him to theorise about 'animal magnetism'. By 1788, after Mesmer moved to Paris, mesmerism had become a highly fashionable pastime with many wild claims for its use. It was said to perform a huge range of feats ranging from the curing of disease, anaesthesia of patients during surgery, ability to sense words and objects without sight of them, and mind-reading. Not surprisingly, the peculiar theories for its mechanism of action and the extraordinary claims for its capabilities combined to tax the boggle-factor of even the most open-minded scientist and medic.

Mesmerism started its road to respectability in the mid-1800s when James Braid, a surgeon and one of the 'puzzled interest' faction, started his own investigations and published his results. He concluded that the mesmeric trance state could be induced without a belief in animal magnetism or the impressive hand passing. It could simply be brought about by means of a bright object suspended above the subject's eyes. By theorising that the trance state was a psychological phenomenon he made it easier to separate any external phenomena produced from the trance state induced in the subject. He also toned down his explanation of some of the phenomena that could be induced whilst in the trance state. Mind reading, and 'seeing' without the eyes, for example, he explained by saying that the subjects had heightened awareness in all their senses. By emphasising the physiological aspects, producing natural explanations for mesmeric claims, and giving the whole thing a new name, hypnotism, he provided the means for the medical profession eventually to accept that the trance state existed.

An article by Dr Milan Ryzl, edited by G. W. Fisk in the March 1962 issue of the *Journal of the Society for Psychical Research*, describes an interesting series of experiments carried out by Ryzl. The idea was to enhance psychic ability by means of hypnotism. The mechanism of how hypnotism works is still unknown, but it is certainly clear that the hypnotic subject is made highly receptive to the suggestions of the hypnotist, and therefore may be helped to overcome problems of distraction, and worries about the phenomena that the subject might be engaged with.

Dr Ryzl experimented with 226 people (73 male, 153 female), of whom none claimed any previous paranormal experience. Of the 226, 27 people obtained good clairvoyant abilities, and another 29 less so. He describes his success rate

Ghostwatching

as 25 per cent, and believes that it could be improved by better techniques. He also thought that better techniques in inducing the hypnotic trance would improve the success rate. His paper describes experiments with one student, a Miss J.K., one of the 13 top-scoring subjects, who, interestingly, were all women.

In one test, J.K. was handed 200 cards of 4 alternative symbols wrapped in stiff opaque paper; the experimenter did not know which card was which. Out of these 200, a 'non psychic' person would be expected to guess 50 cards correctly, by chance alone. J.K. guessed 121 cards correctly. She was then tested without hypnotism, and no attempt at clairvoyance, achieving 46 correct guesses – within only the 'chance' range of results.

Dr Ryzl describes more experiments with J.K. which are equally impressive, and then goes on to describe his training techniques. The process begins with a series of sessions, over which the subject is given more and more training. To start with, the subject may be told that certain limbs cannot be moved; and later the subject may be given an item which he is told is burning. They then pass on to other senses such as hearing and sight, being told that he is hearing certain types of noises, for instance, and seeing certain visions. As time goes on the subject will be able to describe, for example, quite complex scenes. Once this level has been attained, the subject will then be asked to sense the shapes of objects in front of him, without the use of his eyes. Gradually, the ability of the subject improves.

The training of Miss J.K. took place along these lines, and her powers developed to a remarkable level. She could not, however, perform her clairvoyance without hypnosis. In order for her to experiment with her own abilities, she was helped to perform self-hypnosis, and this had a practical outcome. At her office some papers were lost. By inducing self-hypnosis she was able to discern their whereabouts.

Researcher Charles Honorton reviewed 24 studies of using hypnosis to enhance ESP ability. In their book *Explain-*

ing the Unexplained, Eysenck and Sargent, commenting on Honorton's review, point out that

> Of the 24 studies, 12 showed a significantly better scoring rate with hypnosis than without it. Remember that our definition of 'significantly better' is a difference so large that chance says we should observe it only once in every 20 similar experiments (5% of the time). The observed figure of 50% is way higher than 5%, and none of the studies showed a significant superiority of scoring without hypnosis. The results of this body of research, collected by many experimenters, are clearcut; hypnosis is an ESP-favourable state.[53]

Honorton's own conclusion was similar: 'I believe the conclusion is now inescapable that hypnotic induction procedures enhance [ESP].'

SELF-HYPNOSIS AND THE MENTAL MEDIUM

Both authors are struck by the apparent similarity between self-hypnosis and the trances of mental mediumship. In order to perform their work, mediums often appear to go into a self-induced trance state; by the time Dr Ryzl had finished, Miss J.K. was able to do the same.

There is also a similarity between the training methods used by spiritualist home development circles and Dr Ryzl's training method. There are specialist suppliers of development packs for people who feel that they might be psychic and inclined towards spiritualism. Such packs include meditation tapes which can be used to induce light self-hypnosis. The listener is encouraged to free-associate and allow images and impressions to come into his mind. This has comparable aspects to Dr Ryzl's early stages of training where the student is encouraged to form complete mental pictures under instruction of the hypnotist. The authors in their own

Ghostwatching

sessions have experimented with hypnosis as an aid to improving psychic ability, as described below.

HYPNOTISM AND SPOON BENDING

Some time ago our research group decided to experiment with some of the things discussed in this chapter, and decided to add hypnotism to help overcome 'psychic inhibitions'. At the first meeting at Tony's house with Lucien Morgan, a hypnotherapist, the authors discovered that he could bend spoons in a rather unusual way, putting one or more twists between the neck and bowl. The three of us decided to hold an impromptu spoon-bending session. His method of bending was to channel energy from an imaginary point above his head, wait until a 'gateway point' was felt, and then project the energy through his solar plexus towards the spoon he would be holding in his hand. The neck of the spoon would give way. His description of that gateway point was that the spoon's neck 'felt like putty'.

We went downstairs into the dining room and stood around the dining table while Lucien tried to work up our psychic energies with some imaginative exercises. After Lucien had shown us how he did it, we both tried Lucien's method to twist our own spoons. Try as we might we couldn't do it. It wasn't until we tried it ourselves that we realised how difficult it is to twist the neck of a dessert spoon. (There is a method of cheating, which is obvious when the result is seen afterwards. You simply bend the handle of the spoon at 90 degrees to the bowl and then use the extra leverage to wrap the handle around the bowl. The result is a very wide twist.) However, if you try the 'Lucien' way by holding the bowl in one hand and the neck in the other and try to twist, it can't be done without extraordinary strength, or by using a vice and a wrench.

At this point – imagine the scene – two extremely irritated people with sore hands were watching Lucien bend spoon after spoon. One of them, Tony, was also worrying that there would be no spoons left in the house.

After taking a deep breath, Tony suggested that Lucien try hypnotising him to see if this would help. Lucien was able to put him in a light trance, and used reinforcing suggestions as a means of helping with the bending. Here is Tony's description of what happened next:

'After Lucien brought me out of the trance, I walked up to the table, Lucien started the spoon-bending session again, and I stared at the spoon, turning it over in my hands, feeling the metal and the shape, trying to empathise with it. Suddenly I felt that the neck felt softer, and I remember trying to twist it, shouting, "Fuck me, I'm doing it!" at the top of my voice. As soon as I shouted, the neck hardened again. I think the whole episode lasted about one to two seconds. Once the neck had hardened it was again immovable, and I hurt my left hand on the bowl trying to continue to twist it.

'The spoon (with a very neat single twist) is proudly hanging up in the kitchen. Later that evening I tried to bend another spoon of the same type, but simply could not do it, and on trying brute force I simply hurt my hand again.'

Lucien then tried to hypnotise John, and discovered that John is probably unhypnotisable. After all this, the group dynamics had changed. There was now an annoyed and slightly depressed John, an extremely high Tony, and an excited Lucien. We tried another spoon-bending session with John, using positive reinforcement. Any of Tony's neighbours reading this description will know when this happened because of the noise we made in shouting encouragement to John. Unhappily John was not able to bend his spoon despite the other two willing him on, and shouting 'Bend! Bend! Bend! . . .'

Since that time, Tony had one other attempt to bend the spoons, with a larger group, but with no success. That second occasion did not involve hypnotism.

Ghostwatching

USING MEDITATION AND ASSOCIATED TECHNIQUES TO ENHANCE PSYCHIC ABILITIES

We spoke to Graham James who has practised psychic exercises for over twenty years, and who regularly teaches members of a group the techniques set out below. He described his programme of training as:

'You should not eat for at least four to six hours before doing these exercises. Metabolism, dealing with absorbing food, takes away concentration from the mind. In the same way you should not have sex within at least eight hours beforehand; sex sharpens the physical senses, but blunts the psychic ones.

'You should be fully relaxed and comfortable; wear loose, easy clothing.

'The first exercise is breathing exercises to the count of five. You breathe in very, very slowly and fully to the count of five. At five you should have really full lungs of air. Then you hold it for five seconds. Then you exhale for five seconds. You fully deflate your lungs, and hold them deflated for five seconds. You repeat this whole exercise five times. It can make you slightly dizzy, you are probably oxygenating the brain more than usual.

'The second exercise is to do a mantra; repeating a word such as "Aum ... Aum ... Aum ...". Do this for two or three minutes until you feel a vibration at the back of your head. You may have to modify the pitch of the voice to get the vibration right. It should feel like your skull is vibrating, but not unpleasantly.

'Once you have learned these, combine them. Do the breathing and the mantra exercises together. This whole preparation period should never take less than ten minutes; it needs application to make it work.

'All these exercises over time will hone you up for a whole range of psychic activities: clairvoyance; Ouija; table-rap-

14 Are You Psychic?

ping; seeing ghosts and spirits; mediumship; healing; astral projection; and so on.

'You are training your mind, relaxing your body, getting rid of stress. You are also changing the colour of your aura, improving yourself at that level; you become more spiritually receptive.'

Graham's system, based on his belief in a 'cosmic consciousness', is very similar to yoga – which has an increasing acceptance throughout the West as a method of stress control and relaxation, necessary to switch on the right-hand side of the brain.

For over six thousand years yoga has been a way of life for a large number of the world's population; principally in the East. It reflects a view that the human body is an inseparable unit of mind, body and spirit, all needing to be in harmony.

Full devotion to yoga can have extreme, beneficial, effects but – most important for those seeking to develop their psychic senses to even a small degree – even a use of basic techniques is believed to enhance abilities. In addition, there are pleasurable spin-offs: you become better able to resist stress and disease, and create for yourself a tranquil and relaxed attitude. Yoga assists in allowing people to connect with their own energy centres, known as *chakras*. The chakras are positioned along the *sushumna*, the astral equivalent of the spinal cord.

In the modern day such training and practice is no longer the preserve of the 'mystic'; revolutionary training programmes for management and senior executives of large companies now use these methods.

GANZFELD

One theory of enhanced psychic abilities is that there is, for most people, too much interference from the 'everyday' world around us. To test this, or experiment through it,

Ghostwatching

sensory deprivation was used to screen out all inputs to the brain. While it showed that the brain could experience altered states of reality it did not make controlled experiments very effective. Seemingly because the brain cannot exist without stimulus it apparently creates its own, in the form of dreams, nightmares and hallucinations.

As a less aggressive method of screening out the 'outside world' *ganzfeld* experiments were undertaken which did not create sensory deprivation but rather controlled the sensory input. (Ganzfeld is German for 'whole field'.) The brain also appears to respond to *alterations* in environment; when the environment does not alter then the brain ignores that 'line of thinking' and allows itself to concentrate on other matters. Ganzfeld experiments typically consist of lying in a comfortable position, on a soft padded sofa or chair, with eyes covered by half-table tennis balls allowing in only a soft orange or pink light from the room. Headphones are worn which relay a constant sound, either random white noise or regular gentle rhythms.

In this state the mind is able to use its potential.

One successful series of ESP tests conducted by Charles Honorton (discussed by Eysenck and Sargent in *Explaining the Unexplained*) involved the 'sender' focusing on a series of pictures. Afterwards the 'receiver' examines four pictures for each one 'transmitted' and guesses the right match. Over a large sample 25 per cent correct would be the 'chance' outcome. In fact, in all the tests the number was 35 per cent, a significant success.

Appendix A – Organisations

The Society for Psychical Research (SPR)
49 Marloes Road
Kensington
London W8 6LA
Telephone/fax: 071–937 8984
Membership enquiries: Eleanor O'Keeffe, Secretary

Objectives: to advance the understanding of events and abilities commonly described as 'psychic' or 'paranormal', without prejudice and in a scientific manner.

Current activities: the study of such topics as telepathy, clairvoyance, precognition and retrocognition, psychokinesis (paranormal effects on physical objects, including poltergeist phenomena), near-death and out-of-the-body experiences, apparitions, hauntings and the survival of bodily death.

The Society organises monthly lectures, study days, weekend workshops and an annual international conference. The Society's library is one of the oldest and most comprehensive collections of writings on the paranormal in the world.

Regular mailings: members of the Society receive the quarterly *Journal of the SPR*, the *Psi Researcher* (newsletter), and *Proceedings of the SPR* (published at irregular intervals).

Number of members: approximately 1000.

Membership fee: Member or Associate: £33. Joint subscription: £36. Senior citizen: £21. Student: £12.

Ghostwatching

Association for the Scientific Study of Anomalous Phenomena (ASSAP)
Saint Aldhelm
20 Paul Street
Frome
Somerset
BA11 1DX
Telephone/fax: 0373-451777
Membership and other enquiries: Hugh Pincott

Objectives: to study, in a scientific manner, a wide range of anomalous phenomena. The Association also seeks to educate and inform members and the public on these controversial subjects. The Association has no official views on the phenomena and encourages its members to be open-minded towards them.

Activities/Achievements: ASSAP is particularly interested in the active investigation of apparent paranormal phenomena reported to it. Training is offered to investigators. Many ghostwatches have been organised, some with dramatically positive results. ASSAP has also done extensive research into subjects such as hypnotic regression.

Mailings: four issues of *ASSAP News* (newsletter) and two of *Anomaly* (journal) are distributed each year to members (included in membership fee).

Number of members: approximately 300.

Membership fees: £11, or £7.50 for under 21 and over 60.

For those wishing to report experiences/sightings directly the authors can be contacted at the following address:

Paranormal And Close-encounter Experimental Research (PACER)
The Leys
2c Leyton Road
Harpenden
Hertfordshire
AL5 2TL
Telephone: 0582-468592/Fax: 0582-461979

Appendix A – Organisations

The authors also run training courses in the subjects covered in this book; details are available from the above address and telephone/fax numbers.

Appendix B – Sample Interview Questionnaire

This is the sort of questionnaire that you can bring with you to interviews with witnesses. It is not meant to be sent to witnesses for them to fill in, but is a guideline for your own questioning. Each case must be viewed and dealt with individually; therefore this questionnaire is recommended as an outline only.

QUESTIONNAIRE RE POLTERGEIST AND HAUNTING INVESTIGATION

Background
1. Where did the incident(s) happen?
2. When did you first notice them?
3. What is the most recent incident you recall?
4. Has there been a variation in the frequency and characteristics of the incidents?
5. Please supply details of witnesses and other relevant persons, i.e. householders (age/sex/marital status).
6. Have any of the persons in 5 above had previous psychic experiences? If so, describe them.
7. Are any of the people in 5 above interested in the paranormal? If so, indicate areas of interest.
8. Have the witnesses any suggestions for 'ordinary' explanations for the incidents?
9. Have any animals reacted to these incidents? If so, describe their reactions.

Appendix B – Sample Interview Questionnaire

Frequency and location
10 Are there any patterns noticed in the timing of the incidents? (Daily/weekly/monthly/yearly/other.)
11 Are there any patterns noticed in the locations of the incidents? (Certain room/with certain people, etc.)
12 Did the incident(s) happen at the same time as other events? (A death in the family/bankruptcy, etc.)
13 Has anything been known to happen when no one was in the area? (E.g. objects moved during absences from the house.)
14 Have particular objects or kinds of objects been disturbed more often than others? If so, please describe.

Movements and noises
15 Describe the types of incident.
16 Have there been any 'strange' movements of objects? If so, what made the movements strange?
17 Have there been any unusual noises associated with the incidents? If so, describe these noises.
18 Has anyone seen an object move when no one else was near it? If so, describe what happened.

Non-physical phenomena
19 Describe any such incidents.
20 Describe the timing and frequency of such incidents.
21 Who was the first to witness these events?
22 Give personal details of anyone else involved in these events.
23 Is anyone aware of any previous such experiences in this location?
24 Did some people experience these incidents while others did not, even though they were in a position to do so? If so, give details.
25 If sightings were visual (i.e. of ghosts), was anyone able to identify a person (living or dead) that it/they resembled? If so, give details.

Ghostwatching

Investigations

26 Do the witnesses or other relevant people have any suggestions for the direction/course/type of investigation they believe appropriate? If so, give details.
27 Has there been any publicity about these incidents? If so, please supply details (copies of news coverage, etc.).

Appendix C – Style of Reporting

As mentioned in Chapter 8, it is important to collect information about ghost reports (parameters/environment/characteristics/time of year/duration of event, etc.). Even if you do not submit your reports to any of the national societies, having a clear, concise report makes it easier to review your own past cases when either dealing with a current, difficult one, or advising or commenting from experience. Research without application is sterile; your case files will help you – and hopefully others – to create a meaningful database for reference.

REPORT WRITING

Reports should always be written in clear, simple language. They may be widely read by a wide variety of people with a wide variety of backgrounds. They may also be subject to translation into other languages, and the simpler the language style the more effective the translation.

Remember: the one-off time you spend on preparing your report in this useful way saves you and every other researcher time in reading and re-reading it in the future. It also increases the chances that your report will be used.

Remember also: once you have done one report to a given standard, keeping to it in the future becomes easier; practice makes perfect.

The report should clearly indicate the differences between the facts, the research, and the conclusions.

Ghostwatching

Researchers are reminded that confidentiality of witnesses' names is important. It is suggested that in reports for submission to organisations, and certainly for publication by the media, pseudonyms are used. The real names and addresses of witnesses should be kept on a separate document, available for researchers, with the permission of the witness. Remember when 'doctoring' files in this way it is important to consider 'disguising' the addresses of witnesses, their occupation, and even the wider location. People can be identified by facts other than their name.

Presentation is important: it is suggested that reports be prepared on A4 paper, typed, using one side of the paper only, and double-spaced. It helps if a wide margin can be left on both left- and right-hand sides of the page; on the left to enable the report to be 'punched' for filing, and on the right so that margin notes can be made on copies of the report.

Separate sections of the report (e.g. facts, research, conclusions) should be started on a separate page.

Front cover
The front cover should contain:
1 a short, descriptive title for the report
2 the primary researcher's name, and the names of any other contributors
3 important dates, including date of report preparation.

Front summary
The next page should contain a short (no more than one or two paragraphs) summary of the case.

The summary should indicate the preliminary conclusions drawn by the researchers.

Contents
If the report is a long one, include a contents page with detailed numbering to allow for easy re-use of the report over time. Each section of the report should be given a number (1, 2, 3, etc.); each sub-section given a sub-number

Appendix C – Style of Reporting

(1.1, 1.2, 1.3, etc.) and each paragraph within the sub-section further sub-divided (1.1.1, 1.1.2, 1.1.3, etc.) The headings and sub-headings should be listed in the report, the paragraphs should be indicated in the contents page by the opening few words (so make sure that they are usefully descriptive).

Layout
The suggested layout of the main body of the report is as follows:
1. Origin of the report: How you came to hear about the case, etc.
2. Background of the case: Summary of details of the circumstances as presented to you. Include details of reported incidents in chronological order, with cross-references if appropriate. Include any maps, drawings, diagrams, statistics, etc. Include subsidiary research into local history, local geography, geology, etc.
3. Background of the witness(es): Personal information such as sex, age, state of health, medical history where relevant, occupation, hobbies, principal beliefs if thought relevant, religious beliefs, etc.
4. Methods of investigation: Include your own summary of the methods of investigation you employed, why you thought them relevant, and how you approached the case with these methods.
5. Comments: Include any general comments you may have.
6. Conclusions: Your own conclusions, with reasoning. Make clear your supporting evidence for your conclusions.
7. Appendix/References: Include any reading, research and other references you have used during the investigation or in framing your conclusions.

Appendix D – Equipment

Equipment serves two main functions – support for you as an individual when investigating, and as a tool to amplify your own senses. Sometimes the functions overlap, but the two distinct functions should be borne in mind when planning a vigil. And some of the more exotic kit is also fun to play with.

SUPPORT FUNCTIONS

The best way of explaining this in more detail is by giving examples. Typical support equipment includes: Wellington boots, vacuum flasks and, not least, packets of crisps.

The support equipment will of course depend on the circumstances. When staying in a restaurant with a generous proprietor, a vacuum flask will not be necessary. When waiting in a muddy field in the middle of winter, then Wellington boots, raincoat and hood, and possibly even a tent are essential.

Other support items can include, depending upon finances: several torches, Citizen's Band (CB) radio equipment, portable cassette recorder and lastly a portable phone. We have a member in our group who is completely afraid of the dark (a ghosthunter, afraid of the dark?) and so he always carries more than one torch about his person. The portable phone is more in the class of 'nice to have in an emergency but never used'.

Appendix D – Equipment

The cassette recorder is handy to assist with making notes. Some investigators use a portable dictation recorder when interviewing and to make comments during a vigil. The dictating machine approach is useful but beware excess noise levels in the environment (such as music from a sound system in a pub, or from a TV in the home) which can completely drown out speech in interviews.

CB radio equipment is very useful for situations where it is handy to have instant contact with other groups on the vigil. Typical uses are to verify whether the other group 'heard that noise', or to ask for some assistance in the event of a problem. A licence for CB radio must be obtained from the Department of Trade and Industry.

Unfortunately the frequency band used for CB radio is not suitable for dealing with the thick walls of typical castles. Reception of signals may attenuated too much for reliable use, so alternative means of communication may have to be used if available.

TOOLS TO ASSIST THE SENSES

The list is as long as your pocket, and as ingenious as your imagination. Effectiveness is not directly related to technology as we explain below. For some of the items which are not normally available in the high street we have included typical costs, and at the end of this appendix we have included addresses of organisations that can supply this type of equipment.

Torches. For a variety of reasons it is useful to have your own lighting supply. In the case of vigils at public buildings, such as the castles we have attended, the main lights are switched off during the night. In other cases it may be preferable to keep lighting to a minimum. In the case of power failures, torches become essential. Keep spare bulbs and batteries with you for all torches.

Ghostwatching

Candles (and matches). If all else fails a candle is your last source of light. Candles are also very useful for testing for draughts.

'Reminder notes' and 'sticky-tac' are useful for marking key locations on walls and furniture (for example 'the point where the ghost was seen disappearing into the wall . . .'). They are non-marking and easily removed without tearing your witness's wallpaper off the walls.

Sugar/salt. These substances have been used for centuries in ghostwatching. If movement of objects is suspected, then simply sprinkling salt or sugar around the items in question will reveal whether movement has taken place. The sort of items this can refer to includes furniture, ornaments and wedged doors. The sound of the sugar or salt crunching as an object is being moved can help identify when the movement is taking place.

Thin string/fishing line. Tying a thin line to a door, bed or furniture suspected of being moved, and tied loosely to the finger of an investigator is very useful. It can also be used to tie across doorways when it is suspected that children are getting up in the night and causing mischief.

Some sundry items are obvious:
Notepaper and pencils
Measuring tape
Sticky tape
Small portable thermometer(s)
Compass
Containers for any 'items' you want tested later; better to have them in something clean than an old crisp bag you find someplace

GETTING SLIGHTLY MORE HIGH-TECH . . .

Portable Infra-Red Proximity Detectors. Based on burglar alarm technology these items are less than half the size of a

Appendix D – Equipment

VHS tape cassette. They emit a loud piercing noise if movement of a human or small animal is detected within 10 metres of the unit. Costing about £30 they can run from an internal battery for several weeks at a time. They are ideal for proving whether humans or animals are entering a room, or walking down a hallway. Most of the alarms can be set into one of two modes when triggered. The first mode just emits a long siren noise for several minutes before re-arming itself. The other mode, often called 'chime' mode, simply makes a brief (several seconds) siren noise before re-arming. This mode is quite useful in conjunction with a sound-operated cassette recorder. When used in this way, the recorder is set near the alarm unit, and when the unit is triggered the cassette will record the noise of the alarm, and any other noises in the room. The cassette unit can be used, therefore, to keep a record of the number of times the siren goes off.

In one recent case, the authors were consulted by a couple who were bothered by a poltergeist taking food from – and placing it in – their kitchen fridge. We lent them an extremely loud movement detector which was left in the fridge overnight to help determine if a human or non-human agent was responsible for the phenomena. They abandoned using the detector for fear it would wake the neighbours; then found that our detector was being alarmed and left in the fridge by the poltergeist as a surprise for them in the morning.

Portable Movement Detectors. Also based on burglar alarm technology these battery-operated units can be fitted to door-handles and any object which might be suspected of movement. Costing around £30 they make a siren noise when triggered.

Sound Detectors. The most obvious form of sound detector is the cassette recorder. Some recorders, especially those used for dictating, have a sound-activated system. This switches

Ghostwatching

the recorder on when a sound is detected, and continues to record for a few seconds after the noise has stopped.

Wireless Microphones. Some investigators use low-cost wireless microphones from the surveillance industry to help hear sounds from a greater distance than can be picked up by a conventional microphone. A wireless microphone is a microphone attached to a small, low-powered transmitter. This transmitter often operates on the VHF/FM band and can be tuned to operate somewhere between 88 and 108 MHz. It can therefore be picked up by a conventional domestic receiver which receives VHF/FM signals. A variation on this is to use a cassette-radio to receive the signal and record the sounds from the microphone on to the cassette.

Warning: there are three disadvantages to this kind of system. First, in the UK it is illegal to transmit on these frequencies, even on very low power.

Second, the power of these systems is so low that a range of 10 metres is about the most one can expect from such equipment.

The third disadvantage is that the FM frequencies are now so crowded with legitimate broadcast stations that it is difficult to find a free spot on a VHF/FM radio to receive the signal from the microphone.

In the last few years a new type of equipment has been licensed to operate on 49 MHz for low-power microphone usage. The most popular use has been that of wireless baby alarms. These cost £20–£60 and operate with a higher power, better aerial system and suffer from much less interference than low-cost wireless microphones. It is worth remembering that if you pick up a strange sound, you need to be very careful that the signal is coming from your sender unit.

There are other systems which plug into the mains, and use the mains to carry sounds over several tens of metres. They can be baby alarms or intercoms. Be careful about overreacting to sounds from the receiver, as the system is

Appendix D – Equipment

often prone to picking up clicking noises from the mains itself.

Low-cost wire-based intercoms can also be used. They can often operate to 100 metres and more, depending on the length of wire involved.

Lastly, if your cassette recorder has a built-in microphone then you can enhance its sensitivity by plugging in an external microphone. It is possible to buy off-the-shelf microphones with built-in connectors. If the connector does not fit your equipment, then adaptors are also available.

Temperature Equipment. There is plenty of evidence to suggest that just prior to a poltergeist event, and some ghost appearances, a sudden temperature drop may take place. At one haunted inn, it has been reported that in a particularly notorious room an electronic thermometer recorded a temperature drop from 18°C to 6.8°C; then down to −6.8°C.

Thermometers which record maximum and minimum temperature readings tend to be the most useful. With ordinary thermometers, as with all other direct-reading instruments, there is always the fear that while one is looking at something else a team of ghostly laughing cavaliers can cause the temperature to drop to very low values, but because no one is looking no record can be made. Electronic temperature modules are also quite useful as they can react quickly to rapid temperature changes. Some modules can be set to bleep when the temperature goes outside a preset range. The cost is around £12 for a reasonably sophisticated electronic unit.

Vision Equipment. The two most obvious forms of equipment in this category are still cameras and video cameras:

Still cameras come, of course, in all shapes and sizes and in various complexities. When we go on vigils we always take a simple camera with the minimum of controls and which does not let you take a picture with the lens cap on. You can imagine the scene: all present watch a table rise

Ghostwatching

unaided into the air and glide out of the window – one of the group with presence of mind takes a photo – he dashes off to the chemist to get the picture developed – and then finds he had the lens cap on. We always leave the flash unit on, so the camera is permanently ready to take a flash. It tends to mean that a fresh set of batteries is required for the next time the camera is used, but the price is worth paying for the ability to take that instant photo. Simple cameras also have the advantage that they are cheaper than the more complex systems, and can also be taken to quite inhospitable situations without fear of incurring wrath from the rest of the family if the camera has an accident.

A Polaroid-style camera is expensive on film but provides the advantage of instant feedback. The one disadvantage is that you do not get a negative.

Anomalous still photographs: if when looking at your pictures you find something unexpected on the print, send them in to either of the two national societies mentioned in Appendix A, with their negatives and a brief statement of the camera used, the operator and the circumstances of the picture.

Video cameras also come in all shapes and sizes. One of our colleagues has developed the art of acquiring second-hand video cameras and video recorders from boot fairs and jumble sales. Being second-hand, they are not exactly state-of-the-art but a couple of these cameras can be used to cover a large amount of space in a house. Video cameras and recorders acquired in this way can be purchased for around £30–£50 a unit.

It is very useful to have the facility of a clock on-screen so that events on camera can be correlated with other notes of events. If such a facility is not available, then if possible put a domestic clock in the field of view.

There are two main disadvantages to the video camera. The first is that if operated during periods of excitement, the 'lens cap' situation can arise, where mistakes are made and the event is not recorded. The second problem is where the

Appendix D – Equipment

recording has to be analysed after the vigil. It is not much fun staring at a picture of a stairway for eight hours watching to see if the headless ghost walks up the stairs. Watching re-runs of a motionless corridor is only slightly more exciting than watching soap-operas.

Deployment of the video camera: one technique is to use the video camera as a sort of permanent note-taker of the events of the vigil. That is fine, provided that the operator can work the camera properly. An alternative is to site the video camera in a tactical position on site and leave it there. Either method is suitable. The second method is often the more appropriate where bulky equipment is used.

Infra-red sensitivity and low-light level detection: many modern cameras are sensitive to infra-red light and can operate in levels of low light. This is discussed more fully below.

Night vision equipment enables the user to 'see in the dark'. It is usually the size of a portable video camera and amplifies the light in a room. Often the equipment is sensitive to infra-red as well as being able to work at low light levels. Sometimes the equipment is so sensitive that the light from an infra-red TV controller can be used to illuminate a room. When testing his own night vision equipment in his living room one night and using a TV controller as the light source Tony nearly jumped out of his skin when he saw a menacing, ghostly image looking directly at him. It turned out to be himself, reflected in the mirror.

Night vision equipment costs around £200–£300 for a second-hand unit and if the rest of the family requires justification for the expense, it can be used for other purposes such as viewing the antics of nocturnal animals in the garden. The equipment Tony uses is an NT-1 unit made in Russia which includes the facility to use Praktica-compatible lenses and has a facility to mount a camera body on the viewfinder.

Deployment of Infra-Red (IR) Sensitive Equipment: the use of IR equipment adds a new dimension to the investigation of ghosts. In the past, the only kit available to the

Ghostwatching

amateur or semi-professional was still cameras equipped with IR-sensitive film. Nowadays, the two main types of IR-sensitive equipment are modern video cameras, particularly Charge Coupled Device (CCD) video cameras, and night vision equipment.

There are two main uses for IR equipment. The first is to enable the user to see into an area which to an ordinary person appears almost, or completely, dark. This enables the investigator to detect human or animal presences which might be causing mischief. Also, some phenomena seem to want only to appear in near darkness.

Warning: when using this kind of equipment which can see things clearly where the naked eye cannot, remember to conduct yourself in a manner which will not attract allegations of misconduct, such as being a 'peeping tom'.

The second use is based on the possibility that IR equipment may be able to pick up paranormal images which would normally be unseen by the naked eye and conventional video or still cameras. There is little evidence to suggest that this is the case, but there have been so few pictures of paranormal events anyway. When working in this mode, there is no reason why normal illumination (e.g. daylight or ordinary room lighting) cannot be used, as the equipment will pick up images based on a wider than usual spectrum of light.

The usual way to illuminate an area with IR is to use a source of light such as a filament lamp and place a filter in front of it. It is possible to obtain infra-red filters from good photographic suppliers. The cheapest is made of gelatine, and the more robust is made of laminated glass. With most filters, when they are in place only the tiniest glow of dark red light can be seen, but to IR-sensitive equipment the illuminated area can look quite well-lit. If the dark red glow is too bright, Ilford Photographic manufacture a glass filter, type 917, which seems to cut out any breakthrough of visible light.

If you contemplate making your own light-box, beware

Appendix D – Equipment

of using a heat source which is too hot for the filter. Gelatine filters melt at relatively low temperatures.

To determine if your equipment is IR-sensitive is easy. All you need to do is to obtain a remote-control TV unit which when operated does not have any visible light that shines. Simply point the unit at the camera and see what appears at the video output. For cameras which can't show the video image directly, you will have to record the image, and play it back. If you see a pulsating light from the front of the remote control then the camera is sensitive to infra-red.

Advanced equipment. As part of our search to understand the underlying cause of ghost phenomena we use remote sensing equipment plugged into a central unit called EMU – Environmental Monitoring Unit. EMU behaves like a super-intelligent burglar alarm which monitors all the sensors, and when a sensor is triggered it notes the date, time and the sensor which was triggered. We use a range of devices, some based on burglar-alarm technology (passive infra-red, ultra-sonic, vibration sensors etc.). We also have a range of DIY sensors which look for other environmental effects. These include temperature, atomic particles, and electrical charge.

This kind of equipment is ideal for monitoring rooms, stairways and corridors for several days at a time. It can also be used where not enough investigators can be found to monitor premises. We have a radio link to enable us to monitor EMU from a distance, and have used it on several occasions to see what EMU has detected while stationed in locked premises.

It is possible for DIY enthusiasts to make a simplified version of EMU using conventional burglar-alarm systems. All that is required is a low-cost burglar-alarm unit and some burglar-alarm sensors. The burglar alarm can be set to operate a siren which can alert investigators to the fact that something has triggered the sensors.

Warning: domestic pets, even mice, can set off sensors, so be discriminating in your siting.

Ghostwatching

SOURCES OF EQUIPMENT NOT NORMALLY OBTAINABLE IN THE HIGH STREET

Maplin Electronics: huge variety of electronic components and equipment for the hobbyist. Mail order catalogue obtainable in all good bookstores. Several shops in London and rest of UK stock majority of catalogue items. PO Box 33, Corby, Northants, NN17 9EL.

Electromail: mail order catalogue obtainable from head office. Suppliers of professional quality electrical components and equipment. PO Box 3, Rayleigh, Essex, SS6 8LR.

Communications Centre: suppliers of night vision equipment. East Blagaton House, Nr. Quoditch, Ashwater, Beaworthy, Devon EX21 5BX. Tel: 0409–221033.

Ilford Photographic: supply of filter type 917. Town Lane, Moberley, Knutsford, Cheshire.

References

Details of cases cited in this book come from the following sources.

1 From authors' own files
2 From various sources; these are well-known cases and can be found in a variety of books on the subject
3 *I Saw a Ghost*, Ben Noakes, Weidenfeld and Nicolson, 1986
4 *Bugles and a Tiger*, John Masters, Michael Joseph, 1956
5 *Ghost Watch*, Professor Colin Gardner, Foulsham, 1989
6 *Morley Observer*, 30 September 1993, and subsequent news coverage
7 *Phenomena*, R. J. M. Rickard and T. Michell, Thames & Hudson, 1977
8 *Weekend Magazine*
9 *Memories, Dreams, Reflections*, C. G. Jung, Collins, 1967
10 *Apparitions and Haunted Houses*, Sir Ernest Bennett, Faber & Faber, 1939
11 *Journal of the Society for Psychical Research (JSPR)*, 1942 12 The *Daily Mirror*
13 *Portrait of my Victorian Youth*, Alice Pollock, Johnson, 1971
14 *Without Knowing Mr Walkley (Personal Memories)*, Edith Olivier, Faber & Faber, 1938
15 *The Candle of Vision*, George Russell, Macmillan & Co., 1918

16 *JSPR*, 1932
17 *Early Reminiscences*, Rev. Sabine Baring-Gould, John Lane, 1923
18 *Journey from Obscurity*, Harold Owen
19 *Black Beech and Honeydew*, Ngaio Marsh, Collins, 1966
20 *The Airmen Who Would Not Die*, John G. Fuller, Souvenir Press, 1979
21 *A Life at the Centre*, Roy Jenkins, Pan Books, 1991
22 *Phantasms of the Living*, E. Gurney, F. Myers, F. Podmore, Society for Psychic Research, 1886
23 *Det Ockulta Problemet*, Dr John Bjorkhem, Uppsala, 1951 (translated for the authors by Bertil Kuhlemann).
24 *The Evidence for Phantom Hitch-Hikers*, Michael Goss (ed. Hilary Evans), Aquarian Press, 1987
25 *The Seen and the Unseen*, Andrew MacKenzie, Weidenfeld and Nicolson
26 *The Ghost of Flight 401*, John G. Fuller, Souvenir Press, 1975
27 *JSPR*, 1884
28 *Annales Fuldenses Chronicles*
29 *The Poltergeist Experience*, D. Scott Rogo, Aquarian Press, 1990
30 *My First Hundred Years*, Dr Margaret Murray, William Kimber, 1963
31 *Haunted Royal Homes*, Joan Forman, Harrap, 1987
32 *Visions, Apparitions, Alien Visitors*, Hilary Evans, Aquarian Press, 1984
33 *The Story of Ruth*, Morton Schatzman, Duckworth, 1980
34 *Natural and Supernatural*, Brian Inglis, revised edition, Prism Press, 1992
35 *A Hind in Richmond Park* (*The Collected Works of W. H. Hudson*)
36 *JSPR*, 1885
37 *The Ghost Book*, Alasdair Alpin McGregor, Robert Hale
38 *Travels in West Africa*, Mary Kingsley, Virago Press, 1982

References

39 Ball of Light Information Data Exchange (BOLIDE), care of Hilary Evans
40 *JSPR*, 1889
41 *Phone Calls from The Dead*, D. Scott Rogo and Raymond Bayliss, New English Library, 1980
42 *Rösterma Från Rymden*, Friedrich Jürgensen, Stockholm: Faxon & Lindström, 1964
43 *Dr Konstantin Raudive: Unhörberes wird Hörbar*, Remagen: Otto Reichl 1968; UK: *Breakthrough*, Colin Smythe Ltd, Gerrards Cross, 1971
44 *Carry on Talking*, Peter Bander, Colin Smythe Ltd, Gerrards Cross, Bucks, 1972
45 A tape of his voices can be obtained from George Gilbert Bonner, 1 St Helen's Lodge, 369 The Ridge, Hastings, East Sussex, TN34 2RD
46 'The case for EVP', *Anomaly Magazine* (issue 11, 1992, George Gilbert Bonner, published by ASSAP
47 The Enfield Poltergeist was described in the fascinating book *This House is Haunted* by Guy Lyon Playfair. Many elements of this haunting appeared in the famous *Ghostwatch* spoof on BBC television, screened on 31 October 1992, with Sarah Green and Michael Parkinson
48 *If This Be Magic*, Guy Lyon Playfair, Jonathan Cape, 1985
49 *Mediumship and Survival*, Alan Gauld, Heinemann, 1982
50 *The End of Borley Rectory*, Harry Price, Harrap, 1950
51 *Mediumship of the Tape Recorder*, D. J. Ellis, privately published, Fernwood, Nightingales, West Chilington, Pulborough, West Sussex, 1978
52 *Light Magazine*, March 1915
53 *Explaining the Unexplained*, H. J. Eysenck, Carl Sargent, BCA, 1993
54 *The Paranormal, A Modern Perspective*, John Spencer, 1992
55 *Ghost and Ghoul*, T. C. Lethbridge, Routledge and Kegan Paul, 1961

Additional Recommended Reading

Allen, Thomas, *Possessed*, Doubleday, 1993
Evans, Hilary, *Gods, Spirits, Cosmic Guardians*, Aquarian Press, 1987
Gould, Alan, and Cornell, A. D., *Poltergeists*, Routledge and Kegan Paul, 1979
Hole, Christina, *Haunted England*, Fitzhouse Books, 1940
Moberley, C. A. E., and Jourdain, E. F., *The Ghosts of the Trianon*, Aquarian Press, 1988
Perry, Michael (Editor), *Deliverance*, SPCK, 1987
Playfair, Guy Lyon, *The Flying Cow*, Souvenir Press, 1975
The Infinite Boundary, Souvenir Press, 1977
Poole, Keith, *Britain's Haunted Heritage*, Robert Hale, 1988
Spencer, John and Anne, *Enclyclopedia of Ghosts and Spirits*, Headline, 1992
Whitaker, Terence, *England's Ghostly Heritage*, Robert Hale, 1989
Wilson, Colin, *Poltergeist*, New English Library, 1981

Index

A38, near Taunton, Somerset 45, 48
Allington, Miss 29
Alonzo de Benavides, Father 92
American Society for Psychical Research (ASPR) 15
Ancient Ram Inn vii, 139–141
Antoinette, Marie 32, 34
Arkansas 210
Arthur, King 30
Association for the Scientific Study of Anomalous Phenomena (ASSAP) ix, 27, 117, 139, 145, 168–170, 226–7, 232, 252
Australian Aboriginals 8
Avebury 35

Bagnères, Frlance 46, 48
Balfour; Arthur, Elenor & Evelyn 12
Ball of Light Phenomena 95
'Barbour' family 54
Baring-Gould, Sabine 38
Barnum, P. T. 10
Barrett, Professor W. F. 13
Batchelor, K. J. 204–6
Bayliss, Raymond 118, 121
Bearnn Eile 100
Beaulieu Abbey 30
Bell Witch 77
Bélmez faces (*see* House of the Faces)
Belvoir Castle, Denton 53
Bender, Hans 80
bi-location 92, 93
Billing, Northamptonshire 54
Blackmore, Dr Susan 180
Blind Men and the Elephant, The 161

Blue Bell Hill ix, 47, 229
Bonner, George 114–6
Borley Rectory vii, 70
Bormann, Martin 210
Boscastle 29
Bradfield St George 29
Braid, James 243
Bramston, Miss 97
Brookes Smith, Colin 239
Bull, Samuel 37
Butler, Lucie 36

Cambridge Society for Research in Parapsychology 165
Cavendish Hotel 19
Charlton House vii, ix, 64–5, 154, 171, 215
Church of England 176, 178
Citizen's Band (CB) radio 148, 260–1
'Claire' 120
clairvoyance 248
Cocke, J. R. 15
Coleman, Michael 34
Conway family 81–5
Cooke, Dr 73
Cooper, Emma 230
Corfield, Bill & Jimmy 61–4
Corinth Canal 62
Cornell, Tony 165
Council of the Photographic Society of Great Britain 108
Cox, Esther 79
Croatia 26
Crossland, Tony 41

Index

Crookes, William 12
Curl, Tracy 194, 199

Dartnall, Steven & Anne 188–90, 192–3, 195–6, 198
Darwin, Charles 10
Davis, Emma 73
Dawkins, Christopher 230
Deen, Douglass 175–6
Deliverance 178
Deliverance Ministry/Ministers 176
doppelgänger 89, 90
Dover Castle vii, 128–35, 146, 148, 151–2, 227
Duguid, David 108
Dymchurch 189

Earwicker, Simon vii, 165
East Ardsley Conservative Club, Leeds 24
Edgehill, Warwickshire 25
Edwards family 37
88 Newark Street, Whitechapel 81
Eisenbud, Dr Jule 109
electronic voice phenomena (EVP) 111–17
Elgee, Mrs 42, 86
Elizabeth I, Queen 89
Ellis, D. J. 113
Ellis, James 114, 116
Enfield Poltergeist 69, 70, 93, 150, 181, 184, 188
English Heritage 129
environmental monitoring unit (EMU) vii, 25, 184, 269
Epps, Leigh 119
Epworth Rectory, Lincolnshire 71
Erson, Herr 44
Eston-in-Cleveland 102
Evans, Hilary 34, 96, 104, 156
Evans, Priscilla 74
exorcist/exorcism 173, 175
extra sensory perception (ESP) 244–5, 250
Eysenck, H. J. 183, 245, 250

Fairlamb, Miss 12
Fay, Annie Eva 12
Fisk, G. W. 243

Fleur 90
Flight 401 57
Foreman, John 57
Fort Amherst ix, 135–6, 152
Fox family 9, 10, 68
Frank, Sir Charles 38
'Frederick Hannaby' 197
French Revolution 13
Fulton, Roy 50
Futility 60

Gadd, Elizabeth 18, 20
Galla Placidia, Empress 28
Ganzfeld 249
Garrett, Eileen 40
Gauld, Dr Alan 117, 209–10
GCHQ 114
Ghostbusters 63, 178
Ghosts of the Trianon 34
Goodenough, Maurice 47
Gregory, Mr & Mrs 34
Grosse, Maurice 93, 181, 184
Gurney, Edmund 12, 13, 17

Hampton Court vii
'Harold' 90
Harry Price Library 70
Hastead, Professor John 202
Hatton, Mrs Elizabeth 34
Hayden, Revd & Mrs Foster 72
Healey, Denis 41
Henry V, King 30
Hinchliffe, Captain W. G. R. 40
Hind, Cynthia 49
Hodgson, Richard 15, 16, 17
Home of Compassion vii, 18
Home, D. D. 14
Honorton, Charles 244, 250
Horner, Miss G. 97
House of the Faces vii, 105
Hubbell, Walter 79
Hudson, W. H. 106
Hughes, F. S. 73
Human Personality 17
Hunt, D. 239
Hurkos, Peter 239
Hydesville 9, 68

Index

infra-red (and other movement detectors) 262–3
Inglis, Brian 108

Jaarsveld, Corporal D. V. 49
James, Graham 248–9
James, William 15
Jardine, Douglas 38
Jeffreys, Judge 48
Jekyll & Hyde 52
Jenkins, Lord (Roy) 41
Joan of Navarre, Queen 30
Johns Cross Inn 75
Johnson, James 77
Jourdain, Eleanor Frances 32–4
Joy, Algernon 43, 86
Judy 65
Jumano Indians 92
Jung, Carl 28
Jürgensen, Friedrich 111

K., Miss J. 244–5
Keel, John 95
Kent Messenger 230
Kent Today 230
King's Backs Path, Cambridge f165
Kingsley, Mary 101
Kits Coty House 229
Kulagina, Nina 182–3

Lancaster, Mr 26
Latheronwheel, Caithness 98
'Laura' 19, 20
Lawrence, Robin vii, ix, 128–9, 194, 199, 227
Le Grange, Anton 50
Le Surf, Jane 152, 189, 191, 193–4
Leaf, Walter 12
Leeds Castle, Kent 30
Lethbridge, T. C. 94
Lewis, Mike 27, 139, 168, 170
Lodge, Sir Oliver 11, 16
Loft, Capt. Bob 57
London Stock Exchange 242
Luce, Cynthia 101

MacDonald, Kenneth 99
Mackay, Elsie 40
MacNeal, Bob 79
Mãe de Ouro (Mother of Gold) 101
Magdaleniana skeleton 8
Marsh, Ngaio 40, 86
Mary, Sister 92
Masters, John 21
Ménégoz, Mlle 34
Mesmer, Franz 242
Mill, John Stuart 10
Millar, Arnold 98
Moberly, Charlotte Anne 32, 34
Morgan, Lucien 65, 246–7
Moses, Stainton 11
Myers, Frederick 11, 12

Newbury Park 90
News of the World 230

Ogowe and Rembwe rivers 101
'Old Jeffrey' 72
'Old man' of Chancelade, Dordogne 8
Olivier, Edith 35
Origin of Species, The 10
Orwell, George 2
Ouija boards 64, 207, 209–10, 248
Owen, Dr A. R. G. 202
Owen, Wilfred & Harold 39
Owens, Don B. 119

Palace of Versailles 28
Paranormal and Close Encounter Experimental Research (PACER) 252
Parise, Felicia 183
Paul, Philip 114
Paxton Cottages, Burra, Australia 31
Peddar's Lane, Standbridge 50
Pendlton, Elsie & family 119
Pepper's ghost (illusion) 14
Pereira, Maria 105
Perkins, Harry 54–7
Petit Trianon 32
Petty family 12
phantasmagoria 13
'Philip Experiments' 146, 201–3, 210
Phinuit, Dr 16
Piper, Mrs Leonoras 15, 16
Playfair, Guy Lyon 204
Pollock, Alice 30
Polstead Rectory 72

277

Index

poltergeists 67–85
Price, Harry vii, 44, 70
Pritchard, Colonel D. 38
Proceedings of the SPR 17, 251
PSI Researcher 251
psychokinesis (PK) and micro-PK 69, 115, 118, 183, 201–2, 206, 209, 211, 241
Pye, Mr & Mrs 29

Raudive, Dr Konstantin 112, 113
Rayleigh, Lord & Lady 12
red ochre clay 8
Reeves, William 60
Repo, Second Officer Don 57–60
Robertson, Étienne-Gaspard 14
Rochester Castle vii, 137, 143, 152, 160, 227
Rogo, D. Scott 118, 121
'Rohan' 65
Romero, José 105
Rosenheim, Germany 80
Roux, Maria Charlotte 52
Russell, George 35
'Ruth' 89, 90
Ryzl, Dr Milan 243–5

Saegée, Amélie 88, 90, 91
St Albans Abbey 18, 20
'Sally' 237
Sargent, Carl 183, 245, 250
Sax, John Godfrey 161
Schneider, Anne-Marie 80
Scott, Philip & Shelia 179, 198–9
Scott-Eliott, Miss 29
Serios, Ted 109
Sharpe, Ian 230
Sheargold, R. K. 112
Shenton, Pete 53
Sidgwick, Henry 11, 12, 13, 17
'Smith's field' 16
Society for Psychical Research (SPR) ix, 12, 13, 43, 117, 145, 176, 232, 251
sound detectors 263
Souter Fell 26

South East London Paranormal Research Group (SELPRG) 188, 215
Southsea, Hampshire 66
Spielberg, Steven 67
Spuk 67, 78, 80
Steff, Philip 182, 186–7, 196
Stornoway, Isle of Lewis 99
Strong, Dorothy 27
Swain, Mr & Mrs 30
System of Logic, A 10

Table-tilting & table-rapping 146, 203, 248
Taylor, J. Traill 108
Taylor, Police Constable 73
temperature detectors 265
Thomas, Dave 47, 229–31
Thorpe, Jeremy 20
Titanic, RMS 60, 61
Tulip Staircase, Queen's House, Greenwich 23

UFO's 1, 28, 47, 54, 96, 164, 238–40
'Uncle Jerry' 16
Uniondale, South Africa 49, 52
Union Inn 145–6, 151, 179, 188–200
Unsworth, Harry 45
US Air Force 114

vision equipment 265–9

Walker, Canon Dominic 176–8, 180–1, 200
Walton, Chris 75, 127, 165
Walton, Philip 127, 148, 165
Watertown, SS 106
Watson, John 53
Wesley, John 71
White Horse Stone 229
Wilkinson, Mr & Mrs 33
Williams, Helena 102
Wilson, David 121
Wilson, Edith 96
wireless microphone 264
Wood, Miss 12
Wycombe General Hospital 120
Wynne, Ruth 29